THE MANIPULATOR

A Psychoanalytic View

by Ben Bursten, M.D.

New Haven and London
Yale University Press
1973

Designed by Sally Sullivan
and set in Linotype Times Roman type.
Printed in the United States of America by
The Colonial Press Inc., Clinton, Massachusetts.

Published in Great Britain, Europe, and Africa by
Yale University Press, Ltd., London.
Distributed in Canada by McGill-Queen's University
Press, Montreal; in Latin America by Kaiman & Polon,
Inc., New York City; in Australasia and Southeast
Asia by John Wiley & Sons Australasia Pty. Ltd.,
Sydney; in India by UBS Publishers' Distributors Pvt.,
Ltd., Delhi; in Japan by John Weatherhill, Inc., Tokyo.

Permission to quote from certain copyrighted materials was kindly furnished by the following:

The Public Trustee and the Society of Authors: *Heartbreak House,* by George Bernard Shaw.

Times Newspaper Ltd. (London): *The Strange Voyage of Donald Crowhurst* and the logbooks of Donald Crowhurst.

The British Broadcasting Corporation: Transcripts of the tape recordings of Donald Crowhurst.

Archives of General Psychiatry: "On Munchausen's Syndrome" in volume 13 (1965), pp. 261–68, and "The Manipulative Personality" in volume 26 (1972), pp. 318–21.

Mangan. . . . I took your father's measure. I saw that he had a sound idea, and that he would work himself silly for it if he got the chance. I saw that he was a child in business, and was dead certain to outrun his expenses and be in too great a hurry to wait for his market. I knew that the surest way to ruin a man who doesn't know how to handle money is to give him some. I explained my idea to some friends in the city, and they found the money; for I take no risks in ideas, even when they're my own. Your father and the friends that ventured their money with him were no more to me than a heap of squeezed lemons. You've been wasting your gratitude; my kind heart is all rot. I'm sick of it. When I see your father beaming at me with his moist, grateful eyes, regularly wallowing in gratitude, I sometimes feel I must tell him the truth or burst. What stops me is that I know he wouldn't believe me. He'd think it was my modesty, as you did just now. He'd think anything rather than the truth, which is that he's a blamed fool, and I am a man that knows how to take care of himself.

Shaw, *Heartbreak House*

CONTENTS

The late Dr. Maurice Levine, director of the department of psychiatry of Cincinnati General Hospital where I spent two years of my psychiatric residency, was something of a phrasemaker. He had a lively interest in the ways we might approach patients, medical colleagues, and intellectual problems, and he promulgated formulae to guide us. One such formula was the "three-layer approach" to the understanding of the personality. According to this scheme, the outer layer is that of the defenses; this is the layer which is apparent to the observer, and is the layer most often reacted to. Beneath this is the layer of anxiety which promotes the formation of the defensive outer layer. And beneath the layer of anxiety is an innermost layer—the basic goodness of the human being. This layer is most often hidden from view, covered over by conflicts and anxiety and masked by the defenses.

I have always felt that this conception of the innermost layer was less a statement of psychological fact than of a humanistic ethic. Those of us who were privileged to study under Dr. Levine could not fail to grasp, both by this formula and by his own style of relating to people, his conviction that patients are human beings and that being a human being carries with it a certain dignity. His was not a soft-hearted approach that tended to excuse rather than to analyze; he could be quite demanding of his residents and, I believe, of his patients as well. But along with his intellectual rigor and high standards went an attitude of respect for people.

It is against this background that I view certain current trends in psychiatric thinking and practice. Many people in our field see virtually all patient behavior—or at least all aspects of the behavior which they do not like—as manipulative. When they peel off the outer layers of the defenses and the anxiety, they seem to find an inner core of manipulation and exploitation. While I do not agree with this formulation for reasons which I shall explain in this book, differences in point of view can make for stimulating discussion and creative thought. However, I have been increasingly concerned with some of the uses to which this formulation has been put. Some colleagues—residents, teachers, and practitioners—viewing their patients as essentially manipulative, are led to adopt oppositional approaches. They seek to outwit and outmaneuver their patients, or to control them. They seem to maintain a pejorative view of the inner core of their patients; instead of collaborating with the inner goodness, they try to wall off the inner badness.

Manipulative behavior does occur, although not to the extent described by some psychiatrists. And it is probably a reflection of neither inner goodness nor inner badness, but of inner humanness. It deserves the same serious study psychiatrists give to other behavior. This book is an attempt at such a study. It is written from the vantage point of a psychoanalytic theoretical framework because this is the framework which I have found to be most useful in my attempts to understand behavior. And, to some degree, it is written from the vantage point of a libertarian, because it reflects the high regard I have for the right of the individual—even if he is called a "patient"—to be himself regardless of what I may think is best for him.

B. B.

Woodbridge, Connecticut
1972

ACKNOWLEDGMENTS

This book is a product of evening and weekend work. My wife, Jocelyn, and my children, Andrew and Amy, understanding how absorbed I was in the manuscript, gave me the time I needed. A contribution of this magnitude can be only acknowledged here; my thanks must be expressed within the family.

I sought suggestions and advice from several of my colleagues at various points in the writing. Drs. David Dressler, Melvin Lansky, Ira Levine, and Roy Schafer, and Stuart Johnson, M.S.W., contributed ideas and read and discussed with me certain portions of the manuscript. Drafts of some of the chapters were presented at research conferences of the U.S. Veterans Administration Hospital in West Haven, the Yale Department of Student Mental Health, and the Connecticut Mental Health Center; the discussions following these presentations were most helpful.

The workers at NARCO (Narcotics Addiction Research and Community Opportunities, Inc.) in New Haven, and the residents and directors of Daytop in Seymour, Connecticut, had a frankness and openness in my visits with them which allowed me to learn about their operation and point of view. Likewise, in England, Dr. J. Stuart Whiteley and the staff and residents at the Henderson Hospital in Sutton made me so welcome that by the end of my stay I had not only observed their community but had become a part of it.

Nicholas Tomalin and Ron Hall of the London *Sunday Times* and Donald Kerr of the British Broadcasting Corporation graciously made available to me their written materials and their own personal impressions of Donald Crowhurst so that I might better understand that particular manipulator.

I also extend a special note of thanks to Jane Isay of the editorial staff of the Yale University Press, not only for her valuable editorial assistance but also for her encouragement from the early stages of the manuscript to its completion.

CHAPTER 1

MANIPULATION

Generally, one of three conditions impels the clinical psychiatrist to study a particular type of behavior. First, society may find the behavior deviant or unacceptable, and the psychiatrist is called in to "cure" the "sickness." Such behaviors are subsumed under diagnostic labels such as "psychosis," "neurosis," and "character disorder," and they cause distress to the individual or to society at large. The psychiatrist is asked to study the syndrome in order that he may change the unacceptable thought or action.

The second condition prevails when certain personality components are valued. Artistic ability and creativity are examples of highly valued attributes. The psychiatrist studies them, partly in hopes of learning what conditions may enhance these qualities.

The third condition arises in the course of clinical work. Intensive and thoughtful contact with a patient may bring to the psychiatrist's attention certain aspects of the personality which have escaped the more casual notice of society, and these phenomena may now become subjects for study in their own right. Regression, identification, and the oral triad are examples. This condition arises especially when the behavior in question seems to obstruct the treatment process. Reactions which may have been viewed only as curiosities in the nontreatment setting become important objects of investigation when they "interfere" with therapy.

The transference reaction is a classic example of an "interference" which became an object of study. At first, Freud (Breuer and Freud, 1893) observed that his therapeutic efforts were often interrupted by the tendency of hysterical patients to form personal relationships with him. This was felt to be an "external obstacle," one not inherent in the material. The "external obstacle" had to be brought to light and traced to its origin within the treatment hour. "To begin with," Freud said, "I was greatly annoyed at this increase in my psychological work" (p. 304). However, his attention had been drawn to this "interference" and in the ensuing years the intense personal reactions of patients to their therapists became a legitimate and important focus of investigation.

Manipulative behavior, like transference reactions in the 1890s, has been observed mainly as a nuisance. The manipulative patient interferes with the therapeutic plan; he is "uncooperative," and if he is not controlled, we fear that he will not only thwart the treatment effort, but in the inpatient setting, he may destroy the ward. Redlich and Freedman (1966, p. 394) put it this way: "It has often been said that this group [sociopath] [1] makes others suffer while they themselves, in contrast to neurotics, do not suffer. The confidence man, and indeed many charming scoundrels with an ability to overlook inhibitions and normal reticence, and an inability to feel real bonds, irresponsibly stirring the passions and bypassing the inhibitions of others, *leave havoc in their wake* [italics mine]."

Manipulative behavior cuts across diagnostic boundaries. While very prominent in the personality make-up of antisocial personalities, it can also be observed from time to time in psychotics, neurotics, and even in people who will never be classified as patients. Manipulation is not a diagnostic syndrome; it is a way of thinking and acting which, like dramatization, may contribute to a variety of clinical pictures.

The prevalent psychiatric attitude toward manipulation is illustrated by Fromm-Reichmann's (1950, p. 21) description of a possible "interference with psychotherapeutic progress." She wrote:

A very brilliant, clever, and shrewd psychopath, many of whose interpersonal relationships were in terms of power manipulations, was told after the first two interviews that the psychiatrist considered himself to be reasonably intelligent but much less clever and shrewd than the patient. The psychiatrist explained that it would be easy enough for the patient to put something over on him should he choose to use his superior shrewdness and cleverness for that purpose. It was then suggested to him that he try to make his choice between using the

1. The terms *sociopath* and *antisocial personality* will be used when I refer to the works of other writers. I shall use the term *antisocial personality* when I refer to current diagnostic concepts. In chapter 10, I shall propose a change in our terminology.

psychiatrist for what help he had to offer or as a target for his shrewd manipulations. In spite of the warning which the psychiatrist had offered for both the patient's and his own benefit, the patient succeeded more than once in deluding the psychiatrist during the course of treatment.

Manipulation, then, is an annoyance or worse for the psychiatrist. It is seen as a noxious and alien character on the therapeutic stage; it does not properly belong there and we would like to command it to leave. In any active mental hospital, hardly a week goes by without a staff discussion of this or that patient's behavior as manipulation. The word appears in nursing notes and doctors' progress reports to signify a setback, an unwholesome development, and (worst of all) an uncooperative patient.

It is striking, but perhaps not surprising, that although clinical psychiatrists express considerable concern about manipulation, they have accorded this behavior very little serious study. It is true that certain types of persons who often manipulate others have been described in some detail. Most notable here are the antisocial personalities. This prime example of deviant and socially unacceptable behavior has been the subject of many clinical studies. However, to study the sociopath is not necessarily to study manipulation as a behavior pattern. Both Robins (1967) and Cleckley (1959) discuss many attributes of the sociopath—such as shallowness of the emotions, lack of responsibility, impulsiveness, and lying—but they neither list nor study manipulative behavior per se. Likewise, the several studies of malingerers, impostors, and other persons leading fraudulent lives (Abraham, 1925; Deutsch, 1955; Cleckley, 1955) have focused on the descriptions, dynamics, and genetics of these types of people rather than on the mechanisms of manipulation.[2] Indeed, a survey of current textbooks in psychiatry reveals that manipulation has not attained sufficient status as a psychological phenomenon to merit a place in the index of most of them.

It is curious that manipulation has received so little systematic study. It has commanded much of our clinical attention, but per-

2. A noteworthy nonpsychiatric exception stems from a group of sociologists who have studied "Machiavellianism" (Guterman 1970). I find the frame of reference of this book so different from my own that I cannot meaningfully integrate Dr. Guterman's findings with my observations.

haps there have been forces which have interfered with our ability to study it.

The schemer causes us to consider two conflicting values in our society—assertive initiative and honesty. We place a high premium on the clever man who has the energy to put his ideas into action and to succeed in our competitive world. However, our ethical heritage places certain restraints on the exercise of cleverness. A man must not cheat, lie, or hurt others. He is not supposed to take "unfair advantage" of another person's limited capabilities. Willful fraud is frowned upon and often the law requires restitution and punishment if one man has cheated another. The conflict of values is well illustrated in the field of commerce where we encourage and applaud the growth of business and production but decry fraudulent advertising and imperfect merchandise. Whenever the subject of governmental regulatory agencies arises, we see the conflict between the need to protect the public from dishonesty and the desire not to restrain unduly the enterprising businessman.

We psychiatrists, of course, are not free of the values taught by our society. We, too, react with admiration (albeit often secretly) when we observe a successful manipulation, and we react with anger when someone (especially ourselves) gets hurt. When the manipulation does not affect us or "our" therapy directly, we tend to wink at it, to admire it, or even subtly to encourage it; when the fraud becomes too obvious we punish it, often by calling it names. Thus, "You're manipulating!" has a pejorative rather than a diagnostic ring.

The use of the pejorative is more common in psychiatry than we would like to admit. Even our most respected "technical" terms are often used in this manner. "Immaturity" is a case in point. We have a more or less specific idea of what comprises maturity. It is a somewhat technical term used to denote certain ways of thinking and behaving. However, we often hear clinicians describing as "immature" behavior which they find distressing or obnoxious. "Abnormal" and "acting out" also lend themselves easily to pejorative usage. When the patient (or the acquaintance or political figure) acts contrary to the standards of behavior which we set for him, we can condemn him without appearing to pass judgment by the pejorative use of technical terms. And, somehow, it is necessary for the psychiatrist to appear not to judge; technical terms sound scientific rather than moralistic.

When we use "technical terms" as pejoratives, there is no need for intellectual follow-through. The clinician, confronted by the problem of paranoia, is stimulated to think beyond the label; "paranoid" becomes a springboard for an inquiry into the genetics, the family dynamics, the chemotherapy, the nature of projection and delusion, etc. However, when the term is used pejoratively, there is no stimulus for inquiry. For example, in a recent discussion on current race relations problems, a psychiatrist was commenting on the prevalence of depression in the black ghetto. "These people have nowhere to go," he said. "They are exploited by the white businessman, harassed by the police, and kept in poverty by the system. Their depression is probably the number one mental health problem in our city."

Shortly thereafter, the discussion turned to the whites living in the surrounding area. I commented on their fear of the emerging black power and the insecurity of their own newly won status.

"They're paranoid," he retorted, and that was the end of that. He did not wish to consider their feelings. He had used the term to dismiss them as unworthy of further study. There was to be no intellectual follow-through; the technical term was used as an insult, and insults serve their own purposes.

Now, "manipulation" carries with it an even heavier pejorative weight than "immature," "abnormal," "acting out," and "paranoid." It stands for lying, cheating, deceiving, and sneaking, and it has rarely risen to the status of a technical term. With the use of this word we tend to dismiss the behavior as unworthy of scientific study, and we have a vague feeling that there is something unprofessional about the whole business. As Robins (1967, pp. 957 f.) noted in a brief discussion of malingering, "An allegation or suspicion of malingering also implies perhaps not necessarily but at least psychologically, an unprofessional attitude for a physician to take toward a patient. . . . Malingering is a complex phenomenon that has yet to be properly studied."

Not all professionals are quite so uneasy about the pejorative approach. Some humanistic psychologists, using an existential orientation, quite readily take a stand against manipulation and feel that it would be unprofessional to do otherwise. Consider the comments of Moustakas (1962, p. 12): "The lie, the distortion of reality, is clearly one of the most pervasive evils of our time . . . it is inevitably a form of manipulation; and manipulation, at bottom, is responsible for much of the human misery and grief and suffering in the world today. . . . In a sense, the shrewd, clever, sleight-of-hand expert is in command over others, but inwardly, such a person suffers, such a person rots in corruption and immorality. To deceive and manipulate, to trick with shrewd and clever tactics is surely a basic illness of modern society which severs the individual self from its own moorings and eventually destroys any sense of unique identity and authentic existence." This merging of values such as "evil" with diagnostic concepts such as "illness" is not uncommon in psychiatry (Szasz, 1961); what is unusual is the frank and unabashed manner in which Moustakas presents these viewpoints. To him, manipulation is both bad and sick, and he seems not to be uncomfortable in his condemnation. Those of us who are more traditional in our attempts to separate our values from our scientific appraisals are not quite so comfortable studying something we want so badly to condemn.

Coupled with our uneasiness about condemning patients is our pleasure in the cleverness of the manipulation and the wish to be at least as clever ourselves. Having identified an individual as a manipulator we turn our attention to guarding against the manipulation or even to outmaneuvering him. Rather than studying him, we gird ourselves to do battle. This reaction is well illustrated in the nonclinical setting by Singer (1964). Using a test designed to measure "Machiavellian attitudes," he demonstrated that the grades of college men correlated moderately with high "Machiavellian scores" while the women's grades tended to correlate with their physical attractiveness. Singer concluded his report thus (p. 150): "The results imply that the poor college professor is a rather put-upon creature, hoodwinked by the male students . . . and enticed by the female students . . . as he goes about his academic and personal responsibilities. He is seemingly caught in a maelstrom of student intrigue and machination. The picture is bleak. In defense we can only offer the consolation that when 22 male members of the faculty at the Pennsylvania State University were administered the Machiavellian Scale, their mean score was

10.44. . . . The faculty appears significantly more manipulative than the students. . . . *It is hoped that the academics are fighting stratagem with stratagem* [italics mine]."

There are also much subtler psychological forces which interfere with our study of manipulation. Some of these will become apparent in chapter 8 where I discuss the reactions of staff members to the manipulative patient. It is sufficient to note here that manipulative behavior stirs up a variety of impulses and defenses within us professionals—impulses and defenses which we might prefer not to confront. The history of psychoanalysis (and of the resistance to psychoanalysis) is in part a study of man's efforts to overcome his own blind spots—and, as we shall see in our unfolding study of manipulation, there are many possible reasons why this behavior has been more encouraged and condemned than studied.

Now, if we are to engage in the study of manipulation as a psychological phenomenon, we must have some consensus about just which mental activity we are investigating. How do we define manipulation? Definition and denotation are troublesome in psychiatry. Words, of course, are no one's private property. Anybody is free to define a word as broadly or as narrowly as he chooses. Jugglers manipulate balls and rings, and scientists manipulate variables in an experiment. Stocks as well as people are manipulated.

Most psychiatric dictionaries are of no help as they do not even list the word. One exception is in Hildenrich's (1968) *Dictionary of Personality* which describes manipulation as "the dextrous or skillful management or handling of people, sometimes for the purpose of self-aggrandizement." This definition does not quite describe the phenomenon which occupies our interest because it lacks the quality of fraud or deception. A teacher may skillfully handle her students or a plant foreman may skillfully manage his workers. While they may reasonably be called "manipulators," when we psychiatrists speak of manipulation we generally imply deceit. Thus, we turn to *Webster's* (1969) for a definition most closely fitting our concept: "to control or play upon by artful, unfair, or insidious means, especially to one's advantage." And, lo and behold! a synonym for the verb "manipulate" is the verb "doctor." The idea of "doctoring" (rather than "patienting") as deceiving appears in another context also. "Manipulation" is listed in the index of Greenson's (1967) work on psychoanalytic technique, and it refers to the psychiatrist's actions in therapy rather than the patient's. I will discuss this aspect of manipulation in more detail in chapter 11.

I propose that, despite the various definitions of the word *manipulation* commonly in use, we select the Webster definition cited above when we use the word in a technical sense. I believe that this limitation will bring the term into line with what most psychiatrists mean when they refer to "manipulation."

Manipulation in this technical sense has four essential components. (1) There must be an initial conflict of goals. The manipulator must want something from the other person which that person does not want to give or comply with. (2) The intention to influence the other person is a second element. A manipulator must consciously intend to manipulate. Influence which is accidental or unintended is not a manipulation. (3) There must be deception and insincerity. Here is the element of fraud, the "artful, unfair, insidious means." (4) There must be the feeling of having put something over on the other person. These four components are obviously interrelated; they are not offered as separate psychic processes. In some cases, one of the components may be more easily recognizable; in other cases, other components will be more visible. But one must see, or reasonably infer, all of these components for a behavior to be called "manipulative" in the technical sense.

Consider this example of manipulation, drawn from the commercial life of a salesman. This young man was seeing me in psychotherapy. He had a good intellectual endowment; he was pleasant and genial, with a warm, engaging smile. He had come to therapy because of recurrent anxiety and unpredictable outbursts of anger so intense that his friends often had to intervene to prevent a fight.

Generally, however, his ability to function on the job or at home was not markedly impaired. He was interesting company and enjoyed a moderately wide circle of friends. One summer, early in his college career, he had obtained a job as a salesman for a roofing and siding company. "It's the hardest kind of selling, cold canvassing, I mean. No leads—you just go up to a house, knock on the door, and try to sell them a roofing job. There were twelve of us college kids that summer. By the end of the summer, they had all quit. It was too hard for them. I was the only one left. Everyone was amazed; I broke all sales records. My father didn't think I'd make any money, but he said, 'OK, take the job. It'll be good experience, anyhow.' When he saw the paychecks I brought home he asked me if they needed any more help—he'd like a part time job there too.

"I'm lucky; I've got the gift of gab. If I can get my foot in the door I have a good chance to make a sale. Of course, there are tricks of the trade, too. Sometimes I'd look a job over and it was, say, a $600 job. I'd say, 'Well, it's an $800 job, but we're running a contest in the office and I need only three more points to win a trip to Bermuda. I'm not worried about the commission because the trip to Bermuda is worth more to me anyway. So I'll give up the commission and write it up so you can have the job for $600.' Or, I'd say, 'Ordinarily this is an $800 job but we're running a special advertising campaign this week. I can't lower the price for you, but our advertising department will deduct $5 a week from your payments and charge it to their costs of advertising.'

"Some of my best sales were really great, though. What I liked about the job was that it was creative. You took a person who had no thought of buying a new roof and you worked with him, gave him the thought and created within him the need, the desire for your product. I mean, the guy might be sitting in his back yard sipping a mint julep, and you walk up to him and say, 'Good morning,' and he says, 'Hi,' and pretty soon you've got him buying a roof. The best sale, though, was the one where I was walking on the street and I saw an elderly man on a ladder painting his home. I walked over to him and said, 'Hi. Can I see that brush for a minute?' He said, 'Sure' and gave me the brush. I looked at it for a minute and then I threw it down in the dirt as hard as I could. I told him, 'You ought to be ashamed of yourself, at your age, painting your house.' I told him he was overexerting himself, it wasn't good for his health. I made out like I was mad and I got his attention. Then I showed him how I could save him the trouble and how he could really afford it. I ended up with a $2700 order for new siding. Boy, when I got back to the office did we have a laugh over that one! The manager really cracked up; I mean, here I ruin the guy's brush and everything, and I get the order for new siding. He was doing a perfectly good paint job and he stopped and bought the siding."

I asked him about the laughter. "Well, it was enjoyable, I mean it was so creative. I guess I was laughing because I was successful." Further discussion, prompted by my questions, however, pointed up the fact that it was not the success or the achievement or even the creativity that evoked the laughter. There were many other creative achievements in this young man's life which did not evoke laughter; he passed exams, wrote good term papers, and had successes in other jobs—none of these achievements caused him to laugh.

His thoughts turned to the neighborhood barber. This man was known as a Scrooge. The patient recalled, "The only time anyone ever won anything off him was a couple of years ago when I bet him that (a certain hair tonic) was cheaper in a discount store. He was so sure it wasn't that he bet me a dollar. When I took him to the store and showed him and won the buck, I was so excited, I went all over town waving the buck. It was a really big deal; it was the first time anyone had ever gotten anything out of old Scrooge." I pointed out that the sense of exhilaration about the bet might be related to the laughter over the sale of siding. He said, "If the damn fool wants to buy siding, who am I to stop him? I mean, the paint job would have done him fine; he really didn't need siding." The patient was laughing at the "damn fool"—the person who had been made to do something he really hadn't wanted or needed to do—just as he had been exhilarated by extracting money from "Scrooge." He then acknowledged some contempt for customers whose minds are so easily changed. The customers he really respected were those who listened to his sales pitch and then made their decisions on the pertinent facts. "I'll never forget one woman," he said. "I knocked on the door and she was very polite. She told me, 'I don't like door-to-door salesmen. I don't need anyone to tell me if I have to fix up my house. I live here every day and I know when something needs to be done, and when I see something has to be fixed up, I'll call someone.' I didn't get the sale, but she was one of the most intelligent customers I ever met."

All the components of manipulation are to be found in this

salesman's story. There is the initial conflict of goals. The salesman wanted to sell his product, and the customer had no intention of buying. Indeed, he had already chosen an alternative (and less expensive) method of renewing his house. It was the customer's sales resistance which made selling so exciting to the patient. It would not have been "creative" if the customer had called him up saying, "Please come over to my house. I want to order some siding." The commission would have been the same, but the excitement, the "creativity" would have been lacking. Nor would we see anything manipulative in the sale where both the salesman's goals and the customer's coincided all along. It is the conflict of goals which sets the stage for manipulative behavior.

The intent to influence is also prominent. From the beginning, the salesman wanted to change the customer's mind in order to make a sale—and as large a sale as possible.

The element of deception and insincerity is apparent in the solicitous "indignation" that the salesman showed to the elderly man. It was as if he were saying, "I'm not primarily interested in selling siding (*my* best interest); I'm concerned about your health (*your* best interest)." The same deceptions are seen in the sales pitches involving the sacrifice of commission and the advertising campaign. Without this deception, we would not call the transaction "manipulation." If a fair presentation of the advantages and disadvantages of both painting and siding were presented, and, on the basis of fitting the facts to his own needs, the customer decided on the siding, we would not feel that there was a manipulation.

Lastly, there is the exhilaration about putting something over on the customer. The significance of the sale did not lie only in the large commission; the sale was gratifying as a psychological maneuver because the salesman "put one over" on the customer. He made a "damn fool" out of him, and he could not respect him.

While this is a reasonably clear-cut example, in other cases we cannot always discern the four elements of manipulation. At times, for example, we may see the conflict of goals and the intent to influence but not the deception or the feeling of putting something over on someone. A sales clerk in a store can provide a hypothetical example. A customer comes in for (say) a $100 suit. He has neither the intention nor the desire to pay more. The salesman shows him several $100 suits as well as one costing $150. He is quite frank about the price but persuades the customer to try on the more expensive suit to see how much better it looks. The customer agrees, reluctantly at first. He is impressed with the quality of the material and workmanship. The suit does seem to fit better than the $100 outfits. The salesman then explains the "easy payment plan," and the customer decides that he can afford the more expensive suit. He is pleased with his acquisition, and the salesman is pleased with the sale.

In this situation, the conflict of goals has to do with the price of the suit; the salesman wants to sell a suit at a price which the customer does not originally wish to pay. The salesman knows what he is doing when he urges the customer to try it on: he intends to influence the customer to spend more money.

Is there deception on the part of the salesman? It is not obvious. He makes no pretense of not wanting to sell the $150 suit. It is true that he flatters the customer's vanity in order to achieve the sale, but then, that is what buying clothes is all about anyway. True also is the fact that he has sized up his customer and paces his sales pitch to what he feels the customer will tolerate, but this does not have the ring of fraud.

After the sale, the salesman is pleased. Undoubtedly his pleasure does not stem solely from the extra fifty dollars. He probably also derives pleasure from having been a good salesman—skillful at his job. It is very difficult to know whether he feels he put something over on the customer. His exhilaration may reflect this, or it may not.

That our salesman is *persuasive* is apparent, but is he *manipulative*? Is all persuasion a form of manipulation? I have asked you, the reader, to restrict your definition of "manipulation" to situations involving the four components listed above. I have referred to this as "manipulation in the technical sense" to indicate that this is a restricted view of manipulation. Of course, you may not wish to accept my definition; you may use the word differently, and neither of us will be more correct than the other. But to understand what this book is about you must at least temporarily accept my definition of manipulation as defined by the four components.

According to this definition, then, many forms of influence are not manipulative. In their best usage, teaching, psychotherapy, administrative management, coaching a sports team, exhortation and persuasion of many kinds may lack the conflict of goals, the deception, or the feeling of having put something over on someone.

Accepting my definition of "manipulation" does not solve the problem of denotation. If we try to decide whether a particular kind of behavior is or is not manipulative we may encounter two problems—the borderline problem and the problem of evidence.

Nature knows no classifications and our attempts to set boundaries around our classes can only lead to frustration. Where manipulation ends and persuasion begins is a blurred area because the presence or absence of each of the four components is not absolute. Often, it is a matter of degree or prominence. There is some masochism in all of us, but we are not all masochists. So, while I use the label as a convenience in communication, and while in some cases the presence or absence of manipulation is reasonably clear-cut, it is not profitable to ruminate over what to call the borderline situations. It is more fruitful to understand the components, and beyond them the psychic mechanisms involved and the situations in which the behavior occurs. In this regard, even when a behavior is not classifiable as manipulative, some of the processes and reactions discussed in the ensuing chapters may help us understand it.

The clinical researcher is also vexed by problems of evidence. In many situations the four components may not be obvious. In psychiatry we have learned not to rely only on how behavior appears to us or what the person exhibiting the behavior first reports has been going on. Further study and probing may bring out aspects of the patient's psychic position which were not apparent at the outset. An interview with a social psychologist illustrates this point. I asked her to discuss one of her experiments and she recalled with much pleasure the first experiment in which she had participated. She was a graduate student at the time and was assisting in a study of conformity and the need to be liked. Her subjects were told to discuss a particular issue in a group. They then had to rate in writing how they felt about each other. The ratings were collected, and the experimentor told each subject how the others felt about him. However, instead of using the real ratings, the experimentor made up ratings in order, she said, "to maximize the impact on the subjects." Thus, some subjects were led to believe that they had become distinctly unpopular in the group while others were told that they were very well liked. The group was reconvened and the previous discussion was resumed. The experimentor noted any changes in positions taken by the subjects as a result of the "ratings."

Was this manipulative behavior? When the psychologist described it to me she referred to "manipulation" but she was talking about manipulating experimental variables rather than manipulating people, and it is manipulation of people which concerns us here. We must look for the four components which have been outlined above.

Deception is most prominent here. The experiment could have been designed without the deception; the subjects could have been told their correct ratings, but the aggregate ratings about any one individual might have had little impact. A subject who knew that some people in the group liked him and some disliked him might not have changed his position discernibly. In an experiment, which is an artificial and condensed sample of more general situations, it is often necessary to maximize the impact in order to isolate a particular pattern of behavior. Thus, the experimentor had to make the subject feel he was liked or disliked by all the others to a greater or lesser degree. This involved deception.

The other three criteria, however, are more difficult to see in this situation. Was there a conflict of goals? This depends on which goals we consider. We shall assume good faith on the part of the experimentor and subjects; they both shared a cooperative goal of "doing" an experiment. The psychologist told me that she attempted to create conditions which would give the subjects the maximum freedom of reactions to the experimental maneuver. This does not sound like a conflict of goals, nor does it sound like an intention to influence the subjects either to retain or change their previous positions. However, the experimenter knew (or thought she knew) that changes in the subjects' original positions were unlikely without the deception; people usually maintain their original positions throughout a discussion for a variety of personal as well as logical reasons. What is implied here is that the subjects would not want to change their positions and that the experimentor would want them to. This is something different from the "freedom of reactions" which the psychologist had talked about. This interpretation is borne out by our further discussion of the psychologist's feelings during the experiment. When she saw the subjects' positions change directions, she was exhilarated: "I was excited and I had the feeling that it's working." Thus it would not be "working" without the change. She would not have had the exhilaration if the subjects had exercised their "freedom of reaction" by not changing their positions. Despite the scientific value of negative results, they do not excite us the way positive results do. Underneath her apparent neutrality, then, the psychologist was trying to make the subjects change their position in a situation where she felt they would not ordinarily wish to do so—conflict of goals and intent to influence. After some discussion, she readily acknowledged that she had hoped that her design (i.e. the deception) would cause her subjects to change their positions.

The feeling of putting something over on the subjects is also difficult to observe in this example, but we can reasonably infer that it is present. The psychologist described her exhilaration when the experiment was "working." I asked her to elaborate on this exhilaration, and she spoke about a sense of power over the subjects: she could deceive them and control the situation. "These were high school students," she said. "You couldn't get away with it with college students; they're too sophisticated."

This example is instructive in yet another way. Because of our pejorative bias, we are accustomed to rejecting the use of manipulation. However, experiments of this type are socially acceptable, and psychologists are particularly careful not to let their manipulations cause lasting harm. Often, extensive debriefing sessions are held with subjects to ensure that they will not be uncomfortable after they have left the laboratory. Deception or manipulation need not necessarily be "bad" or "harmful" (the humanistic psychologists such as Moustakas would disagree). If one is going to judge their value, it is not the manipulation per se but the manipulation in a context which should be judged.

Our psychologist's excitement in doing and seeing experiments has now greatly diminished. She no longer enjoys participating as she did in that first experiment. She now much prefers to consider theoretical issues and to design experiments to test her hypotheses·

she would rather have her assistants actually run the experiments with the subjects. The pleasure of the experimental interaction has diminished with experience and professional maturity. Manipulation, then, was only one aspect of her psychological situation; intellectual curiosity was also important. To attend only to the manipulative aspect may be useful to us as a focus of our study, but it by no means describes the situation of the experiment or even the total psychological situation of the experimentor. And by placing the manipulation within the context of the experimentor and experiment, we see that it may indeed have a social function generally considered acceptable and useful.

One further example will illustrate the use of manipulation, through bluffing, in a socially acceptable context. A lawyer recounted the use of "courtroom technique." The witness, in a sworn affidavit, had maintained that only he and one other person had been at a certain meeting. Our attorney had good reason to believe that Mr. X. and Mr. Y. had also been at the meeting, but he had no admissible evidence to prove it.

The lawyer recalled, "I asked him, 'Mr. A., are you sure only the two of you were at the meeting?' The witness insisted that there were only two people there—himself and one other man. I asked him again and again. Contrary to what you see on television, in real life when you press a witness he doesn't usually break down; he hardens his position. And this is just what I wanted him to do. I wanted him to insist that there were only two of them at the meeting. Then, at the right moment, I turned to my table and reached into my briefcase. I took out a paper, I didn't even know what was on the paper—it might even have been blank for all I know. I looked like I was reading from it and I said, 'Mr. A., isn't it true that Mr. X. was also at the meeting?' He became pale—that's the value of building up the tension—and said it was true. Then I said—still looking at the paper—'And wasn't Mr. Y. also at the meeting?' He said 'Yes.' The judge was furious at him for having lied, and we won the case. And the funny part about it is that if he had stuck to his story, there was nothing I could have done; I would have put the paper back in my briefcase and rested my case." This last was said with an outburst of laughter.

I asked the attorney why he was laughing. "Well, it worked," he replied. "The deception worked."

"OK," I said, "the deception worked. Why does that make you laugh?"

"He was the enemy," he said. "We floored the bad guy." His pleasure in "flooring the bad guy" was obvious. He went on to recount other situations where he had tricked his opponents and he said, "We usually get a good laugh out of it back at the office."

The elements of manipulation are easily discernible here. The conflict of goals was the attorney's desire to present the true story and the desire of the witness to withhold it. The attorney intentionally influenced the witness to change his stand by a deception. The feeling of putting something over on the witness is evident in the "good laugh" about "flooring the bad guy."

The context of this bluff, and indeed of many bluffs, is a socially acceptable one, and the manipulation would generally be considered socially useful. The ethical and moral considerations involved in using deception for a socially useful end are outside the focus of this book. I have shown, however, that manipulation can occur in a variety of contexts, some considered socially undesirable and some socially acceptable. Let us now turn to an example arising in the context of clinical psychiatric practice inasmuch as this is the context which will be the center of our attention in this book.

A young man was admitted to the hospital because of a fear of dirt which had led to a marked limitation of his activity. He felt safe only in very familiar surroundings, and he refused to leave the hospital ward. Although he was a bright young man, he found himself unable to apply himself to his schoolwork. This was not because of difficulty in concentration; indeed, he could and did read novels alone on his bed and was able to discuss them very intelligently with friends. The problem stemmed from the schoolroom situation where he had to fend off bothersome feelings about the schoolteacher by refusing to cooperate with her.

The patient had little difficulty with his peers. Despite the many limitations his phobia placed on his activities, he was accepted and liked by other patients. They especially appreciated his sarcasm and they rallied around his clever, satirical portrayals of staff personnel.

I was a psychiatric resident at the time and the patient was assigned to my care. He took an instant dislike to me and lost no time in presenting his views to the hospital community. If I were inclined to grant one of his requests and was overruled in a staff meeting, he ridiculed my ineptitude. If I refused to grant a request, he went to a "court of appeals"—either other staff members or the patient group—to show how mean and unfair I was.

The early psychotherapy hours with him alternated between silence and insults. The insults pointedly illustrated the conflict: I was dirty, ugly, perverted, syphilitic, mean, and dangerous. At a later period of therapy he was able to discuss his desire to look at my genitals and his need to keep his sexual interests and impulses in check. The regression to anal sadistic pleasures was also made explicit. The insults, then, could be seen as expressing the pleasure in dirty and sexual ideas and the need to keep me at a distance by denying any attraction to me. At the time of the following incident, however, we had not yet come to this understanding.

The patient had become increasingly antagonistic toward me and had adopted a mocking tone. He lost no opportunity to put me in ridiculous situations. For example, on one occasion, he told the chief resident that I had tried to hypnotize him and was gleeful at the prospect of my being chastised.

One morning he had unwittingly left his bedroom door open while dressing. A nurse, passing in the hall, had observed his nakedness and had reported that he was exposing himself. Such issues were commonly brought up at patient-staff meetings where often an attempt would be made to help the community and the patient understand what impelled this behavior. When the issue was raised in the large meeting, the patient was mortified. While the nurse's understanding of this behavior was probably accurate, the patient was by no means aware of his desire to exhibit himself. To him this was just an accident, and he became quite agitated as the discussion proceeded.

It had become apparent to several of us how disturbing the meeting had been to the patient. After the meeting, the patient came over to me in the hall and requested a tranquilizer. I acknowledged how upsetting he had found the meeting and suggested that we talk about it. He became very angry—no longer agitated in the anxious manner of a few minutes before—and stomped off.

An hour or so later, he came into my office for his regular therapy appointment. He was smiling, very well composed, and he said, "I have a surprise for you."

"What is it?"

"That's for me to know and you to find out. You're so stupid you could never figure it out anyway."

My inquiries about the surprise or about his agitation earlier in the day were met with silence or with taunts, such as "What makes you so ugly?"

Suddenly the telephone rang. It was the hospital director. "I saw John in the hall a few minutes ago," he said. "He's very upset and he says you won't give him medication."

"He was upset," I replied, "and I decided that it made more sense to discuss it with him than to give him medication." The patient could hear my end of the conversation, and his grin revealed that he knew what the other end was like.

The director's voice became stern as he told me once again how agitated John was and that I had better give him medication. I replied that John was sitting right there in my office and was well composed. However, the director would not hear of this; he had just seen a terribly distraught patient in danger of psychotic decompensation. In no uncertain terms he insisted that I write the medication order, and he hung up.

I was annoyed and crushed, and it certainly showed on my face. The patient laughed as he said, "Like my surprise?" He gleefully taunted me by describing what a scene he had put on for the director and how he had timed it so that the call would come during the therapy hour and he could watch me "get it" from the director. He had outsmarted me, he had gotten what he wanted. All this proved how dumb I really was.

Let us look at this episode from the standpoint of the four components of manipulation. The situation had conflicts of goals. The patient wanted medication while I was disinclined to give it to him. The hospital director would not have given the medication either had he known how well put-together the patient was. The patient wanted to ridicule me; neither I nor the director would have approved of this goal.

The patient took deliberate action to influence the director and to force me into a situation which he found satisfying. He was aware of what he was doing and he proceeded as he had planned —intentional influencing. This was amply demonstrated by his announcement that he had a surprise and his subsequent glee over how well his plan had worked.

Deception in this situation is blatant. Although originally agitated, the patient was much less upset after our encounter in the hall. Indeed, in rather typical fashion, he handled his anxiety around sexual issues by picking a fight and becoming contemptuous and insulting. When I had refused the medication, his agitation was quickly submerged under his anger. However, he did not reveal this change to the director. Instead, he must have put on quite a show of imminent disintegration. The director, having observed how mortified the patient had been during the patient-staff conference, was probably feeling compassionate (as were we all) and was more receptive to the patient's subsequent display of anguish.

Deception played another important part in the plan. The patient's display of anguish to the director had to be kept from me. While John gloated about the surprise, he would not tell me what it was. He knew that if I had been aware of his plan, I would have contacted the director and discussed the situation in a setting of calm deliberation. It was important for the patient to keep the excitement up, to keep everyone off balance so that the staff could not get together.

There is no doubt that the patient felt that he was putting something over on me. His taunting me with the "surprise," his glee when "it worked," and his pleasure in calling me stupid all attest to this fact. He probably also felt that he had put something over on the director. He showed such pleasure as he described the scene he had played for the director.

There are two further points about manipulation which we can learn from this situation. First, manipulation does not exist in isolation. When we identify the four components cited above, we may call the behavior "manipulation"; however, it may also be defensive and expressive of a variety of motives and conflicts. Behavior has multiple determinants and the aspect which captures our attention may reflect as much our own interest as the importance of this aspect for the patient. In this clinical example, the behavior, clearly manipulative, had very important economic and dynamic[3] determinants. The patient had loosened his defensive hold on his sexual impulses and "accidentally" exposed himself to a nurse. Having been caught at this, he felt the need to redouble his defensive efforts by denying intent. The patient-staff meeting was on the side of making his impulse conscious; indeed, by making it public, patients and staff were further exhibiting our patient, and his rickety defenses were sorely tried. The dangers associated with the impulses were imminent—hence the anxiety and the wish for medication. My refusal of medication served as a nidus for bolstering his defenses. He could now deny his interest in men (and their genitals) by opposing them. He could make me impotent and stupid and thus could be safe from my power. As we saw at a much later time, by rendering me powerless he was castrating me. Now he need not fear that I would either attract him or attack him sexually. There were still other determinants of this manipulation, but these illustrate the point to be made here.

Now, those who incline toward a pejorative view of manipulation may say at this point, "Oh, well, if all these dynamics and economics were involved, then he really wasn't manipulating at all; he was expressing an unconscious conflict." This is as if to say, "We can't really blame him (call him a 'manipulator') if we understand the forces behind the action." Of course, I am not blaming him; I am using the term "manipulation" to describe a constellation of thought and behavior which is only one of many psychic activities all going on at the same time, each contributing to the elaboration of all the others.

The second additional point has to do with the cast of characters. The patient is identified as the manipulator, but who was manipulated? Was it I, was it the director, was it the whole hospital system of well thought-out and coordinated therapeutic activity, or was it all of these? If we try to trace just one person who was manipulated, we get into difficulty in our analysis. It was really primarily the deception of the *director* which enabled the

3. These words are used as terms of psychoanalytic metapsychology (Rapaport and Gill, 1959).

patient to feel that he had put something over on *me*. And if he had not hidden his plan from me, he would never have been able to fool the director.

When we consider manipulations, we often deal not just with two people but with a whole system. Frequently, there are manipulative plans involving a goal conflict with one person, a deception of two or three others, and a feeling of having put something over on the whole system.

This brings us to a final preliminary consideration in our understanding of the term "manipulation" as it will be used in this book. Currently, there are two major vantage points from which behavior is studied in psychiatry—the intrapsychic and the interpersonal.

Traditionally, psychiatry has focused on the individual as the object of its observations and the subject of its theory. It was, after all, the individual who was out of step with his environment; it was he who had to be cured (i.e., brought back into harmony with the rest of us). Freudian psychoanalytic psychology in particular is a psychology of the individual. It deals with the intrapsychic; the structures and forces within the mind of the individual occupy the center of its investigational stage.

Neo-Freudian psychiatrists and many other contemporary workers have placed increasing emphasis on interpersonal relations and on the balance of forces between an individual and his environment. The concept of roles which an individual assumes within an environmental setting has facilitated the elaboration of the transactional approach. "Essentially a field approach," wrote Spiegel and Bell (1959, p. 139), "the transactional point of view postulates that the events involving the sick individual with his family occur within a total system of interdependent subsystems, any one of which—for example, the individual, the family, the community, the value system—may become, temporarily, a focus of observation." The transactionalists study systems of individuals; this is reflected in their tendency to treat groups, wards, families, etc., while de-emphasizing treatment of the individual. The psychoanalysts place greater emphasis on the forces within the individual.

Implicit in this difference in viewpoint are assumptions about the influence on thought and behavior of biological and genetic[4] factors and the relative stability and persistence of the influence of these factors. The psychoanalysts emphasize the tendency of the individual to be governed by relatively stable internal regulating mechanisms (Schafer, 1968a), and they focus their attention on these. The focus of the transactionalists is primarily on external and currently active forces in the systems of which the individual is a part. They place less emphasis on the importance of the genetic background and the stability of internal regulators.

Now, when I define manipulation and discuss its four components, I do so from the vantage point of an intrapsychic psychology. Regardless of how many people or systems of people are involved in the behavior complex, the psychological components of manipulation are in the mind of the manipulator; manipulation is viewed as a psychological process, not a transactional one. Thus, a person may be manipulating if he is employing the four components, regardless of whether the manipulation "works." Even if no one is manipulated or if the manipulation is justified or socially useful, if we can detect the four components *in the mind of the individual actor,* we shall term the mental process "manipulation." I do not intend to ignore the interacting system in which the manipulator finds himself, nor do I downgrade the importance of interactional or system factors. However, while manipulation may be *influenced* by what goes on around the individual, in the technical sense in which I use the term in this book, it is *defined* by what goes on within the individual. And thus, it is to these intrapsychic processes that we must now turn for a deeper understanding of the phenomenon.

4. See above, n. 3.

CHAPTER 2

THE ROLE OF CONSCIOUSNESS

Throughout our investigation of manipulation and its four components, we shall be concerned with the role of consciousness. By this I mean that I shall place some emphasis on that portion of mental life which is conscious and I shall highlight the distinction between conscious and unconscious mental events.

This focus on the conscious mental life might seem to be an unusual stance for a psychoanalyst to take. Psychoanalysis, after all, opened the gateway to the understanding of the unconscious mental life and Freud (1917, p. 380) took special pains to warn of the danger of laying too much stress on observable behavior and conscious experience. He wrote, "There would be the risk of not discovering the unconscious . . . and of judging everything as it appears to the ego[1] of the neurotic subject." Indeed, we must stress and restress the importance of unconscious mental events in order to understand human behavior. A psychology which treats only what is conscious and directly and immediately observable ignores the larger part of mental life. And a psychology which, ignoring the forces of repression, assumes that all mental life is readily available to consciousness, tends to become an intellectualized psychology, teaching patients to express psychodynamic formulations while their affective life becomes isolated.

The case for the study of what is unconscious needs no elaboration here. However, in our pursuit of that which is unconscious, we may err in the other direction; we may de-emphasize that which is conscious. Or more particularly, we may fail to distinguish between what is conscious and what is unconscious.

This distinction occupied the center of the stage early in the development of psychoanalysis. During that period, Freud's (1900, 1915b) psychological description separated the mind into three

---

1. At this point in the development of psychoanalytic theory, the word "ego" implied consciousness and volition.

systems; the Conscious, the Preconscious (containing material relatively easily available to consciousness), and the Unconscious. This separation was known as the "topographical point of view." There were several problems with this scheme. For example, mental processes which were supposed to characterize the system Unconscious could become conscious. "Conscious" and "Unconscious" were being used in three ways: as a quality of mental life referring to the state of awareness, as a mental structure referring to the systems of the mind, and as a reference to the degree to which some mental contents are actively repressed. Because these three uses of the terms did not have a one-to-one correspondence with each other, there was considerable theoretical confusion.

In 1923, Freud introduced his new structural point of view—id, ego, and superego—and the topographical viewpoint was no longer the center of psychoanalytic focus.[2] However, Freud by no means intended to abandon the distinction between that which is conscious and that which is not. He wrote, "The property of being conscious or not is in the last resort our one beacon-light in the darkness of depth psychology" (p. 18).

In this book, I shall use the terms "conscious" and "unconscious" to refer to the state of the quality of awareness and the degree to which mental contents are firmly repressed. "Conscious," then, will refer to those mental contents of which the individual is aware or which are relatively easily accessible to awareness; "unconscious" will refer to those contents which repression keeps firmly from awareness because conscious acknowledgment of them would constitute some danger in the person's eyes. I do not claim to have solved the problems of topography or to have presented a rigorous classification of the phenomena of consciousness by this use of the terms; I adopt this use as a convenience in order that we may proceed with our study with some common understanding.

Now, this use of the terms raises two problems which we must

2. Rapaport and Gill have eliminated the topographical approach from their list of metapsychological points of view. Whatever the merits of the logic of their argument, I believe that it is an unfortunate deletion as it tends to de-emphasize the importance of the role of consciousness in the approach to the study of mental events. This was undoubtedly not their intention, since they themselves devoted considerable energy to the study of consciousness (Rapaport and Gill, 1959; Gill, 1963).

consider. First, we must recognize the fuzziness of my definitions. Where does "relatively easily accessible to awareness" end and "firmly repressed" begin? Can we always be certain that we can gauge this in another person? As we have seen in chapter 1, in all our attempts at classification we are confronted with the grey area of borderline cases. We must acknowledge that at times judgment of whether something is conscious or unconscious is very difficult, and in our clinical work we must try to be as sensitive and perceptive as we can. We must be content to do our best. But we shall gain nothing if we define the problem out of existence by ignoring the distinction between conscious and unconscious because the grey area seems too difficult to cope with.[3]

The second problem has to do with various qualitatively altered states of consciousness (Gill and Brenman, 1959; Rapaport, 1951; Klein, 1970). Fugue states are a good example. Here there is awareness but it is a different type of awareness from that of the usual waking state. It is as if another self has taken over in the fugue state and the conscious experience of this self is separated and disconnected from the usual self. When I refer to consciousness, I shall, for convenience, refer to the usual waking state. Thus, for example, in our discussion of intentionality, the conscious planning to which I shall refer is that thought which is fully experienced as belonging to a self which is continuous with the individual's predominant sense of self. In the discussion of deception, the consciousness of the lie will refer to the individual in his usual state of reflectiveness, not to the transient condition where, in his excited state, he "loses himself" in the drama of the situation.

With these guidelines in mind, let me make clear the role of conscious mental life in manipulation as I define it. Each of the four components which I listed in chapter 1 must be conscious if we are to term the behavior "manipulative." The conflict of goals to which I refer is a conflict perceived by the manipulator. He may misunderstand the actual situation; indeed, the whole conflict may be only in his own mind. It is his understanding which will indicate whether there is a goal conflict. The intention to influence is also to be judged by what is conscious. In chapter 4

3. We shall return to the problems of the "grey area" in subsequent chapters.

I shall differentiate between intentions, which are conscious, and wishes, which may be conscious or unconscious. The deceptions which are involved in manipulative behavior as I define it are those perpetrated by a person who knows they are fraudulent. Self-deception, where an individual keeps some knowledge from himself or believes something erroneously, will not be considered one of the components of manipulation. Likewise, the sense of having put something over on someone, with its exhilaration and feeling of contempt for the "victim," elusive though it may be to the outside observer, must be a conscious feeling in order for us to call the act "manipulative."

Now, this is not to imply that we will be interested only in the conscious aspects of manipulation. In our discussion of the four components we shall stress their unconscious underpinnings and some of the factors which determine whether these conflicts, wishes, deceptions, and pleasure in putting something over are allowed into consciousness. However, I shall attempt to distinguish between what is conscious and what is unconscious, and I shall diagnose behavior as manipulative only when the four components are conscious.

Many writers seem to have ignored the importance of distinguishing between conscious and unconscious mental events. They would balk at my restricting the term "manipulation" to those cases where the four components are conscious. If there is a goal conflict and someone is influenced (they would say "coerced") to react to the patient in a certain way because of symptoms which are "unreal" (deception), then they would say that the patient has put something over on the other person; it makes no difference whether the patient is aware of what he has been doing—he is playing a manipulative game. In this way it is possible to reduce all psychiatric conditions to the framework of manipulation, and that is precisely what some psychiatrists have done. Such simplistic reductionism flies in the face of logic and common observation. The various psychiatric syndromes are different, both to the patient who experiences them and to the psychiatrist who observes them. To label them all "manipulative" is to ignore these differences and to discard the rich diversity of mental life. Let us look at some of the psychiatric syndromes which have been called "manipulative" in order to sharpen the differences among them and to illustrate the value of restricting our use of the term to those situations where the components are conscious.

Consider first the conversion reaction. The patient develops a disabling bodily symptom (such as paralysis) for which there is no physiological pathology. Sullivan (1956, pp. 216 ff.), emphasizing the interpersonal aspect of this syndrome, wrote, "Now, when there is this conversion, it performs a useful function . . . [which is an] almost juvenilely simple type of operation set up to profit from the disabling symptom." He pointed out the way the patient uses his symptom to influence others for his own benefit, and he concluded that the patient "has a rather deep contempt for other people." Szasz (1961, pp. 259 ff.) is even more explicit about this aspect of the conversion reaction. He referred to it as a game—particularly a "coercive game." He wrote, "Viewed as a game, hysteria [conversion reaction] is characterized by the goal of dominance and interpersonal control. The typical strategies employed in pursuing this goal are coercion by disability and illness. Deceitful gambits of various types, especially lies, also play a significant part in this game." Here are the components of manipulation; the patient desires some benefit which he feels might be denied him, he seeks to influence by deceit, and he is contemptuous of the other person. Are we, as Szasz suggests, dealing with a highly manipulative person? I do not feel that this approach adequately describes the state of mind of the person with a conversion reaction. Even Szasz acknowledges that the patient "is unclear, first about what sort of things he values in human relationships, and second, about the relationship of his values to his actions." The patient is indeed "unclear," and here is where the role of consciousness comes in; the transaction may well be coercive and others in his environment may feel coerced, but the patient is not aware of desiring to play a "coercive game." He feels weak, afflicted, unlucky, and perhaps even embarrassed about having to inconvenience others. While the line between malingering and conversion may be difficult to draw, many people with conversion reactions are convinced of their disability; they are not feigning disability in order to deceive others. When the person with the "paralyzed arm" asks us to write for him, he is happy when we help him (help him write and satisfy his dependency needs); his happiness is not derived from the conscious satisfaction of having coerced us, having deceived us, or having put something over on us any more than it is derived from an awareness that we have helped him repress his conflicted impulses.

This is not to say that the patient cannot manipulate. At times, he may consciously wish to dominate us. He may be angry at us, or envy us; he may, for example, not want us to go out to have a good time while he is "crippled." He may then exploit his "paralysis" chiefly in the service of interpersonal control. "Don't go," he may say. "I must get this letter out right away and I can't write it myself." While he may be unaware that there is nothing neurologically wrong with his arm, he may be well aware that he does not have to get the letter out right away, or that he is more interested in detaining us than in the letter. This (and not the "paralysis") is the deception as defined in this book, and here the conscious feelings may be those of controlling us and fooling us, and (perhaps) the satisfaction of vengeance.

The need to consider the role of consciousness is even clearer in the case of the depressed patient. Bonime (1966) considered depression a "practice, rather than a reactive or endogenous response." He wrote, "The basic outline of this concept is that the depressive is an extremely manipulative individual who, by helplessness, sadness, seductiveness, and other means, maneuvers people toward the fulfillment of demands for various forms of emotionally comforting responses . . . (the depressed patient) feels gypped and is angrily determined to get what is rightfully his" (pp. 244 f.). However, Bonime (1960) has acknowledged that the satisfactions of manipulation are disguised from the patient himself, and the angry, sadistic approach toward others is not within his awareness.

In contrast to the manipulators described in chapter 1, the depressed patient does not feel exhilarated by his "practice"; he is depressed. He may be unconsciously exhilarated, as Bonime implies (and which I doubt), but this is quite a different mental situation from the conscious feeling of putting something over. And what about his lack of energy and his low self-esteem—the very criteria on which we base the diagnosis of depression—are these merely pretense and deception? There can be no question that the depressed patient consciously experiences a lack of power in contrast to the inflated sense of power felt by the manipulator.

His self-esteem is low while the self-esteem of the manipulator is high. Where the manipulator feels contempt for the other person, the depressed patient is usually conscious only of contempt for himself. To ignore these differences by overlooking the distinction between conscious and unconscious is to throw away important data.

Masochism, also, can be viewed as manipulation, but only if we wish to oversimplify. The demonstrative feature (Reik, 1941) of masochistic behavior propels the patient into the center of the stage and tends to evoke sympathy and the impulse to take care of or comfort the victim.[4] The provocative feature "forces" others to hurt the masochist and thus to set up the demonstration. However, if we look more closely at an example of masochism, we are again impressed by the fact that the psychological situation is quite different from that of the person who consciously sets out to coerce and tyrannize.

Years ago, I had the following experience. One cold, snowy winter's day, I went down to the superintendent's quarters in the basement of an apartment house to make an inquiry. As the door was ajar, I walked in to find Mrs. Jones, the superintendent's wife, sitting in the livingroom. She was wrapped in blankets and she had a box of tissues in one hand. A pile of used tissues overflowed a wastebasket by her side. I asked for the superintendent and she informed me that Mr. Jones had been gone for several days. Apparently, every so often, Mr. Jones would disappear to have an affair with a younger girl. He would leave without notice and return when he was tired of the fling. Having told me this story, Mrs. Jones got up and, with a sigh, announced that it was time to shovel more coal into the furnace. Noting how sick she was, I offered to do the shoveling, but Mrs. Jones would not accept the offer. And while this wretched-looking woman was shoveling the coal, she exclaimed, "What can you do when you love a man!"

That she propelled herself to center stage and invited sympathy is apparent. But if she were attempting to coerce and tyrannize,

4. While the demonstrative feature may evoke pity, Reik stressed that its dynamic meaning was more focused on the secret display of strength: "Look, what I can endure." I have often seen clinicians ignore this aspect and focus on the patient's desire for attention. I agree with Reik's emphasis.

the effect was lost on her husband, and she could not accept the help from me.

What she was doing was presenting herself as the object of her husband's contempt. "Look how he treats me!" she was saying. Reik has carefully analyzed the unconscious mechanisms behind this presentation and shown how the masochist has reversed the situation. She has contempt and scorn for her "lover" which she is afraid to display, or even to feel. The opposite condition is experienced and presented as a safety device; *she* is the object of contempt, and she "loves" the man. But, in contrast to the depressed patient, she is still able to feel proud. "Despite my cold, despite my suffering, I can endure! I can shovel the coal." The disappearance of the husband would be a narcissistic blow to the depression-prone patient; it is a narcissistic spur to the masochist. However, while the masochist may be aware of feelings of strength and power, she is not *aware* of her contempt; her attitude is not one of putting something over on the other person despite her feelings of nobility.[5]

Turning now to mania, we find patients with this disorder described thus (Janowsky et al., 1970, p. 260): "A primary issue seems to be the fulfillment of dependency needs. However, a manic feels that it is threatening, unacceptable, and dangerous to rely on others or to wish to be taken care of. As a way of maintaining self-esteem, and feelings of power and strength, the manic instigates a situation in which he is able to control and manipulate those people on whom he must rely. . . . He professes to be totally autonomous and self-sufficient; yet his actions belie his words. By constantly testing, racing, manipulating, dividing, over-committing, and expanding, the manic patient increases his 'independence' to a point where he involves the resources and life styles of those around him so that they have no choice but to control him and take care of him." And how do staff members react? "Those dealing with the manic patient frequently find themselves on the defensive, attempting to justify their actions and mo-

---

5. This does not mean that masochists cannot manipulate. If the neurotic pattern striving to place the patient in the position of being the object of contempt is frustrated, the patient may manipulate others to achieve this position, and she may feel triumphant about having fooled those who frustrated her. This situation will be illustrated in chapter 3.

tivations. Commonly, they feel 'outsmarted' and 'outmaneuvered.' They may 'know' that their judgment and actions are appropriate, yet he outargued and manipulated them into positions which they consider unacceptable."

Now, indeed, in hypomanic and manic states, we are more likely to see true manipulation. Unlike the depressive, the manic patient has a strong sense of omnipotence and often a biting contempt for others. I do not agree that manipulation is necessarily a central feature of the manic state, or that the influence the manic patient exerts on others is always intentional. Nonetheless, the feelings of power, superiority, and contempt for the other person are so much a part of the manic picture, and are so ego-syntonic, that there is a fertile field for manipulation. While Janowsky seemed to indicate that manic manipulations are aimed at coercing others to control (take care of) him, my impression is that the enhancement of his self-esteem at the expense of the other person, the satisfaction that the manipulation "works" and he has put something over on the other person, is a crucial driving force behind the activity. There are other factors, however, which limit the manic patient's ability to manipulate. His flight of ideas often makes it difficult for him consciously to plan and carry through a deception with any finesse.[6]

It is in the antisocial personality that we see the champion manipulator. These patients have no difficulty in openly displaying contempt for the other person and in feeling powerful and superior. They delight in putting something over on the other person, not only because of what it gets them, but also because it feeds their vanity and reinforces their contempt for others. One such patient once boasted to his therapist that he was the most powerful person in the hospital. He said that he could make his parents dislike the therapist and there was nothing the therapist could do about it. And the therapist, from bitter experience, believed that the patient was right.

One of my antisocial patients caused so much havoc in the

---

6. It is true that limit-setting and controls may help diminish manic behavior, but that does not mean that this was the goal of the behavior. It may indicate that when the manipulation fails, the inflated narcissism is punctured and the manic, at least temporarily, is brought closer to the experience of his underlying depression.

hospital that unusual measures were instituted. Not only were patients restricted from leaving the hospital (except to go to work), but the men and women were enjoined not to mix. Men were not allowed on the women's side of the ward, and women could not visit the men. Even in the dining room, men and women had to sit separately. This highly unusual state of affairs was largely the result of my patient's sexual adventures with several schizophrenc girls—adventures which had so stimulated the patients (and staff) that chaos seemed imminent.

At the next patient-staff meeting, my patient was contrite and the picture of respectability. He acknowledged his role in disrupting the hospital. He said that he had not meant to disturb the girls; he had just needed to support his masculinity. "Being locked up in a hospital is a castrating experience," he told them. "All your independence and all your responsibility are taken away. You have to do something to be a man. But I guess I shouldn't have done it this way and I'm really sorry I caused all this trouble."

The next day, he came to his therapy session in a jovial mood. "Do you know what those idiots did?" he asked. "They put me up for proctor (for the school examinations). They said I needed a sense of responsibility and a constructive outlet." He laughed derisively. "I screw up the ward, and I make one little speech, and they put me up for proctor. How about that!" Here is the pleasure, the exhilaration derived from the feeling of having put something over on the other person; here is the sense of superiority and the contempt for others.

Now, I do not imply that only people with antisocial personalities manipulate; I have already indicated that people with other psychiatric diagnoses can also manipulate at times. But by examining the psychological state of this antisocial manipulator we see a markedly different mental state from that of the patient with the conversion reaction, the depressed patient, the masochist, and the manic patient. And the role of consciousness gives us an important key to these differences. This antisocial patient had clearly in mind what he intended and what would be allowed. He clearly used deception to influence the patient-staff group, and he was able to experience and enjoy his contempt and the exhilaration of having put something over on them. The patient with the conversion reaction could not allow himself to realize that his paralysis was "unreal" (in contrast to the "contrition" of the antisocial personality). The depressed patient could not savor the "victory"—indeed, it might even make him guiltier and more depressed. The masochist could not allow himself to be aware of the scorn and contempt. And the manic patient might well have difficulty in the conscious formulation and execution of the deception.

To enumerate the various internal factors which govern whether the components of manipulation will be conscious or repressed would require writing an entire psychiatric text. Some of these factors will be described in the ensuing chapters. What is important here is that we not obliterate these various factors and the differences in the conditions to which they lead by calling everything a "manipulation." By restricting the definition of "manipulation" to those situations where the components are relatively accessible to consciousness, I call attention to the different states of internal mental organization which lead to different syndromes and different behaviors.

While the emphasis in this chapter has been on the role of consciousness in differentiating various mental conditions, I must mention one other consideration. Patients with various psychiatric diagnoses may consciously employ the four components of manipulation, and their behavior may be manipulative by our definition. This does not mean, however, that manipulation is necessarily the central or major feature of the behavior or syndrome. As I indicated in the previous chapter, manipulation does not exist in isolation and often the other aspects of the behavior and the mental processes underlying them are of crucial importance both in understanding the behavior and in planning our therapeutic approach. We shall return to this consideration in chapter 13. At this point, bearing in mind the idea that in manipulation the four components are readily available to consciousness, let us look at them in more detail.

CHAPTER 3

THE CONFLICT OF GOALS

When we consider the component of conflict of goals from an intrapsychic standpoint, we immediately encounter a problem. What could be more transactional than a conflict of goals: two or more individuals relating to each other in an incompatible manner? My hospitalized patient wants to do something, and I do not wish to allow him to do it. He feels he needs medication, and I feel it would be unwise for him to have it. He wants me to lower my fee, and I am unwilling to do so. Can these conflicts be viewed from an intrapsychic vantage point?

What will concern us in this chapter is the conflict as the patient sees it. Where his understanding of the actual situation is reasonably accurate, the conflict of goals will reflect a real conflict—one which he perceives. Where his understanding is inaccurate, the conflict may exist only in his own mind, or the conflict of goals which he perceives may be different from that seen by others. His construction of reality is determined not only by the actual events in his surroundings—these will be considered in chapter 8—but also by *his* own needs of the moment and by *his* background and *his* relatively stable internal regulating mechanisms. Thus, when we speak of the conflict of goals, we shall refer to the individual's construction of reality.

Let us take as an example a hypothetical case of a rather typical masochistic woman in a hospital setting. She may have been greatly disturbed by her repetitive involvements with men who use her and then abandon her. She may realize that there is something within herself that causes her to re-enact these painful involvements. She hopes that therapy will change this pattern of behavior. But when the next man appears on the horizon, she is irresistibly drawn to him. We, the staff, see this budding romance as "nontherapeutic" and "self–destructive." The masochism is apparent and the patient is warned against the involvement or even restricted from seeing the man. How do we explain this to the patient? We do not ordinarily say, "You want to associate with Mr. X, but I don't want you to." We pose the conflict to her in terms of therapy: "Instead of re-enacting your pathological behavior patterns," we may say, "you should give us a chance to analyze them." This involves both a clarification and an injunction. The clarification is that her desire for the association is a part of a recurrent pattern of behavior (masochism), and the injunction is, "Analyze, don't act."

Often, the patient is not emotionally ready to receive the clarification. "True," she will say, "all my other romances ended in disaster, but this one is different." She will point out what a fine, gentle, and generous man X is, etc., etc. "And besides," she may add, "you have helped me see the pitfalls in my relationships, so I can keep my eyes open and I won't get into trouble." Then comes the "clincher": "If you don't let me associate with men, how will I ever learn to have good relationships?" She then convinces the nursing staff that her doctor did not *really* mean no contact with X—just no sexual contact.

Not having been able to assimilate our clarification, she cannot accept our injunction, and a conflict of goals has arisen. While we may see the essential conflict of goals as between our desire to treat the patient and her desire to obstruct the treatment, this may be incomprehensible to the patient. In her mind, the conflict is between her desire to associate with X and our "arbitrary" or "doctrinaire"—but certainly unrealistic—opposition.

One of the common errors in clinical psychiatry is that of losing sight of the way the patient sees things. Our interest in the therapy of masochism is important, as is our concern that the patient is manifesting a resistance. Our analysis of the antitherapeutic effect of the romance is probably accurate. But when we attempt to understand the psychology of the patient as she manipulates the staff in order to associate with X, we must also examine the conflict of goals as it looks to her. She does not understand the subtleties of psychotherapy, nor can she see the relevance of masochism to the present situation. She is not being obstructive. All she wants is a "normal" association, and it is *we* who are being obstructive.

Thus, in this situation, the conflict in her terms is that she wants to associate with X, and we do not want her to. Her perception that there is a real conflict is accurate, but her *understanding* of that conflict differs from ours. To study her manipulative behavior, we must know about her understanding of the conflict, and this will lead us into a consideration of her insistence on expressing her masochism, and the dangers she fears if she does not enact the masochistic pattern—as well as the role of the action as a resistance.

We often accuse such patients of "sabotaging" the treatment. This accusation overlooks the fact that the patient is expressing her illness. As she understands the conflict of goals, she is behaving quite reasonably. And since from her point of view, we are behaving quite unreasonably, we deserve to be tricked and outwitted. In the words of our attorney in chapter 1, we have become the bad guy," and she will gladly see us "floored."

We must remember, too, that patients may view treatment differently from the way we do. When they find that therapy may not necessarily make them feel better quickly and that the road to improvement is paved with frustrations, anxieties, and discouragement, resistances may arise. The desire to resist treatment may not be at all apparent to the patient. We may see the conflict in terms of resistance, while they may see us as having reneged on our "promise" of making them feel better. Indeed, in their view, it is sometimes we who are the saboteurs.

What I have just described is a conflict of goals arising primarily from acting-out—a patient repeating "without insight an unconscious psychic situation out of the past in terms of current reality" (Weiss, 1942, p. 487). To the degree that the conflict of goals in manipulation arises from acting-out, our understanding of the former is enhanced by our understanding of the latter. At times, but not always, acting-out has a very strong relationship to what is going on in psychotherapy. This is especially true in intensive psychotherapy where the resistance aspects of acting-out are particularly important. When the therapeutic work has diminished resistance to a point where an inner conflict threatens to become conscious, the patient may act-out in order to strengthen his defenses. Again, with the intensification of the transference, the threat of eruption of impulses vis-à-vis the therapist may make the patient sufficiently uncomfortable for acting-out to occur as a preferred form of discharge. It is not uncommon, for example, to see patients initiating active heterosexual adventures in order to avoid realizing the homosexual implications of the transference. As Fenichel (1941) put it, "The patient wishes through [acting-out] gratification of impulses instead of their confrontation with the ego . . . in order to spare himself further surmounting of resistances" (p. 71).

Thus, when we observe a patient who is manipulating, it may be instructive to examine his goal and the reasons why he is unable to understand our objection. If we ask ourselves the further question, "Why the manipulation *at this time?*" we may find the answer partly in the recent events of therapy. And, conversely, if we are aware of the anxiety generated by the intensification of the transference, and/or the imminent emergence of an inner conflict into consciousness, a well-timed clarification or interpretation may further the therapeutic work and simultaneously reduce the sequence "need to act-out leading to conflict of goals leading to manipulation." This is not to imply that clarifications and interpretations should be made in order to ward off manipulative behavior. Many factors intrinsic to the therapy must govern the timing of our interventions. When our clarifications are poorly timed (as in the case of our masochistic lady), the interventions will not contribute to the patient's understanding and, indeed, may reinforce the resistances against understanding.

A special instance of manipulation in the service of resistance is seen in the denial of illness. This situation, not uncommon among hospitalized patients, occurs when the patient is sufficiently frightened about the implications of being mentally ill to deny that he is sick. This may occur early in the treatment when the impact of being hospitalized helps the patient mobilize his defenses (or gratifies his need for punishment). Or it may occur any time during treatment when he is sufficiently threatened to adopt the position that he is now recovered and should not be in treatment. His goal is to leave the treatment situation, and he cannot understand our objections. He accuses us of being mercenary or of having other ulterior motives for wanting to keep him as a patient. He may then manipulate in order to flee from the threatening situation.

A young man was being considered for discharge from a mental hospital. Almost as a matter of policy, this hospital expected its patients to obtain jobs and suitable living quarters and to arrange to have "intensive" (i.e., three times weekly) therapy with an "outside" therapist as a prerequisite for discharge. He was referred to me for "outside" therapy.

The patient had had a severe agitated depression, and for a while his hospital course had been shaky. His depression had lifted, however, and he was once again able to function, although his rather marked character pathology placed limitations on what he could allow himself to accomplish. While recognizing these limitations, the patient was afraid of further therapy because he recalled how devastating the depression had been. He did not want to "rock the boat." However, he correctly understood that the hospital would not discharge him if he had not arranged outside therapy. He was aware that he could legally leave the hospital, but such outright and obvious defiance made him too uncomfortable—this would be "rocking the boat" in another way.

His attendance at our therapy meetings became spotty because he always managed to have a job interview during the appointment time. ("After all, doctor, they won't discharge me if I don't have a job.") He then proceeded to obtain a job which precluded the possibility of his keeping reasonable appointment hours. He told the hospital staff that I could not see him and that he would have to see a resident until discharge. He continued to maintain that he liked therapy (thus satisfying the hospital's need for his allegiance to treatment) and simultaneously ensured that I would not conveniently be able to see him by not telling me of his new time requirements until it was too late for me to rearrange my schedule. The hospital, contrary to its usual policy, accepted his arrangement as the only practical one in this instance, and the patient expressed considerable amusement at how he had handled the staff. He was subsequently discharged without firm arrangements for intensive therapy.

This case introduces some important issues. Under the law, most patients have the right to refuse treatment, although we put many obstacles in their paths. There are many pressures forcing the patient to remain in treatment even when he does not see the need for it. He both respects and fears the doctor. He will not dismiss a professional opinion lightly, and he will be uncomfortable taking the responsibility involved in going against the doctor's advice. How much safer it is to manipulate the doctor into changing his advice, or to arrange a situation where it is fate, rather than the patient, who has gone against the doctor's suggestion. Even when the patient knows he has "forced" the doctor to change his opinion, there is a part of him which feels that the doctor has now given him the go-ahead, and the patient will feel less responsible should things not work out well.

Another issue which is raised is that of whose assessment is the more realistic for the patient. The conflict of goals ("I want to do something and the doctor does not want me to") is not always primarily a result of acting-out or a flight from treatment. A psychoanalyst is said to have made this statement in casual conversation to a friend: "You know, after practicing psychoanalysis for thirty years, I have come to the conclusion that what we analysts call 'acting-out' other people call 'living.'" There are many situations where nontreatment may be realistic and appropriate, and where the therapist's devotion to an unattainable therapeutic ideal may set the stage for the conflict of goals (Coleman, 1969). And there are many situations where activity represents a vigorous and productive confrontation with reality which, while perhaps in part acting-out, is much more than acting-out: it is action. Erikson's (1962, p. 463) comments on reality and actually are relevant to this point: "Reality . . . is the world of phenomenal experience, perceived with a minimum of ideosyncratic distortion and with a maximum of joint validation, while actuality is the world of participation, shared with a minimum of defensive maneuvers and a maximum of mutual activation."

What I am discussing here is the situation where the patient's view of the goal conflict may represent a close approximation of the real situation. While the inequities of some of the real situations in which our patients find themselves will be considered in chapter 8, I shall present one example at this point in order to emphasize that our focus on the *perception* of the conflict by the patient does not necessarily imply that his understanding always proceeds primarily from neurotic distortions or the need for neurotic acting-out.

A lawyer had been hospitalized because of a panic state. His panic quickly subsided in the hospital, and he wished to return to his home and his law practice. He was interested in starting therapy as an outpatient. He was told by the hospital staff that he was not ready to leave because he had not engaged in a sufficiently intensive therapeutic experience in the hospital. His conflict of goals was between wanting to leave the hospital (under conditions of "honorable discharge") and being prevented from doing so.

He decided to bring pressure on the hospital to change its stand. He had heard of me through a friend, and he called me to request a consultation. He told me that he felt well enough to leave the hospital and had indicated to his doctor that he would seek therapy. The doctor had warned him that if he left the hospital against medical advice no respectable psychiatrist would accept him as a patient. He suspected that in part he was being kept in the hospital because they had a shortage of patients.

On the telephone, he sounded quite reasonable despite his suspicions. I could detect no flavor of gross psychosis. I asked him what he wished from the consultation, and he acknowledged that he was really looking for a witness to prove his point to the hospital. Perhaps I could force them to change their minds. I told him that my opinion carried no special weight and that the hospital generally decided issues such as discharge quite independently of "outside" opinions. I also informed him of his legal right to leave the hospital and indicated that, in my opinion, many psychiatrists would evaluate his current status and judge whether to treat him as an outpatient on this basis alone. I was skeptical about the consultation because at that time I would have been unable to consider treating him, and I doubted whether my being used as a witness was a useful role for me to assume. I suggested that I call the hospital and discuss his request with his doctor to see if there would be any use in arranging such a consultation. At first the patient was reluctant to have me call the hospital as this would reduce the element of surprise and the effect of my witness. When I told him that his discharge should be decided on its merits rather than on surprises, he agreed to have me call the hospital.

The first reaction of his doctor was that this patient was manipulating. I agreed. "This shows," he said, "how sick he is. The more he uses these kinds of manipulations—the harder he tries to get out of the hospital—the more convinced I am that he is not ready."

The doctor acknowledged that the patient was not psychotic; he was functioning well and could probably get along adequately out of the hospital. The disturbing thing, however, was how the patient was maneuvering and manipulating, a sure sign that he was avoiding some internal conflict.

I suggested that while I knew very little about the patient's inner conflicts, he saw a real conflict between his desire to leave and the hospital's prohibition. He was a lawyer; maneuvers and manipulations were part of his stock-in-trade, just as analysis is part of ours. I saw little intrinsic pathology in his attempting to use me as a witness and his desire for secrecy and surprise. Indeed, I suggested that his manipulation might just be a sign of strength, a sign of his ability to function adequately. The doctor reflected on this possibility and said that he would reconsider the situation.

I do not know enough about the patient to come to any firm conclusions about whether his understanding of the conflict of goals was realistic or distorted by a need to flee an uncomfortable situation. I had heard from other staff members that there was a shortage of patients in the hospital, but I do not know if this consideration entered into the doctor's reluctance to let him leave. Likewise, I cannot say whether the manipulation was primarily defensive flight, or if it was actuality in Erikson's sense. Nonetheless, this example again illustrates our need to be aware of our therapeutic bias when we assess the conflict of goals.

The examples we have considered thus far represent instances of manipulation in the service of some conflict or gratification. The patient may desire something, he may need to act-out, he may want to deny his need for therapy, or he may realistically want something which his doctor refuses to grant. He hopes to satisfy these needs and desires through a goal which he sets up; he is thwarted in his attempt by his doctor's antagonistic goal, and he sets about to win his point through the manipulation. There are other situations, however, where the manipulation itself largely fulfills the need or desire; the stated goal of the patient is less important to him than the act of manipulating. Some of these motivations and gratifications of manipulation itself will be discussed in chapter 6; I shall discuss the matter briefly here to serve as a focus for further consideration of the conflict of goals.

For a variety of reasons, a patient may not be able to tolerate the feelings of closeness and affection which an intensive psychotherapeutic experience may evoke. As he becomes increasingly attached to his therapist, his anxiety may mount. One method of handling this anxiety has already been discussed: the patient may act-out by forming a relationship with a third party, thus distracting himself from the therapeutic relationship. However, a more "direct" path may be chosen: the patient may ask for something —almost anything—which he knows the therapist is likely to oppose. He may set up this conflict of goals which will lead to a struggle and manipulation in order to put himself at a distance from the therapist. The struggle and the manipulation may contain all the elements of the forbidden sexual impulses which the patient is trying to keep out of consciousness, but as far as the patient is aware, he is displaying (and experiencing) nothing but antagonism and dislike for the doctor. Here it is the manipulation itself, rather than the stated goal, which relieves the anxiety.

This situation brings us to yet another consideration regarding the conflict of goals—whether there is always a real conflict. In all the illustrations I have presented above, there was a real conflict of goals even though each party may have understood the conflict differently. The patient wanted something which his doctor prohibited. While the understanding of the doctor's position may have been distorted, the position itself was seen correctly. Now in situations where the patient needs the manipulation itself, either for gratification or defense (usually for both), he must have a conflict of goals. And, if a conflict of goals is not readily available, the patient may perceive one even where it does not exist. The patient may incorrectly believe that his therapist opposes his wishes—indeed, he may refuse to believe the therapist even when the doctor reassures the patient that he goes along with the wish— in order to enact the manipulation. This can lead to a situation where the patient has been manipulating but the doctor and staff do not feel manipulated. The staff may be oblivious to manipulations in such circumstances. Nonetheless, the patient has engaged in manipulative behavior—there was a conflict of goals in the patient's mind, even if the conflict had no basis in reality.

A young man with an antisocial personality had been brought up in a family which placed a high value on appearances. His father, a local politician, emphasized the appropriate "American values" of hard work and devotion to God and family, and he wanted his family to set an example that could be held up as a model for the community. The patient's mother had been trained as a nurse, and although she was not working at that time (she was the model housewife and mother as well as being active as a community service volunteer), she maintained a lively interest in health matters. This provided a nidus for her sexualized relationship with the patient; when he was younger, she had engaged in a considerable amount of exploration and handling of his body under the guise of "attending to his illnesses."

The patient had caused his parents grief for many years. He had gotten into all kinds of trouble, and it was only through the father's political influence that public scandal had been avoided. Hospitalization was in part the family's method of getting the patient out of town and "salting him away" somewhere so that their public image would not be completely ruined.

While the patient had spoken to me from time to time about obtaining a job or going to school, his interest seemed quite half-hearted, and I had never pressed the issue. Thus, at what may be arbitrarily called the outset of the present episode, I took no special notice of his remarks about going out to look for work. To my mind, whether he worked or not was less important at this time than his inability to look at himself. He often tended to focus on external issues, and I could see the possibility of his immersing himself in job-seeking activity in order to avoid the self-investigation of psychotherapy.

One day he came to my office about 15 minutes late. He was walking slowly, and he sat down very carefully. He winced once or twice. He said that he had been undecided about coming because he was not feeling well. He had pain on urination; at times he was seized with a sudden urge to urinate, and found himself going to the bathroom seven or eight times a day. He thought he had a fever, but he had not taken his temperature as yet. There was a vague discomfort in his lower abdomen, and he was sure he had a urinary tract infection.

He missed his next appointment, but he did call to cancel it because of illness. On the following visit, he told me he was feeling somewhat better; the nurses at the hospital had reported his temperature as 103°, and he was being treated with antibiotics. He would probably be his old self in a few days.

Shortly thereafter, the patient played a prank on me. After leaving my office, he flipped the latch on my waitingroom door so that no one could come in from the outside. He laughed about the prank on the next visit and this led into a discussion of how he enjoys outsmarting and tricking me. By this time, one of my periodic conferences with his "administrative psychiatrist" in the hospital had revealed that he had never had a urinary tract infection; there had been no temperature of 103° and no treatment with antibiotics. Indeed, to the knowledge of the ward psychiatrist, the patient had not made any medical complaint whatsoever. Thus, when our discussion led to his pleasure in tricking me, I brought up the deception of the urinary tract infection.

Now, some of the dynamics of this deception were quite obvious from the nature of his complaint and my knowledge of his family. Here was an invitation for me to become concerned with his urinary (and genital) system; perhaps I, like his mother, would play nurse with him in an exciting, sexualized atmosphere. On a deeper level, he was probably reflecting his struggles and inability to become a man—especially an ambitious man—as required by his father.[1]

Interpretation of themes such as these would have been useless. The patient was easily as adept as I at formulating dynamics about transference, sexuality, and the like. He had been in contact with a succession of psychiatrists during his life, and he knew how to talk the language. I doubt that he was acquainted with the implications of urethral eroticism, but he would have been delighted to learn about them and to use them with my successor. Clearly, such interpretations would have no therapeutic impact at this time.

Instead, I tried to explore with him the implications of his playing tricks on me. "I screwed up your plan," he said.

"What plan?"

"You thought I was going to get a job." He went on to tell me

1. The relation between exhibitionism, shame, ambition, and urethral eroticism is summarized by Fenichel (1945).

that he "knew" I wanted him to get a job. In this way, I could show off to the hospital; his working would be a tribute to my therapeutic skill. He did not want to work, nor did he want to be used to build up my reputation. He could undercut "my" goals by being sick and thus he could gain a "reprieve" from me. I would not use him to show my worth to the public; he would get me to drop "my plan" and to become sympathetic. Then he could laugh at my stupidity and the tables would have been turned; instead of my using him for my pleasure, he was using me for his.

Of course, the deeper dynamic elements discussed above are reflected in his explanation, but what is missing above is the fact that there was not only a deception to express these dynamics; there was also a manipulation. Even after I had learned from his "administrator" about the deception, I had been unaware of the goal-conflict aspect of the behavior because it had not been my intention to get him to work. What at first had appeared as a transference reaction based on displacements from his nurse-mother, was later seen as stemming from his need to thwart me and to express his contempt and superiority. In a sense, he was running to me, his mother, in order to thwart me, his father. However, if I failed to realize that I had been outsmarted, the effect would be lost. Therefore, he played the second trick on me which drew my attention to the manipulation. We were then able to see how he was utterly unable to believe that I was interested in *him* and his inner life rather than in his *performance* and my reputation.

Thus far we have considered the conflict of goals which initiate a manipulation from the point of view of the patient who must adapt to a frustrating reality and the patient who distorts his understanding of a real conflict or creates a conflict in order to play out aspects of his neurosis or character pathology. We now turn our attention briefly to the psychotic patient.

The world of the psychotic patient is filled with a confusion of real objects, part objects, objects which have only a most tenuous degree of separateness from the self, objects whose characteristics or whose identities are projections and delusions, etc. While the neurotic's ability firmly to distinguish the inner and outer world may diminish at times, the renunciation of some of his reality-testing functions is only partial and temporary. The psychotic patient is subject to a more massive, severe, and lasting breakdown of ego boundaries. The conflict of goals is subject to all the delusional distortions in his repertoire.

I shall describe two particular types of goal conflicts which might arise when the patient is psychotic. First, under the sway of his psychosis the patient may wish to do something which the more reality-oriented staff may object to. In a persecutory panic, for example, the patient may wish to jump out of a window. Or he may want to cut himself in order to break through the numbness, feel something, and become a person again. It is indeed remarkable how parts of the ego can so split off from one another that a patient who cannot really experience himself without hurting himself can, nonetheless, accurately perceive the reality of the conflict of goals and can cleverly devise a manipulation involving a complicated interaction with the staff in order to obtain a pair of scissors to be used as an aid in restoring his ego-boundaries.[2] For example, a panicked young lady was brought to the emergency room of a municipal hospital. The ambulance attendants who accompanied her felt that she was highly suicidal and was not to be left alone. A nurse was instructed to wait in the room with her until the psychiatrist came. The patient said to the nurse, "Would you just look outside and see if my husband has come yet?" The nurse, caught off guard by the patient's reasonable request, took her eyes off the patient long enough for the patient to smash a bottle and cut her wrist. After this action, the patient was calmer, and when the psychiatrist arrived she said that she felt much better now and was ready to come into the hospital.

The second particular situation with psychotic patients occurs where the patient uses the goal conflict itself as a means of redefining reality. And here, as in the case of our antisocial young man, the conflict may exist only in the mind of the patient.

While the variations of this situation are many, they stem from the fact that the psychotic patient is so often in danger of losing the boundary between self and object and returning to a state of fusion (Lewin, 1950; Searles, 1965; Jacobson, 1964). Burnham (1966) has pointed out how patients with tenuous ego boundaries and poorly integrated senses of identity may attempt to make some order out of themselves and their worlds by split-

2. Freud discussed this process in two of his last works (Freud, 1938a, 1938b).

ting their ambivalence.[3] In a primitive manner, they come into conflict with part of the staff (bad: to be extruded) and appeal for help from other staff members (good: to be introjected). In this way, Burnham maintained, patients act as agents in promoting staff dissension, and the "bad" staff often feels manipulated by the patient's use of the "good" staff. I would add that not only do staff members *feel manipulated,* but these patients often are *manipulating*—and the goal conflict and manipulation are in the service of helping the patient define himself vis-à-vis the outside world.

Mrs. Smith, a chronically schizophrenic woman, had been hospitalized intermittently over a period of several years. When not in the hospital, she lived with her daughter and managed to function "adequately." She had been deserted by her husband some years earlier and, while she had a few acquaintances, she did not really get along well with anyone. She was particularly resentful of her in-laws for their "unfriendly attitude." Nonetheless, when she again began to hallucinate actively she went to their house for help, and they arranged for her hospitalization. It was characteristic of Mrs. Smith to turn eventually to the "unfriendly" relatives in time of panic; she did not go to her own family, although she felt closer to them.

In the hospital, she tended to be isolated. She was very critical of the staff and promoted confusion by telling different stories to different people. As her acute episode subsided, she was allowed to do more things, although the staff never had the feeling that she was cooperative or that they could get close to her. Even her individual psychotherapist felt that Mrs. Smith would only go so far in the relationship; then she would draw back and be unreachable.

A staff conflict came to light one morning during a patient-staff meeting. The patient, feeling she was ready for discharge,

---

3. The followers of Melanie Klein have placed great emphasis on splitting as characteristic of the paranoid-schizoid position. Because they postulate a greater degree of ego organization at birth than do the more traditional Freudians, splitting is seen not primarily as a fight against fusion, but as a defense against annihilation of the introjected ideal objects. Nonetheless, they do also feel that splitting plays an important part in helping the immature ego make order out of its experiences. A succinct description of these views can be found in Segal (1964).

had told the staff that she wanted to get an apartment. While staff agreed that Mrs. Smith would be discharged soon, they felt that arrangements should be made gradually. It was staff's opinion that Mrs. Smith tended to take on too much at once and that she would be overwhelmed. Mrs. Smith had taken matters into her own hands; she had obtained an apartment in nearby Appleton and, with the help of her father, had put down a deposit on it. Now she was complaining bitterly to the hospital population that some of the staff didn't want her to keep the apartment. The apartment was perfect, her daughter liked the school in Appleton, the price was right, and apartments were hard to find. Some staff members were angry that Mrs. Smith had deliberately disobeyed their instructions and was now presenting them with a fait accompli. Had they known she would do this, they would not have allowed her to go out by herself.

Mrs. Smith maintained that other staff members were not so unreasonable. There were some, at first reluctant to speak up, who felt that the patient's initiative was a sign of health; they were less concerned with the fact that she had not informed the staff of her intentions. Mrs. Smith tried to enlist the help of the "good" staff to win over those who objected, and in the ensuing days she shuttled back and forth between the two factions, at times conveying truths and at other times, distortions. Ultimately, the staff agreed that she could keep the apartment, and she felt victorious. I talked with her shortly thereafter, and she made it plain that she thought very little of the opposition; she knew all along she could win them over. However, now she refused to count them as friends or allies; she promptly ran away from the hospital, without accepting any proposals for follow-up treatment.

I would like to be able to report that intensive psychotherapeutic work revealed unequivocally that she needed the manipulation and the staff split in order to strengthen her sense of self vis-à-vis an object world. Unfortunately, such neat evidence does not often arise in real-life hospital situations and, at times, we must rely on reasonable speculation. I do know from this patient's psychotherapist that she had frequent blurring of her ego boundaries, evidenced not only by the hallucinations, but also by feelings of depersonalization and occasional loss of a sense of whether she or her therapist were thinking a thought. Division of people into "good" or "bad" had been a constant feature of her life and particularly at times of stress, she felt more comfortable with the "unfriendly" relatives—possibly because of firmer reality-definition. Likewise, finally having maneuvered all the staff into her corner, she abruptly ruptured relations with them. It is quite possible, therefore, that manipulations, object-splits, and disdain for others played an important part in her ability to order herself and her world.

The use of a goal conflict and subsequent manipulation in order to restore ego boundaries may be more direct than the projections and introjections involved in splitting the ambivalence. Mahler and Gosliner (1955) referred to the negativism employed by the developing child in "the process of disengagement from the mother-child symbiosis." With some psychotic patients, this negativism may take the form of a kind of catatonic stubbornness; in better integrated psychotic patients it may take the form of purposely contrived goal conflicts.

Thus we see that the conflict of goals involved in manipulation may have deep, personal, and idiosyncratic meaning to the individual patient. In one man it may mean the difference between intactness and dissolution. In another, it may be chiefly a vehicle for acting-out. For some, the conflicts exist only in their own minds; others go out of their way to set up real conflicts. Others recognize the real conflicts which do exist, and some of these patients utilize the manipulation in an actualizing and adaptive manner to overcome a conflict which may also be a legitimate and realistic difference of opinion or even an injustice.

CHAPTER 4

INTENTIONALITY

The broad problem of intentionality must be limited if it is to be of use to us in the study of manipulation. We shall not consider here the question whether *all* behavior is purposeful or determined, or if some actions are accidental or a result of free will. Nor shall we consider whether all determined behavior is *psychologically* determined, either consciously or unconsciously. While these are intriguing and important questions which must be confronted in order to have a full understanding of intentionality, they are not immediately pertinent to our specific purpose. What occupies our interest in this chapter is the search for a convenient way of thinking about whether an individual intended to influence another person by his behavior—the behavior being a rather global and complex social action.

The major question which will confront us in our clinical work is this: Which influencing behavior shall we call "intentional"? If we remain unaware of the influence, the question never becomes a pratical one. However, if we do become aware of the influence, either because the patient tells us about it or because we feel the pressure of the influence, the question of the patient's intentions does arise.

Not all behavior which influences was necessarily intended to influence, or to influence precisely in the manner in which we may react to it. Ruesch (1959, p. 899) has discussed the place of intention in communication thus: "In discussing communication, communicative intent is frequently confused with communicative effect. Any action, be it word, gesture, or practical implementation, has an impact if it is perceived. Both sender and receiver are influenced by it, regardless of the sender's initial intention. . . . The context, a previous situation, or incidental events may shape the effect of a message as much as the intentional expressions of the sender.

"Frequently, too, verbal communication is identified with intentional expression and non-verbal communication with unintentional expression. Unfortunately, this division cannot be maintained either, and the reverse is often true."

There are several intentions involved here. First, there is the intention to communicate. Some theorists take the position that every expression is an intentional communication. Like Mahl (1968), I do not subscribe to this view. There may be vocalizations, gestures, etc., which do convey meanings to another person, but this does not mean that the one who vocalizes or gestures *intends* to communicate.[1]

Next, even if there has been an intention to communicate, we must determine what the message of the communication was intended to be. One message may be sent and another received. In common parlance, we call this "misunderstanding."

Then there is the question of the intention to influence. The message may be received correctly and the receiver may be influenced, but this does not always mean that the sender *intended* to influence, and it certainly does not mean that the sender intended to influence in the way in which the receiver was influenced. We have a common expression for this disparity also: we say, "His plan backfired."

Now, there are psychiatrists who interpret the intention of the patient in terms of the response it evokes. Thus, if the psychiatrist hears or sees a patient's expression, he may feel that the patient intended to communicate; if the psychiatrist interprets the "meaning" of the expression, he may believe that the patient intended to convey that particular message; if the psychiatrist feels pressure to do something, he may feel that the patient intended to influence. Ruesch, for example, goes on to say (p. 899), "As a matter of fact, the only way to infer intention is to study the impact a message has had, because the conscious intention of the speaker may

1. Freud (1911) distinguished between communication and intention to communicate in his discussion of earliest mental life. "[The infant] betrays its unpleasure, where there is an increase of [internal] stimulus and an absence of satisfaction, by motor discharge of screaming and beating about with its arms and legs, and then it experiences the satisfaction it has hallucinated. [That is, the mother realizes the baby needs something and she cares for it.] Later, as an older child, it learns to employ these manifestations of discharge *intentionally*" (italics mine).

not have been his unconscious intention, and often the speaker himself discovers his own intention only after having observed the impact he has created upon others."

In clinical practice, this view can lead to ludicrous and sometimes antitherapeutic situations. I have often heard clinicians say, "I could feel myself getting angry so I knew the patient was trying to make me mad," or, "I felt attracted to her so I could see she was trying to seduce me." Psychiatric residents, in particular, being unsure of their status in the ward hierarchy, are apt to feel controlled and put-upon by patients, and they frequently think this feeling is evidence that the patient is manipulating.

But, suppose that our patient is in (say) a patient-staff conference, and he addresses himself to an issue which does not directly involve either Dr. A or Dr. B. Dr. A responds with anger while Dr. B does not. What, then, can we say about the patient's intention? Did he really want to make Dr. A angry but not Dr. B? Possibly, but then again, perhaps Dr. A is too sensitive, or is displacing his anger from another patient. The impact on Dr. A may be misleading in terms of the patient's intentions—even in terms of his "unconscious intentions." We sometimes employ a curious double standard in psychiatry. When a doctor interprets a patient's intentions in terms of the impact on him, we call it "clinical intuition"; when the patient interprets the doctor's intentions on the basis of the impact on him, we call it "projection" or even "paranoia."

Should we abandon the use of the impact on the observer as an indication of the intention of the patient? Of course not—without an impact we could never be aware of the intention. Often it is the impact that provides the doctor with the first clue about the patient's intention.[2] But, while communication may be an interpersonal phenomenon, intentionality is an intrapsychic phenomenon. Whether one communicates is a matter involving two

2. This situation of inferring the patient's intention on the basis of the feelings of the therapist has been discussed by the followers of Melanie Klein in their descriptions of projective identification—a process whereby the patient is supposed to project part of his impulses on to the analyst (in a real sense—i.e., an actual communication), thus inducing that impulse (or its emotional derivatives) in the analyst. Heimann (1950, p. 83) for example, wrote: "The analyst's counter-transference is not only part and parcel of the analytic relationship, but it is the patient's *creation,* it is part of the patient's personality" (italics mine).

or more people; whether one *intends* to communicate is a matter involving the psychic state of the individual (although this psychic state may be determined in part by situational factors). Thus, we must look to the patient to check our intuition and to verify our impressions about his intentions. We must hear from him what he intended.

Admittedly, this is not always easy to do. At times, the patient may readily reveal his intentions. At other times, it may take prolonged questioning and probing to elicit the information, as in the case of our social psychologist described in chapter 1. And, at times, particularly with manipulators whose actions are based on deceptions, a frank statement of intention may never be elicited. Much depends, of course, on the atmosphere surrounding our inquiry. If it is a contentious and potentially punitive one, if we are *accusing* the patient of intentionality, he is less likely to acknowledge it. If we can encourage a working alliance (Greenson, 1965) and convey an interest in the patient's intentionality as a psychological phenomenon to be understood, we are more likely to learn about his intentions. As with many intrapsychic phenomena, whether the patient intended to influence or not may often not be revealed to us. We may postulate intention on the part of the patient on the basis of the impact, and whatever other evidence is available, but we must be less certain of our understanding of the patient without confirmation from him. Unfortunately, we cannot always take his assertion of intentionality at face value either. Again, much depends on the relationship we have developed with the patient.

Now let us look a bit further at intentionality in order to arrive at a common understanding of what psychic phenomenon the word connotes. Indeed, the words "intent" and "deliberately" are often used in the current psychiatric literature with virtually no attention given to their meanings. This was not always the case. "Intent" and "deliberately" imply volition, and volition (will) was a major area of study in the psychology of William James (1907).[3] To a great extent, the study of volition has become outmoded. As psychoanalysis threw light on unconscious mechanisms,

---

3. It is striking how, without the benefit of a psychoanalytic psychology, James discussed many of the issues which I am about to present. In part, this is due to the conscious nature of intentionality as will be presently discussed.

much which had heretofore appeared spontaneous and "willed" was shown to be directed by unconscious forces. And the psychoanalytic study of the unconscious forces led to a focus on instinctual drives. As Hartmann (1939, p. 74) noted in 1939, "Psychoanalysis, concerned as it is with the regulation by instinctual drives and thinking, has lost sight of the regulation by the will. . . . We know much about the dependence of the will on the needs, but little about its independent, specific psychological significance, though we recognize that it is steered by the external world more than the instinctual drives are."

The study of intentionality was further inhibited by the concept of psychic determinism. If we adopt the view that no behavior is accidental and that all behavior is in part determined by impulses, motives, and wishes, we may come to the conclusion that all behavior is intentional. This conclusion is implicit in the concept of unconscious intentions as expressed, for example, by the statement of Ruesch quoted above: "The conscious intention of the speaker may not have been his *unconscious intention,* and often the speaker himself discovers his own intention only *after* having observed the impact he has created upon others" (italics mine). While this is certainly a tenable position to take, if we do consider all behavior to be intentional, there may be little impetus to focus on intentionality because it does not help us understand differences in behavior.

An alternative approach to the definition of "intentionality" arises from Knight's (1946, p. 255) discussion of determinism and "free will." He pointed out that "determinism is . . . a theoretical construct which fits the observed data, as demonstrated by predictions which were fulfilled. . . . 'Free will,' on the other hand, is not on the same conceptual level as are these constructs. It refers to a *subjective psychological experience"* (italics mine). Free will or choice refers not to a theory of causality, but to an individual's experience of being free to choose.

I propose that we confine the word "intentional" to that behavior which is experienced as voluntary—in great measure freely chosen[4] in Knight's sense of the term "free will." Behaviors which are experienced as accidental or not under one's own control will

---

4. "Free choice" does not mean that the patient feels uninfluenced by other factors such as the obligations to or the demands of his environment. It refers to his feeling that, given the circumstances, *he* is deciding to act.

not be considered intentional. This is not to say that they are not motivated or do not serve some purpose both in terms of the internal psychic economy and the social situation. The intentional aspect of an action may be only the smallest aspect; unconscious guiding and regulating processes are of very great importance, but let us not call them "intentions." I suggest that we speak of "wishes," "motives," "aims," and "purposes" which may be conscious or unconscious, but that we reserve the term "intentions" for conscious purposes.

We gain two advantages by having a term reserved for purposes which are experienced as being freely chosen. First, as I showed in chapter 2, whether the desire to influence by deception is admissible to consciousness and whether the patient has the capacity to see or feel himself as actor makes a great deal of difference in the clinical picture he presents. Secondly, as a matter of therapeutic strategy, it is important to assess whether the desire to influence by deception must be so repressed that if we call attention to it our intervention will serve no useful therapeutic purpose and may, instead, drive a wedge between us and our patient. Or conversely, we must try to recognize when the aim to influence by deception and the need to put something over is conscious, as it may be of prime therapeutic importance to focus on those aims and needs.[5]

Thus, I define intentionality as a conscious process and bring it into line with the discussions of volition by James and other psychologists[6] who emphasized the conscious aspects of the process.

The crux of intentionality is not only that it is conscious, but also that it is anticipatory and carries with it the sense of activity. Eissler (1951), in his discussion of malingering, acknowledged the role of consciousness, and he put considerable emphasis on "the attitude of deliberate and persistent planning."

Not all anticipatory thought is conscious. For example, Freud (1926) described the thought processes which produce phobic

5. These therapeutic issues will be discussed in chapters 13 and 14.
6. See, for example, Murphy (1947) and Rapaport (1951). Rapaport specified that the consciousness involved in "willing" is *waking* consciousness. "The more closely the dream state is approximated, the less it is possible to exert voluntary effort" (p. 29).

anxiety as unconscious. In essence, the unconscious thought of his example can be schematized this way: If I gratify my desire to compete with my father for my mother, I will be castrated. Therefore, I shall avoid my father and thus escape his revenge. Here, the unconscious anticipatory thought has to do with avoiding father. However, the anticipatory thought of which I speak in intentionality is not this unconscious anticipation; it is the conscious anticipatory thought which we call "planning" and "deliberation" to which I refer. In the example of the phobia, the fear of the father is displaced by fear of an animal. While the child remains unaware of his Oedipal conflict and his fear of a castrating father, he becomes very much aware of his fear of animals and he deliberately plans to avoid them. In the example of the phobia, then, the anticipatory component of the *intentional* act is not the unconscious contents of the Oedipal drama but the conscious plan to stay away from the street where the feared animal is.

The other central feature of intentionality is the sense of activity. This feeling, of course, is intimately bound up with consciousness and anticipatory thought.

The many uses (and misuses) of the concepts of activity and passivity were described explicitly by Schafer (1968b) who pointed out that these concepts can be examined from various points of view. In terms of instinctual aims, we speak of Freud's (1915a) "polarities": if the aim of the instinctual drive is to act upon the object, it is active; if the aim is for the individual to be acted upon by the object, it is passive. Another context described by Schafer is in terms of psychic structure (e.g., the ego being passive with respect to demands of the id). A third context is in terms of object relationships. A helpless, dependent person craves a passive and receptive relationship with others. The fourth context, and the one of prime importance in the present discussion, is subjective experience, while the fifth context is trauma—that is, to what degree a trauma was experienced because of internal factors (active) as opposed to external factors (passive).

Now, if we do not define our viewpoint when we discuss activity and passivity, we can become hopelessly confused. Freud (1932, p. 115) implicitly recognized this when he wrote about the passive aims in femininity: "To achieve a passive aim may call for a large amount of activity." And Rapaport (1953, p. 537) cautioned, "In the description of (activity and passivity), the dynamic condition of activity and passivity and the patient's subjective experience of them must be kept apart. While the two often coincide, they must never be unquestioningly equated."

What we are concerned with in intentionality is the sense or subjective experience of activity. Thus, a patient may be aware of his activity in influencing someone (intentional) or he may be unaware of his part in the influence (unintentional). From other points of view, the patient may indeed have played an active role in influencing the other person—he may have unconsciously wished to bring about the influence—but, if he has been unaware of his activity, if he does not *feel* active, we will not call the activity "intentional."

This sense of activity is a global phenomenon. In the terms of our discussion, intentionality involves a sense of *doing* something to achieve a *goal*—that is, both a consciousness of activity in the motility and the setting of the goal (result). However, many of the minute component activities which comprise the global action depend on preconscious automatisms (Hartmann, 1939). Separately these components carry no *sense* of activity and are thus not intentional.

We use forms of the word "intention" in two ways. We call an action (present or past) "intentional," and we also say that we "intend" to do a future action. We may not carry out this future action, but we may still have intended to do it. Thus, intentionality does not depend on the carrying out of the activity. In the future sense of the word, the sense of activity does not accompany action; rather it is a sense of future activity. The person says, "I have planned this, and *I* will carry it out."

The role of consciousness, anticipatory thought, and sense of activity in intentionality can be illustrated by contrasting two patients. The first patient had great difficulty with intentionality. She was a middle-aged high school teacher who had had a long-standing feeling of listlessness and bleakness. Although she was able to be reasonably effective in her teaching, she felt that she had a severe work inhibition. She had many ideas for teaching and for further studies which she could not muster the energy to implement. Her home life was filled with arguments with her husband upon whose physical presence she seemed to depend in order to function at all. For example, if she had to grade papers and her husband took a nap, she was incapable of functioning and she bitterly resented his lack of consideration. It was not that he actually helped her with the papers; when he was asleep, she ran out of energy.

The husband was a man of extraordinarily low self-esteem. He constantly berated himself for not being able to support his wife and live up to her demands on his time and energy. Then, every once in a while, he would explode in a temper tantrum ("I can't take it any more; you'll drive me crazy") and storm out of the house to stay with a friend for awhile. During his absences, the patient would be in what could best be described as a kind of suspended animation; she was dulled, and she plodded through day after day with wistful fantasies of "someday, somehow" finding a more satisfactory husband. She did not lose her ability to function: she still taught, kept house (as well as usual), cooked and ate meals, etc. However, it was as if she were "on automatic pilot"; ordinarily her life was bleak and routine, but when her husband was absent, it was like being in a daze.

During one of these separations, the patient acknowledged her longing for her husband's return. The idea of calling him occurred to her, but she never seriously considered it. She hoped he would call her, but it was a wistful hope; she really didn't expect that he would, and she had no idea of how they would be reunited. She knew they would come back together as they always had in the past, but she could not imagine the *process* of coming back together.

During the next session, the patient said she had received a gift from her mother. The gift, a casserole dish, had arrived in the mail quite unexpectedly. What was remarkable was the fact that the patient had not spoken to her mother in over a year. Whenever the mother telephoned, the husband answered, and it was understood that the patient would not talk to her. In fact, the patient never answered the telephone in order to make sure that she would not be faced with talking to her mother. There had not been a definable argument—rather a drifting away; it was as if an "understanding" had developed that there would be no direct communication. Thus it was all the more striking that her mother, who had tacitly accepted and complied with this arrangement, suddenly sent the casserole dish—something the patient had needed and wanted for a long time but could not buy for herself. The patient reported that she was very pleased with the gift and had had thoughts of calling her mother to thank her and perhaps even to resume a more cordial relationship with her. These were just passing thoughts, however; the patient could not actually go to the telephone and make the call.

The remainder of the hour centered around the themes of the emptiness of the house and her life with her husband away. Should she call him? She wished he'd call her. This was really her chance to meet another man, now that her husband was away; someone who would really love her and take care of her. But it would never happen; it was only a dream.

In the following session, the patient told me that her husband had called. "I was afraid to answer the phone—I was afraid it might be my mother. But then I thought, 'What if it's my husband?' If it were my mother, I could hang up. When I heard my husband's voice, I was very pleased that he had called. But then he spoiled it all. He asked me if I wanted him back home and that spoiled everything." The patient explained that she wished he were home, but she couldn't tell him to come home. In their usual manner of talking past each other, the question of whether he would return that day was left unsettled.

Another disturbing thing happened during the telephone conversation. The patient had told her husband about the casserole dish, and the husband informed her that he had told her mother some time ago that she needed one. This "ruined" the gift. It was no longer a spontaneous action of her mother's; it was as if she, through her husband, had asked for it.

When we examine this series of events from the standpoint of the patient's intentionality, we see that the problem was not one of not knowing what she wanted (although she sometimes put it that way). She knew what she wanted. She wanted the casserole dish and she wanted her husband back. Moreover, these wishes were conscious. In our subsequent discussion, it was not difficult to establish that her pleasure at having these various wishes satisfied came as no surprise to her. She had known all along what she wanted. Her problem was that she could not actively seek the gratification; it had to come to her without her participation.

Now, there are some psychiatrists, proceeding from a transactional point of view, who would call this patient an extremely able manipulator. They would focus on her passive needs, or her need to maintain herself in the dependent position. By presenting herself as "indecisive," they would say, she influences others to do things for her and to give her things. This would be very much like Freud's description of activity in the service of passive aims.

There is no doubt that our patient participated in a communicative process, and that people were influenced to satisfy her wishes. But while she did consciously wish for the results, it is very unlikely that she intended to influence others to grant her wishes. Indeed, it was especially clear when we discussed her wish to have her husband back home that she could not consciously anticipate any process designed to bring this goal about. She could not attend to the question of *doing,* she could not plan. In contrast to the manipulator, who gloats (openly or secretly) over the masterful way he has handled a situation, this patient lost her pleasure in the satisfaction of her wishes whenever she learned that she might have played a part in obtaining the satisfaction. Satisfactions had to be given spontaneously, without any sense of activity on her part. Thus, the communication of her desires, while sometimes effective, was not intentional.

Impairment of the patient's sense of activity was displayed in many facets of her behavior. Most striking were her reports of how she depended on her husband to be awake in order for her to do work. When he was asleep, all her energy was gone. She had no clear sense of self; a symbiotic relationship with her husband provided her with the ability to act. When she was away from him geographically, but not emotionally, she could still use some of his (their) intentionality; when there was an emotional breach or he was obviously asleep (gone), her intentionality was severely crippled.

The patient's mother was a dreaded object, seen as a seductive and destructive woman with an all-devouring mouth. The patient had to keep emotional distance between herself and her mother in order to preserve some sense of boundary between them. Otherwise, the mother would be introjected, and the patient would become evilly purposive, conniving, and destructive. This was one of the genetic and dynamic elements involved in her battle against activity; to be active from within was to be propelled by the introject of her mother with all its destructive consequences.

We may contrast this schoolteacher with a businessman who came to analysis because of multiple problems in his marriage. He sensed his inability to love and his need to provoke an endless series of confrontations with his wife; he could no more let her love him than he could love her.

He was quite successful in business, and he derived special pleasure from business deals wherein he had tricked his adversary. This tendency to play tricks on people pervaded his personal life as well. He recalled with relish such schoolboy pranks as handing in to his teacher a paper which had considerable literary merit. It was only after the paper was displayed on the bulletin board that the class became aware that the initial letters of each line combined to spell out an obscene condemnation of the teacher.

He loved to use other people, both for what he could get out of them and for the pleasure of "besting" them. During one hour, he explained his late arrival by telling me how he had arranged to have luncheon with someone, not because he enjoyed his company, but because he knew the other man would like to play the part of the gentleman by picking up the check and offering to give my patient a ride. In the same hour, he recounted how as a youth he had a girl friend who lived across town. Not having a car, he used to visit another boy who lived near him. He did not like this boy, but after a short visit, he could persuade the boy to drive him to the girl friend's house.

These tendencies to manipulate were woven into the course of the analysis as well. He saw the entire treatment as a kind of secret defeat of both his wife and me. While he would spin intellectual delights, his dreams were filled with absurdities which showed his laughter at the analysis. This laughter was not unconscious; he readily acknowledged his attempts to fool me and was astounded and dismayed by my "coolness" when I did not respond with anger or throw him out.

He used to play a "game" during the early years of the analysis. When he became convinced that he could not provoke me with his contempt, he would lapse into silence to wait for me to say something. Or he would say something with a double meaning, apparently oblivious to the second meaning, hoping that I would pick it up. Then he would laugh because I thought I was so clever in detecting the hidden meaning when he not only knew it all the time but had purposely set it up.

What is important for our discussion at this point is the fact that he did all these things consciously. He planned them, he enjoyed them, he felt active in setting up the situations, and was proud of his ability to tease and to use others in this manner. In contrast to our schoolteacher, the businessman intended to influence the other person.

Here, as in all behavior, there were aspects which were unintended. The unconscious wishes involved in rape fantasies, the Oedipal wishes underlying the fear of loss of power, the anal pleasures in "dumping" on the other person, and the unconscious themes more specifically underlying the need to put something over on other people—themes which will be described in chapter 6 —were all present as repressed wishes serving to impel his behavior; these were not intentions. But the maneuvering in order to place the other person in an inferior position was intentional.

To recapitulate, then, intention is one kind of purpose. It is conscious and involves conscious anticipatory thought and a sense of activity.

Now, most of our clinical situations are far less clear-cut than these illustrations. In some cases, the desire to influence, while not actually conscious during the course of the activity, is reasonably accessible for consciousness. In some of these situations, the desire easily becomes conscious, and when it does, it is firmly grasped and the patient has no difficulty in feeling that he intended to influence. However, we often encounter other situations where the desire to influence comes into consciousness only fleetingly— either spontaneously, as a consequence of our pointing it out, or when the patient has observed the result. In these situations, the patient may have a conscious grasp of his purpose, but it is as if he cannot hold on to it long enough to integrate it usefully into his conscious sense of self.

A bright and pretty teenager with a fresh, lively personality was in psychoanalysis with me. She had been in both individual and group therapy for brief periods before coming to me. Thus, she had picked up considerable intellectual knowledge about subtle messages that transpire between people. Indeed, she and some of her friends seemed to enjoy "analyzing" each other's motivations: it was like a game to see who was cleverest or quickest.

Early in her treatment, she began one hour by telling me that when she was sitting in the waiting room she had been thinking of how her dress had "hiked up" in the back as she sat down. When I had come into the waiting room, she had gathered her packages and coat to bring them into the consulting room with her. It now occurred to her that her dress might have "hiked up" when she leaned over to pick up the packages. "Not that I would care if you'd see my beautiful legs." She laughed sarcastically at the word "beautiful" because she did not feel that she had a good figure. She felt that she had a chunky, unattractive build. "But," she continued, "what if I want to be seductive? No, I wouldn't want to be seductive towards you, that would be just awful. If I was being seductive, it wouldn't be conscious, but I wouldn't even want to do it subconsciously."

She went on to talk about her current boy friend. She was losing interest in him as she had lost interest in a string of boy friends before him. It seemed that whenever a boy friend became interested in her, her own interest waned. She no longer found him sexually attractive, and she became bored when he became passionate.

Her thoughts then turned to a girl friend, Emma Carlon. Emma had recently met a young man whom she found interesting. She had phoned him when he was out, and had told his roommate to tell him that Emma Carlon had called. The young man had received the message incorrectly, and when he dialed the number, he asked for Mr. M. Carlon. Emma responded by saying it was she, Emma, who had placed the call. The young man acknowledged that he had thought it might be she, but he had returned the call in the manner in which he had received the message. Emma had been quite distraught, feeling that he had known all along it was she, but for some reason of his own he was playing a trick on her. My patient mused about this for awhile, finally deciding that the young man had not intended to play a trick; it was an error, not intentional.

Other topics were brought up, all related to the issue of whether effects were really intended. I pointed out her concern about intending to do things.

"Especially tricky things," she responded. "I don't like to lie or deceive people. Look at me," she continued, "I really pursued my boy friend. I thought I wanted him more than anything in the world, and then when he responds, I lose interest. Isn't this tricky? And yet I say I don't like to deceive people. I don't know, I don't mean for it to work out this way, it just does. I don't want to tease. My mother tells me when I was a little girl, I used to tease my brother, but now I wouldn't consciously tease anyone."

After a thoughtful pause, she went on. "Yes, I guess I do manipulate my environment for my own ends. I guess I do pursue men; every time I conquer one boy friend, I lose interest and turn to another. I make them want me, and then I don't want them anymore."

Another pause, and then she remembered the Duke of Windsor. How touching his abdication speech had been. He could not reign as king without the woman he loved. He gave up his throne for love. "That would never happen to me."

And then, "Already I'm looking at another boy. I'm sure I'll meet him and then it will all start over again. In ten years, I'll leave a string of men behind. I do love them at the time. And then they fall in love with me, and I lose interest."

Now, what was this girl's attitude toward men? Did she wish to lure them and then crush them? Did she want to tease, to influence them by arousing their interest in order to deflate them by withdrawing hers? Did she wish to be deceitful and cruel? The answer to these questions must be "yes." Not only did the wish show up in the repetitive theme of the hour—seduction, trickery, teasing, and the sacrifice of the king's throne, but subsequent events in the treatment made very plain her intense rivalry with men and her desire to use her "femininity" as a weapon in her competition with them. In part, her penis envy had led to intense phallic strivings, and she was driven to make men impotent.

She *wished* to do all these things, but did she *intend* to do them? Most of the time she did not. Often, she had not the slightest inkling of what she was doing or how provocative her behavior was. It was only much later in the treatment, for example, that she realized how often she drew my attention to her body, and how she resented the fact that I did not respond. It later became apparent that she really wanted me to "interpret" her behavior, and then she would come up with faster and cleverer interpretations.

We can understand the state of her intentionality by examining her anticipatory thought and her sense of activity. Often, neither were present. She usually felt quite involved with her boy friends at the outset and was not aware of how the relationship would develop, let alone her attempt to create the teasing situation. It had begun to dawn on her, however, how repetitive her relationships were. In addition, her friends had "interpreted" her behavior to her. The hour discussed above is remarkable for its vacillation; now she knows what she does, now she doesn't, now she employs negation—"I don't want to tease." She ended the hour with good evidence of anticipatory thought; she knew what would happen. But there was no real sense of activity. These things were beyond her control; she was involved in them, but she was not doing them. Very often this is the situation when patients employ negation. Freud (1925) pointed out that in negation much of the work of repression goes on; only the ideational content of the repressed is admitted into conscious. Affective components may still be repressed, and, in terms of our discussion, the wish remains repressed, and there is no consciousness of a feeling of active participation.

The condition in negation is often reproduced by premature interpretations, whether given by a psychiatrist or by members of a therapeutic group. The patient may become aware of the content of repressed wishes and thus may be able to experience anticipatory thought. But because the affect and sense of activity are lacking, the behavior may show no change—indeed, how could it change? The patient can see the consequences, she may even *know* that she does these things, but she does not *feel* that she does these things.

This very common situation falls within the grey area referred to in our discussion of consciousness in chapter 2. When the conscious grasp of the desire to influence is as fleeting as it was in the case of this teenager, we can see that there must be some active mental forces seeking to keep it out of consciousness—albeit forces not so strong as if she were unable to have any inkling of her desire altogether. It is when we analyze her consciousness in terms of anticipatory thoughts and sense of activity that we see how little intentionality she has. At times she may know what she is doing, but the firm and enduring sense of the self which is doing it is lacking. This is why if we tell her she is "manipulating" she may "see" what we mean and, if she is compliant, may agree with us; however, there is little prospect that this clarification will have any generalized effect on her behavior.

There will be many clinical "grey area" situations where we will be hard-pressed to say whether the patient has sufficiently integrated the anticipatory thought and the sense of activity into a firm and enduring self-image that we can term the purpose, the "intention," and the act a "manipulation." Often, however, our therapeutic task in these situations is clear. It lies not in a premature labeling of the act as "manipulative"; rather we continue our policy of not being influenced—in this case not being sexually interested or in engaging in a contest of interpretive skills—and we try to explore with the patient those mental forces which prevent her purposes from becoming intentions. For an unconscious purpose is pressing for conscious expression; if the need is not gratified, it may press even harder. And if we can help the patient come to grips with the dangers which prevent the purpose from becoming an intention, an enduring conscious understanding and feeling of the purpose may emerge. At this point we can discuss the act as intentional and perhaps as manipulative.

In our young woman, the theme of activity and passivity was a central one. In the hour, she frequently raised the question of whether things were done intentionally (active) or by error or accident (passive). Again, this was a consciousness of the content of activity without the appreciation of being active. To *be* active for her was to acknowledge her phallic strivings which in turn would expose her to the pain of her penis envy. She was not ready for this as yet. She could only allow herself to behave in an active manner if she waived the feeling of activity.

Thus, at the point of this hour, we could say that while she wished to use and abuse men, she did not intend to do so, and thus she was not manipulative within our definition. During the course of treatment, it is at the point that the wish becomes the intention that the process of working through and internal change can take place.

This view of intentionality and manipulation has sometimes led to a misunderstanding among hospital staff personnel. Confronted with a patient who feels himself helpless, they may label him a "manipulator." While he may not be manipulating in the sense of the word as used in this book, this conclusion should not necessarily lead us to cater to his helplessness. Indeed, as I have suggested above, even if the need for attention and being cared for is not conscious, it may be wise not to gratify the need in order that it may emerge more clearly. In addition, to gratify it may be to perpetuate it. As we shall see in chapter 13, I do not propose that we oppose all manipulations or gratify all those needs which are not manipulations.

Now, our interest in intentionality is focused on its role in manipulation, or more specifically, on the attempt to influence others in order to resolve a goal conflict to one's advantage. Confronted with a conflict of goals, a patient's reaction may be primarily autoplastic (producing a change in himself) or alloplastic (producing a change in the outside world). Among the autoplastic changes, he may gratify his wish in his dream or fantasy life or he may develop a symptom which expresses both the wish and its prohibition. If he is psychotic he may disavow reality and fail to realize that there is opposition to his wish, or he may satisfy his wish through delusions or hallucinations. In yet another autoplastic reaction, the patient may put aside his wish and yield to the other person's desire, i.e. *he* may be influenced.

While the autoplastic reactions de-emphasize intentionality, the alloplastic solutions involve the intentional carrying out of work to resolve the goal conflict by changing others.

What are the factors which determine whether an alloplastic solution will be employed? It must be clear by now that intentionality is a function of the ego, and whether a patient will intend to influence another is governed in great part by the ego's relationship to the id, superego, and reality (Freud, 1923). Reality factors are inherent in the various systems and subsystems in which the patient finds himself, and thus they must be analyzed from a transactional point of view. This aspect will be examined more thoroughly in chapter 8. One example will be cited here for illustrative purposes. We can look at a rather typical attempt at manipulation seen in student health services—the student who wants to be excused from class just before vacation despite the fact that the college requires attendance. He might confront his professor directly, but he knows that herein lies an unyielding reality. Perhaps the health service might be more compliant. Maybe, if he goes to the infirmary early in the morning, complaining (falsely) of a sore throat, the doctor will advise him to rest and not to go to class. If the doctor on call is known to yield easily to these requests, the patient is likely to use him in the manipulation; he will influence the professor by influencing (through deception) the easier object, the doctor. On the other hand, if the infirmary is known to refuse virtually all such requests, the student will suppress his intentionality and go to class—i.e., yield to the professor in the conflict of goals. While in class, he may ignore the lecture and daydream about where he really would like to be. The intention has been replaced, in part, by a fantasy. Thus, the degree of alloplasticity depends partly on the pliability of the environment.

The id and superego play an important role in determining whether there will be intentionality. Our businessman illustrated this quite clearly. Although generally successful and manipulative, he did suffer occasional periods of work-inhibition. These became more pronounced during one period of his analysis. As he became more aware of his jealousy of my women patients, it began to dawn on him that many of his manipulative provocations were in the service of getting me to take care of him as a man takes care of a woman. Simultaneously, he began to realize that he wanted to stir my wrath so that I would verbally attack him as he had imagined his father had angrily attacked his mother in intercourse. As his passive-feminine longings threatened to erupt into consciousness, he manipulated (intended) more and more furiously. Then he began to feel guilty in part because of the aggressiveness underlying his behavior. The provocations stopped, and he became anergic and sleepy on the couch. At one point, he unwittingly rubbed his eye. I called this to his attention, and he immediately thought of his childhood fear that if he used his eyes too much he might damage them. Although during this period his work-inhibition was accompanied by a marked diminution in sexual activity with his wife and his masturbating activity, it was not until much later that the Oedipal wishes and castration anxiety which underlay the waxing and waning of his intentionality became conscious. Even at this point, however, he became aware of his fear that to *do,* to *act,* was to risk punishment just as looking (at this time looking was accompanied by a sense of activity) was to risk damage to the active organ. The passive role was far safer, but now he could not even actively pursue it. Thus, the intentionality involved in the manipulation was bound up in the vicissitudes of his Oedipal wishes and guilt.[7]

Schafer (1968b) has shown us that self-representation is central to intentionality. He has pointed out that the sense of activity is dependent on the existence of stable internalizations. With well-established identifications there is a firm representation of self; thus there is a self which can act (a representation of self which can experience volition or intention). Individuals with less stable internalizations tend to feel at the mercy of inconstant introjects and have difficulty pulling together an "I" who can intend. We have seen this phenomenon earlier in this chapter in the description of the schoolteacher whose intentionality was most severely impaired when her husband was absent.

Self-representation, of course, goes hand in hand with self-object differentiation and the relationship to reality. We recall the discussion in chapter 2 which described how manipulations (involving intentionality) are sometimes used to define boundaries between self and object and how a conflict of goals may be necessary to preserve or strengthen the self-object distinction. The clinical implication here is that manipulations may often be indicative of (or in the service of) the patient's attempt to organize his sense of self. The theoretical implication is that we see a confluence of several ego-functions: self-representation, reality-testing, and intentionality.

---

7. I have selected this particular theme out of the complex of determinants involved in this patient's intentionality for illustrative purposes. Of course, conflicts from other psychosexual stages are also represented in the behavior. Nor do I mean to imply that intentionality must proceed from feelings of masculinity. One woman, near the end of her analysis, became increasingly intentional as she realized she *did* have a sexual organ—a vagina—and that this organ was useful and could be used.

We may add one further ego-function to this confluence—the state of consciousness. I have stressed that intentionality depends on consciousness—the consciousness of anticipatory thought and the sense of activity. Rapaport (1951), using himself as the subject, attempted to record his impressions of dreams, hypnogogic hallucinations, and reveries while remaining in as drowsy a state as possible. He noted that "writing under these conditions becomes, to a considerable extent, automatic. . . . The hand writes without any subjectively experienced decision or intent. . . . The more closely the dream state is approximated, the less it is possible to exert voluntary effort" (pp. 27 ff.). Schafer (1968b), too, noted the relation between the sense of activity to the state of consciousness.

Elsewhere (Bursten, 1967) I have put forth the hypothesis that the infant emerges from the undifferentiated state to a great extent by virtue of motility. Motility invites the cathexis of bodily boundary which may serve as the basis for psychic structure-building as well as self-object differentiation. In that essay, I referred also to some evidence that motility is involved in progression from one kind of dream state to another or to wakefulness. Thus motility, which underlies the development of intentionality, also may underlie the state of self-representation, reality-testing, and consciousness. Indeed, further study may show that we are not talking about four ego-functions but four aspects of one ego-function, and that alterations in one aspect are accompanied by alterations in all. Thus the state of consciousness, firmness of self-representation, and reality-testing may depend on the dynamic interplay of forces affecting intentionality.

A clinical example may illustrate this interplay. In her first year of therapy with me, a young borderline salesgirl who had had previous psychotic episodes became less and less able to talk. She began to bring in samples of automatic writing. She described states where, sitting at her desk, her hand would write without her guidance, and it was only later, on reading the material, that she realized what she had written. The subject matter centered around an accusation that she was a bad child, but she could not say why. The episodes sounded like dissociative reactions, but other examples of disturbed reality-testing indicated that her ego-functioning was indeed precarious. At times she knew where she was but was unable to do what she wanted to do. At other times, she had frightening experiences of unreality. Although she had been in similar states from time to time previously, she was alarmed about the fact that, since starting therapy, they had once again become frequent and pronounced.

I suggested that the automatic writing or drawing might help provide a clue to her present difficulties, and she eagerly accepted my suggestion to set up an easel for use in the hours if she wished.

Her initial drawings were full of self-condemnation and "shit for brains" pictures of herself. Blood and knives were often featured. Much of her hate, based partly on an introject of a dangerous mother, was reprojected on to me, and at times she left the office in terror, afraid that I would harm her.

Soon, her drawing activity diminished and her difficulty in intentionality came more into focus. She was unable to turn the page of the drawing pad. She asked me to turn it in what at first appeared to be a manipulation—a feigning of inability in order to "make" me treat her as "sick," or to evoke pity. It soon became apparent that she was terrified of turning the page for fear she might tear it.

Then began a period where she would start the hour by asking, "What do you want to do today?" The hour was punctuated with such questions as, "What do you want to talk about?" or "What would you like me to draw?" During this period, also, she often had to ask me if she had actually done such-and-such or had just thought it. A variant was, "Did I say that, or did you say it?"

One day she recounted an intense episode of derealization which had occurred the previous evening. She was changing clothes preparing for a relaxing evening at home when a "fog" came over her, and she became confused. She was unreal, objects in the room were unreal, and for a while she had no sense of being able to do anything. Having described this episode, she talked briefly about current events in her life and then lapsed again into the "What do you want me to do?" pattern. I commented on her need to have thoughts and ideas come from me rather than from her. She said that she had become less and less competent over the past year; she used to be a very creative person. I said that her coming into therapy seemed to be related to her shutting off her creativity and competence; in part this must reflect her struggle to avoid becoming aware of her inner thoughts. She acknowledged (as she had on other occasions) that there was something seductive about therapy and that asking me to set the therapeutic stage was a way of avoiding the temptation to reveal herself.

I then brought her back to the incident of the previous evening. "What," I asked, "were you changing into?" She said she was changing from a dress into slacks. I pointed out that her wish for a penis and her need to conceal this wish played an important role in her ability to intend. It was as if she saw having a penis as being competent; by renouncing activity and competency, she was concealing her wish and was parading her "disguise" of being a girl.

She listened attentively and then suffered a few moments of intense embarrassment. After much hesitation, she told me of two childhood events. One was a fantasy of standing and urinating through a large piece of macaroni which could protrude through the unzipped fly of her dungarees. The other was her secret childhood practice of stuffing one of her father's condoms to make an artificial penis. She would secure this "penis" to her pubic region and conceal it under her dress, thus appearing in public as a girl—but with a secret penis.

These, then, were some of the dynamics underlying her loss of intentionality. And with the loss of intentionality came alterations in her state of consciousness, reality-testing, and representation of self. One might postulate that the anxiety generated by the threat of awareness of her infantile wishes in some way produced a disintegration of these ego-functions. But it may well be that the anxiety is ancillary to the process, and that the restriction of intentionality involves the alteration of these "other" functions because they are not "other functions" at all, but all aspects of the same function.[8] And it may be that self-object differentiation involving manipulation, such as I described in chapter 3, may depend in great part on the dynamics of intentionality. Thus, intentionality, which is central to my definition of manipulation, is central as well to much of ego psychology.

8. It is interesting to speculate whether psychotic episodes precipitated by homosexual or aggressive panics may also be examples of dynamic shifts in intentionality.

CHAPTER 5

DECEPTION

A favorite story of mine relates that many years ago two men from the same small town in Russia were bitter enemies. One day, they found themselves sitting near each other on a train. "Where are you going?" asked the first man.

"I'm going to Minsk," grunted the second.

"Ha!" shouted the first man gleefully. "I happen to know from a reliable source that you really are going to Minsk. But you're telling me you're going to Minsk so I'll think you're going to Pinsk. So! Why are you such a liar?"

Was the second man lying? What is lying and how does it relate to deception? If lying is the verbal expression of the negation of the truth, then the second man was not lying; he was telling the truth. If, as Eck (1965, p. 25) maintained, lying is the putting forth of "an untruthful proposition (or the equivalent of a proposition, e.g., writing or gesture) with the intention of inducing another into error," then our Russian was not lying; the information he was expressing was accurate.

And what about the first man—was he lying? He did not make a statement at all; he asked a question. But in asking that question, he made the *implicit* statement, "I don't know where you are going"—a statement which was patently untrue. Nonetheless, there was no verbal expression of untruth.

Consider now this childhood joke: "They say that George Washington, father of our country, never told a lie. But he really did, you know. When he chopped down the cherry tree, his father asked him who did it. He answered, 'Pop, I did it!' and Popeye wasn't even living then."

Is an ambiguity a lie? Did George Washington verbalize a truth or an untruth in the story? Or did he do both simultaneously?

Are there lies of omission? If a teacher asks her class who rolled the marble down the aisle, and the culprit remains silent, is he lying, despite the fact that there has been no verbalization at all? And what about the rest of the class—is their silence a lie? Eck continues (p. 34), "To lie is to refuse to tell the truth to someone who has the right to hear it."

Of course, the answers to these and many similar questions rest on one's definition of lying. I prefer to distinguish between a lie and a deception. I define lying as the expression of an untruth with the intent to deceive. Deceiving is the intentional setting up of circumstances in order that the other person will not possess sufficient knowledge of the reality of the situation to allow him successfully to pursue his goal. As nearly as possible, these definitions are worded in psychological rather than in moral terms.

Lying, then, is seen as one kind of deception. It is not merely dependent on the verbalization of an untruth. Indeed, when we see the actor on the stage, he utters all kinds of untruths. "I come to bury Caesar," proclaims the man portraying Mark Antony, but he knows and we know that Caesar was buried years ago and that his words deny reality. However, this is acting and not lying; the actor is not trying to deceive the listener. He is not trying to deprive us of realistic knowledge in order to prevent us from successfully pursuing our goal. Our goal is not to see Caesar buried; if it were, the actor would be lying. Our goal is to enjoy the play and to be put in a certain mood. The actor distorts reality in order to help us realize our goal.

Another area where we see verbal distortion of reality is in the use of tact and social convention. The polite expressions we voice almost automatically every day are not to be taken at face value. The busy executive may become irritated at a visitor who talks on and on. Finally, with both tact and firmness, the executive stands up, opens the door and says, "It's been very nice having this talk with you." The statement itself is not true, but neither is it a lie as the term is used here, because there is no real attempt at deception. Both men know that the words are being used as a signal for the visit to end: it is a social convention used by both parties, and the visitor realizes he is being politely dismissed. Indeed, if deception were likely in this situation, the visitor, thinking the executive really enjoyed the talk, might be impelled to prolong his stay in order to give his host even more enjoyment. Then, the executive would have to be more blunt: "That's all the time I have," or more truthfully, "Get out and stop bothering me!" But the social convention works and the message gets across with a modicum of harmony between the two parties.

A college professor recently told me of an amusing social convention. "At Yale," he said, "When you're no longer interested in talking to someone, you say, 'We must have lunch together sometime.' That's the Yale 'Good-bye!' "

Of course, tact and social convention can also be used in the service of deceit, and then it becomes a lie. If the executive, for example, has been interviewing the visitor with reference to the latter's application for a job, the executive may have various reasons for not wishing to turn the man down directly. He may wish to make the applicant feel that he has a real chance even though another man may already have been selected. This occurs quite frequently, for instance, with government jobs under civil service regulations where all qualified applicants must be reviewed even though there has been a favorite contender all along. Then, the executive's "It's been nice talking with you, we'll be in touch" is more than a social convention; it may be a lie, and it certainly is a deception intended to make the applicant believe that the interview was to be taken seriously.

Returning now to our earlier stories, we see that neither Russian lied—that is, distorted the truth. But both of them tried to deceive. Indeed, as the first Russian remarked, the second man tried to deceive, not by lying, but by telling the truth. As every good poker player knows, the essence of good deception is knowing when to lie and when to tell the truth. The consistent liar will not deceive the same person for long, and given a record of lying, the most effective deception may, at times, be accomplished by telling the truth.

As for the second story, I would consider the "Pop, I—Popeye" ambiguity a lie. The speaker fashions the intentional ambiguity out of not only the truth, but also the distortion of the truth; he means to convey the distorted fact, and he relies on the true fact as a cover or an excuse.

The students (including the culprit) who remain silent when the teacher asks who rolled the marble are deceiving, but not lying, according to my definitions. They have not distorted the truth, but they have set up circumstances whereby the teacher is deprived of sufficient knowledge of the reality of the situation to allow her to discipline the culprit.

The many circumstances and motivations for lying and other deceptions, including situations in which these deceptions might be considered not only justifiable, but even obligatory, are discussed by Eck and by Durandin (1957) and will not be gone into here. Nor is it my purpose to distinguish too finely between lying and not-lying or between lying and other deceptions. The working definitions I have proposed and the examples I have furnished will serve as a platform from which to launch a discussion of the psychological factors involved in deception.

At the outset, we note that deception occurs in a social context, and that a conflict of goals exists between the participants. "Deception is a symptom of social friction," wrote Hartshorne and May (1928, p. 19) at the beginning of their work on deceit. As I said in chapter 3, when we examine the psychology of the deceiver, we are interested in *his* understanding of the conflict of goals, realistic or not. In order to deceive, the individual must be in a psychological position not only to assess the conflict of goals, but also to intuit the other person's goal with a high degree of accuracy. What I describe here was discussed by Fromm-Reichmann (1950, pp. 87 f.) when she considered the role of interpretation in the treatment of antisocial personalities. She wrote, "In psychotherapeutic work with psychopathic personalities, it is indicated that great thriftiness be used with interpretations in all areas. These people make an attempt to counteract their insecurity . . . by compulsively paying lip service to the acceptance of interpretations offered. They try their hand at doing some seemingly astute interpreting of their own as an intellectual maneuver designed to placate the psychiatrist. . . . Their *intellectual alertness and their marked sensitivity to the expectations of others* equip them for it far too well for their own good" (italics mine). While antisocial personalities are frequently masters at deception (and manipulation), I have indicated in chapter 1 that these maneuvers are not limited to any one diagnostic category.

This ability to intuit the other person's goals, this "intellectual awareness and marked sensitivity" is called "empathy." Speaking about the "born psychologist" and the "practical psychologist," Fliess (1942, pp. 212 f.) described empathy as an "ability to put (oneself) in (another's) place, to step into his shoes, and to obtain, in this way, an inside knowledge that is almost first hand." Following Reik (1937), Fliess stressed the importance of this ability in the psychoanalyst; however, in contrast to Reik, Fliess described empathy as "trial identification."

Manipulators, like psychoanalysts, are practical psychologists, although there are crucially significant differences, some of which will be described in chapter 6. Most often, manipulators must be intuitive, they must be empathic, in order to deceive successfully.[1] This empathy does not refer only to an ability to understand the other person's goal (which may be in conflict with his own); the expert deceiver must also be able to intuit the other's character, his interests, his prohibitions, his propensity for guilt, his anxieties, loyalties, etc. For in addition to recognizing the goal conflict, the deceiver uses empathy to fashion the nature of the deception—that is, the technique of influencing the other person. One person will be influenced by an appeal to his vanity, another by an appeal to his ambition or loyalty to the values of some group. One person will change his goal if made to feel guilty; another, anxiously fastened to the need to maintain rigid logical congruities, will change his position if the manipulator gives him false but convincing information which produces discordance in his logical system. The most effective manipulations are accomplished where the deceiver knows and understands the other person (and beyond the other person, the total situation) well, and this knowledge and understanding is, to a large extent, dependent on empathy. It is in this sense that empathy "may enhance the object's reality (Schafer, 1968 a) and it subserves adaptation.

Like Fliess and Schafer, I feel that empathy is a type of identification. Schafer has referred to it as "identification in fantasy" which may or may not spill over into the actions of the

1. Guterman (1970) has indicated that there is an *inverse* relationship between "empathy" and Machiavellianism; however, a study of his scales and test suggests that his use of the term "empathy" is vastly different from the psychoanalytic one.

person. It requires the concurrent occurrence of three levels of psychological activity—trying to be like the other person, trying to be the same as the other person, and merging with the other person. While Schafer has elaborated to some degree on each of these levels of activity and their relevance for identification in general, what is important for our consideration is that empathy requires the ability, simultaneously, to experience different types of relatedness to the object—relatedness which preserves the object as separate, relatedness which magically transforms the self in part into the object, and relatedness which tends to obliterate the boundary between self and object.

In an earlier article, Schafer (1959) compared aspects of empathy with aspects of the aesthetic experience described by Kris (1952) and he concluded that empathy is dependent partly on regression in the service of the ego. This, of course, is implicit in the discussion of object-relatedness involved in empathy, and it has implications for our understanding of different types of patients seen in clinical practice. Some borderline patients may be made so anxious at the prospect of relaxing their rather rigid but brittle ego-boundaries that they cannot regress comfortably to earlier forms of object-relatedness; indeed to do so might lead them to a point where they could not re-erect the boundaries. For them, empathy might be too risky a business, and thus their ability to deceive effectively will be limited.

The regression involves changes in other aspects of mental organization as well. Defenses must be relinquished in order for certain empathic experiences to occur. The patient with an overly severe superego often cannot allow this to happen, and thus, his capacity for experiencing and using empathy (and his capacity for deception) may be curtailed. Hysterical naïveté may be cited as an example. At times, our hysterical patients may display an amazing degree of naïveté about the motives of others and about the social situations in which they become involved. They may be prevented from deceiving in part because their superegos will not allow them to feel the forbidden wishes which characterize the other person and which might make him vulnerable to deception. There are people who cannot take advantage of someone else's lust, not only because of a moral position that it is wrong to take advantage of people, but also because they cannot fully comprehend that people really do have lust; to fully grasp another's lust would require empathic identification with a momentary realization of one's own forbidden lust.

This is not to imply that lust is absent from the interactions of the hysteric—far from it. But you will recall that manipulation and deception require intentionality, a phenomenon involving consciousness. In order deliberately to plan to take advantage of another's lust, one must allow the empathic understanding to enter into consciousness, and it is here that the superego may cause the processes to be intercepted. Thus, the sexual aspects of the hysteric's interactions occur largely outside of consciousness; the hysterical woman expresses surprise and disbelief when informed of the sexual interest of the man. She may be seductively responsive to his advances without being manipulative—i.e., without being aware of his interest, let alone consciously desiring to take advantage of this interest.

Is empathy, then, a phenomenon of consciousness? Of course, no psychological phenomenon is dependent on conscious factors alone; our discussion of the superego illustrates one possible unconscious determinant. But need the *content* of the empathic identification be conscious? Does one have to feel the hate of the other person in order to empathize, or can the empathy take place outside of consciousness? I suggest that much empathy is not available to consciousness; we may react to someone's hate (thus showing our empathic understanding of it) although we may not be able to be aware of his hate even when someone else points it out to us. However, when we consider the role of empathy in deception and manipulation, there can be no doubt that the most successful manipulators (like the most sensitive psychoanalysts) are able to become aware of the contents of empathy and thus are able to plan their actions deliberately and with a maximum of knowledge.

Let us return to the "intellectual alertness" and "marked sensitivity" mentioned by Fromm-Reichmann, for they comprise the two aspects of empathic understanding which Schafer (1959) described in terms of cognitive and affective components. There must be a balance between these components. The overly intellectualized obsessional patient often is prevented from deceiving, again, not only out of moral considerations, but also because he cannot grasp the affective aspects of the other person; frequently his attempts to influence the other person are limited to the use of intellectual argument alone. Having to isolate his own affect, he is unable to identify with the affect of the other person and thus his grasp of the situation is impaired, and his attempts to influence may miss the mark.

On the other hand, it goes without saying that an intellectual understanding of the situation is necessary for any effective action. A dull person will be much more limited in his understanding of the other person and the total situation than a bright individual. And a person who has been briefed about another's vulnerability will be in a better position to empathize and to deceive than one who has no prior knowledge.

Among the factors which may limit the success of the use of empathy in deception, we must include also the person's relative lack of freedom from some compelling unconscious impulses and/or defenses. We have already encountered this situation in chapter 3 where I described conflicts of goals which were not real conflicts. You will recall the case of the antisocial young man who was driven to see me as being chiefly interested in his work performance which would be a testimonial to my therapeutic skill and enhance my reputation. Ordinarily a very empathic young man and a skilled deceiver and manipulator, he was, in this instance, blinded by his own needs, and he misread the major thrust of my interest. This does not mean that he was not manipulating; the intention to deceive was present, but without the empathy it was a private affair with its effect lost on me.

The empathy involved in deception is a kind of identification, as I have already mentioned. It differs from some other kinds of identification by virtue of its being transient. Fliess (1942) referred to empathy as "trial identification." In order for the empathy to be useful to the manipulator, he must be able to sample it, to try various plans out on it, and then to relinquish it. As an identification, it occupies part of the ego, but it is under the scrutiny of another part of the ego;[2] it is observed, recognized in its relation to the object, worked with, and released. We may contrast this process, for example, with another type of identifica-

2. Fliess ascribed this self-observing function to the superego, as did Freud in several of his writings. Hartmann and Loewenstein (1962) placed this function within the ego, although they pointed out that it is heavily influenced by the superego.

tion—suggestibility. Here, the identification is not so critically scrutinized by the ego and the proper relationship of the identification with the object is lost. The person more completely becomes the other person, and the identification is not so readily relinquished.

The ability to relinquish the empathic identification plays a role also in determining whether the person will manipulate or be manipulated. In any conflict of goals, the person may empathize with the other person's goal and find it so in accord with his own feelings, guilts, etc., that he ceases to preserve its relation to the object, and he adopts it as his own. In this case, he immerses his actions in the framework provided by the other person; that is, he is influenced by the other person. Clearly, whether he is more or less likely to influence or to be influenced depends in part on his sense of self and his state of activity or passivity, as described in chapter 4. A person with a strong sense of self and the ability to acknowledge his activity will work upon the empathic identification and, in part, will retain it as a foreign body, an introject. This will be coupled with his desire to be active in the relationship, to use the understanding in the process of acting upon (influencing) the other person. A person with a less well-defined sense of self will be less able to prevent the identification from spreading over much of the ego; his lower level of activity sense will allow him to work less on the empathic "sample," and a preference for passivity may promote his tendency to be influenced by his understanding of the other person (and hence, in the social sense, to be influenced by the other person).

These, then, are some of the psychological considerations regarding the individual's ability to deceive and manipulate successfully. Now, we must turn to the contents of deception itself in order to examine some of the processes in the construction of the deception. Although these processes are generally the same for all types of deception, I believe that it will be easier to illustrate them in terms of the lie.

We may start once again with the comments of Eck:[3] "Lying is negation and cannot exist independently of negation. To lie is

---

3. Eck emphasized the existential aspects of negation and denial, having to do with the relation to the other person.

to deny what is, and deny it intentionally. That is to say, with the desire to deceive" (p. 18).

A lie, then, occurs when a person is aware that he is distorting[4] reality; it is the intentional expression of this distortion in a conscious and deliberate attempt to deceive. Note that I have said that the *expression* (of the unreality) is intentional, not that the *distortion* is intentional. The distortion itself is a thought which occurs to the conscious part of the ego; its occurrence is a passive phenomenon not at all under the conscious control of the ego. What the ego does with this thought may be more or less under its conscious control (intentionality). For example, the ego may fit this distortion into its empathic assessment of the other person and the individual may then express this distortion as a lie. Or, alternatively, the ego might use this distortion in the elaboration of a wish-fulfilling fantasy but not express it to another person; that is, not lie.

Now there are still other types of situations where distortions reach consciousness and may be expressed without being considered lies according to our definition. I refer to cases where the person is unaware that he is distorting. Psychotic disturbances where projections force distorted perceptions of reality are a case in point. Neurotic disorders also occur and may produce situations where the patient is unaware that the thought represents a distortion. One example is the transference neurosis where the patient's perception of the analyst is molded to fit his Oedipal wishes. Another example is the hysterical conversion symptom where the patient distorts the reality of his own body. "My arm is paralyzed," he says, and by this he means that he is unable to move it but that he has a physical disability. Here, again, the patient is unaware that what he is expressing is a distortion. Yet another example of distortions reaching consciousness without the individual's awareness that they are distortions is provided by Geelard. (1965) She has written about "denial in the service of the need to survive." With this defense mechanism, the ego wards off anxiety by ignoring certain real dangers and thus is free to participate with courage in interaction with an uncertain, and at times hostile, environment.

4. The term "denial" has considerable ambiguity, as Altschel (1968) has shown. I use the term "distortion" at this point to avoid certain theoretical considerations which, while important, would be for us a digression.

In other words, there is a whole gamut of conditions wherein individuals employ distortions of reality. As Stewart (1970) has maintained, some of these conditions are severely pathological (as in the psychoses), some are less disabling (certain neurotic patterns), and others may be quite adaptive and of questionable pathologic significance (some lies and "denial in the service of the need to survive").

Historically (Freud, 1927, 1938 a, 1938 b), the fetish has provided psychoanalysts with a good vehicle for the study of the distortion of reality because it lends itself to the observation of both the acknowledgment of reality and its simultaneous distortion. The fetishist knows that women do not have penises and yet (unconsciously) believes that all people have penises. Briefly and schematically, the situation can be described thus: A little boy of about four observes a naked woman and is startled to discover that she has no penis. He finds this observation so unacceptable that he persists in his belief that all people (women included) have penises. If he were never to be confronted again with the reality of sex differences, he might retain his misunderstanding and that would be the end of it. However, he is exposed in hundreds of ways to the reality of the situation—by observation, discussion, etc.—and reality wins out; he learns that, indeed, women do not have penises. However, his contrary belief persists, although it is now pushed from consciousness (repressed). By displacement, the imagined penis of the woman is portrayed by a shoe, a garment, etc., and, thus disguised, the infantile belief can again be admitted to consciousness without appearing to contradict reality. The fetish, representing the penis, *is* real and sexually exciting, and can exist side by side with the conscious knowledge of sex difference.

Now, why did not the boy just accept the reality of sex differences in the first place? Again, schematically, we say that, being an Oedipal age child, he placed tremendous value on the penis and feared that, as punishment for his sexual urges, his own penis would be lost. But wait! All he had to do was to check to see that his penis was intact; it was someone else who lacked one. Here we must posit another mechanism—identification (Bak, 1953)—in order for the story to make sense. In part, our little boy must have been unable to keep proper distance from the

woman. He must have identified with her on whatever combina-
tions of the three levels of relatedness were available to him.
The lack of a penis thus became a very personal thing, and a
personally dangerous thing. The idea was rejected in favor of a
more pleasurable idea: "I have a penis and nothing can happen to
it." Then, this idea (really a wish involved with phallic narcissistic
and Oedipal impulses) was projected onto everyone: "They all
have penises and nothing can happen to them." And as the
child's reality-testing increased (and in part, this means a sturdier
differentiation between himself and others), he was better able to
accept the fact that the woman (not he) lacked a penis.

There are then two opposing fantasies (Jacobson, 1957), one
more nearly attuned to reality and the other badly distorting
reality. In the fetishist, the realistic idea prevails while the distorted one is repressed and expressed only symbolically. A
psychotic patient might be more conscious of the distortion while
paying less attention to the realistic one. On the other hand, a
person with little castration anxiety would have less need to
retain the distortion or its derivative, the fetish.

These processes also occur in the formation of the content of
the lie. Like the other types of distortion, two ideas sit side
by side in the mind—the realistic one and the distorted one.
However, in the case of the lie, both are conscious. The balance
between the two ideas determining which will reach consciousness,
which will undergo disguise, which will be believed by that part
of the ego most closely involved in intentionality is an intriguing
question of economics. I shall return to economic considerations
later in this chapter. At this point, I wish to draw your attention
to these issues to show that the contents of the lie are fashioned
from the same psychic mechanisms as other distortions and to
emphasize that, rather than being merely an abrogation of reality
(a kind of negating of the truth), they are the expression in
consciousness of impulses and wishes. We can easily infer some
of these impulses in some of the deceptions employed in examples
of manipulations described earlier in this book. For instance, we
may recall the salesman described in chapter 1. Coming upon
an elderly man painting his house, he asked to see the man's
paintbrush, feigned anger, threw the brush on the ground, and
then expressed concern for the man's health. He thus convinced

the prospect to stop painting and purchase $2,700 worth of siding. "I made him mad, and I got his attention," he told me. You will recall that temper outbursts were part of the reason he came for therapy. In part, these outbursts were rage reactions stemming from feelings of deprivation. His parents had been very active in business and social affairs, and as far back as he could remember the patient and his younger brother had been given makeshift meals, often meals left for them by a mother who had gone off to meetings. No one was at home to greet him when he returned from school, and he had developed strong resentments about being neglected. I do not know many of the intimate details of his early life or his unconscious impulses and feelings of frustration because he was not in intensive psychotherapy with me; I can speculate, however, that oral strivings and anger directed against an ungiving mother and a usurping sibling were prominent features underlying his temper outbursts. So, it is quite probable that, wanting to sell siding, he unconsciously registered the painter and his implements as a competitor and a potential source of deprivation. His hold on reality, however, counterbalanced this in at least two ways. First, he could not consciously distort reality-testing sufficiently to allow the idea of malevolent intent on the part of the environment to hold sway; a paranoid person might have thought consciously that the man was painting the house purposely in order to deprive him of a living. Second, our salesman's goal was to sell siding; he focused on the realities of the situation and adapted to them. He could both express and deny his anger by feigning it. The content of the deception (anger) was an expression of unconscious psychic truth, but it was adapted to the realities of the situation, and the salesman used it rather than being ruled by it. The further deception of concern for the painter's health also reflected personal concerns as the patient had a prevailing fear that his own father would fall ill and die. Presumably it was an admixture of Oedipal and oral themes which found expression in the deception, but, as I noted above, firm evidence is lacking.

A more apparent example of the part played by unconscious themes in producing the idea for the content of the deception was described in chapter 3. The antisocial patient who feigned a urinary tract infection was reflecting his earlier mode of relating to a sexually stimulating nurse-mother, and his conflict about ambition.

Imposture, with its rich and lasting quality, gives us an especially good opportunity to study some of the psychological elements of the contents of the lie. The deceptions of impostors are striking examples of the way lies are fashioned from unconscious thought. As Greenacre (1958, p. 521) has noted, "The ability of the impostor to put on convincing acts of impersonation, including facsimilar reproductions of special skills . . . may seem to be almost miraculous and inspired. Indeed the impostor may bring his latent fantasies into a vivid living form in the assumption of his impostured character." Both Greenacre and Deutsch (1955) have described how the contents of the imposture reflect the patient's struggle against feelings of genital inferiority and passivity; the potency and narcissism which the patient's "real self" is unable to display finds expression in the contents of his deceptions.

Not only do impostors portray the reflection of unconscious impulses and infantile dangers, but they also show the existence of multiple identifications. You will recall that in my brief discussion of fetishism, I pointed out how the little boy must partially identify with the naked woman and it is this that makes the possibility of castration so personal and so frightening. The impostor, too, as Deutsch has described him, puts forth at least two identities. One, the "real self," is often fashioned out of identifications with those aspects of people which are less able to pursue a "masculine" goal. This passive self is unable to make solid achievements. The second self, the imposture, often reveals identification with active, heroic attributes, and all of the impostor's often considerable talents are pressed into the service of this self. Deutsch has noted that the impostor is unable to pull these various identifications into a fluent self "and to achieve a reliable degree of inner stability." There is a disjointedness about the "real" self and the imposture self: the "real" self knows that the imposture is not "really me" or "me as real."

This situation is present to a greater or lesser degree in many lies. Where the content of the lie is meant to deceive the other person into thinking the liar is someone (or has done something), some of the elements of the identification are often obvious. Where the lies involve other people and events, the identification patterns may not be so apparent.

A young adult, a student, had a predominantly phallic-narcissistic character structure. He and some fellow classmates skipped classes one day to go golfing. His wife knew about the outing and approved of it as long as he would be home by 6:00 p.m. so they could go out for the evening. In his hour with me on the following day, he started by describing what a great success the outing had been. The fellows had played 18 holes of golf and then proceeded to get drunk in the clubhouse. They joked, each man tried to outdo the others in his stories about successes with women; there was general disparagement of women, and a sense of masculine conviviality pervaded the day. Because of their reluctance to end the day at 6:00, my patient called his wife to say that his car had broken down and he would arrive home late. His wife accepted this excuse, and he went home three hours later. "We stayed for another three hours," he told me. "Man, what a time! When we finally left, it was so late, I drove 110 miles an hour to get home as quick as I could." In my own mind, I doubted that his Volkswagen could go 110 miles an hour, and this exaggeration alerted me to the possible significance of the contents of his lie to his wife. The car had suddenly been transformed from a defective thing to a superthing. I asked him about the 110 miles per hour, and he acknowledged that it was an exaggeration on the order of the tall stories of the day before: "Like when you first learn to drive when you're a kid. You think driving fast shows courage and manliness." He then proceeded to recount another aspect of the day. He had felt funny about the group's boisterous behavior. "Who were we trying to impress?" he asked. "Like, on the way down, some of the guys were talking about people on welfare, and how they'd like to shoot 'em all. Now, I don't really feel that way, but I went along. I had to show that I was one of the group. We all made fun of our wives. I really respect my wife, but I had to be one of the guys."

Toward the middle of the hour, the patient discussed the difficulty he was having with his mother who insisted on over-indulging his children despite the fact that the patient and his wife repeatedly asked her not to ply the children with sweets and gifts. He displayed an air of frustration and helplessness against the desires of a strong-willed mother who refused to listen.

Returning, then, to the events of the previous day, the patient wondered why he had lied to his wife. She probably wouldn't have minded too much even if he had told her the truth: that they were having such a good time that they had not wanted to come home. But the other fellows wanted him to lie; they were afraid of their wives. "No," he went on, "that's not entirely true either. I was a little afraid of mine, too." I noted the difference in attitude between the boasting manliness he exhibited in a group of men and thread of fear woven into his relationship with his wife, not only suggested on this occasion, but earlier in the analysis as well. We discussed his feeling that women were secure and independent, and that they belittled men. I called his attention to his frustration with his mother earlier in the hour, and he agreed that she was a prime example of secure, immovable, and at times frightening independence. She made him feel "like a little kid; somehow that's the only way I can be with my mother." The dynamics of the contents of the lie to his wife were now apparent; it was all right to have a supercar (superpenis) with the boys, but with a potentially dangerous woman one must appear weak and defective. I noted how he had changed his emphasis during the hour from one of manly conviviality in relating the events to me at the outset to an "I'm not really so masculine" approach after I had asked about the speed. He acknowledged that he knew I wouldn't be moved by his exaggeration. He saw me more as a woman (this theme had been emerging for some weeks previously in the analysis): I would stand firm on my decisions and be immovable. Lying on the couch was infantalizing for him, while I had a kind of inner strength that was sometimes frightening to him. When I asked about his driving 110 miles per hour, he knew that I was not prepared to join him in pseudo-masculine boasting; he was afraid he had gone too far and had to retrench by undercutting his masculine strivings as he had by announcing to his wife that his car had broken down.

To say that all lies contain in their contents elements of unconscious impulses, defenses, and unintegrated identifications would probably be theoretically correct but clinically meaningless because all behavior reflects these elements. The lie emerges as a fitting of these themes into the empathic understanding of what the other person might believe and what the situation requires. However, many lies are so predominantly geared to fitting in with the social situation that the underlying dynamics of the liar as reflected in the contents of the lie are obscure and not at all reasonably accessible to clinical analysis. Nevertheless, lies arising in the clinical situation often are not so obscure, as we have already observed. Understanding that the contents of the lie reflect these personal themes may help the clinician avoid reacting only to the fact of the lie or to the intention of the lie, an aspect which I shall discuss presently. To say that a patient's statement is untrue and to focus only on his need to lie (or to get angry at him for manipulating) can cause the therapist to ignore important clinical data which may be woven into the lie's contents. The clinical approach to the lie, then, must embody considerations about the *fact* of the patient's lying and the *contents* of the lie as expressive behavior. Where the immediate focus of inquiry will be directed will, of course, depend in part on what is to be accomplished in the treatment [5] and on the therapist's assessment of the patient's position at that particular time. In the case of the antisocial young man (chapter 3), I chose to focus on the fact of the lie because I felt that discussing the contents of the lie (the urinary tract infection) would lead only to an intellectual game. In the case of the phallic-narcissistic young man, the contents of the lie figured heavily in my helping him to understand his need to play down his masculine strivings in his relationships with threatening women.

Let us now consider some of the economic aspects of lying. Fenichel has shown that pseudologies have the function of aiding repression. When the contents of the lie emerge into consciousness, the liar, by judging them untrue and by making others believe that they are true, creates a situation where truth and untruth are interchangeable; in this manner he can doubt his own inner truths.

Fenichel (1939) hinted at the genetic origins of the lie. The lie seems often to have the quality of "I'm making it up." This seems to be the reverse of infantile magical thinking: "I think it,

5. The issue of different therapeutic goals will be discussed in chapter 13.

so it is true," or "I think it, so it will happen." I believe that the prototype of the lie must arise in part from the conflict between these primitive modes of understanding the world and the developing sense of reality as outlined by Ferenczi (1913). These omnipotent fantasies must be relinquished when they fail to work; there must be many instances of "I think, so it's not so" or "I think, so it won't happen" as an intermediate phase (negative omnipotence, if you will) before the more reality oriented "I think and it may or may not be so," or, "I think and it may or may not happen." The liar, then, gains support for his repression in part by "knowing" that he is just "thinking, so it's not true or it won't happen." And, as Fenichel's formula tells us, the liar gains support for this by seeing that the "other" person's thought means nonreality.

A young unmarried woman consulted me because of dissatisfaction with her social life. She was gay, flirtatious, and generally popular, but had a nagging feeling of restlessness and an inability to take men seriously; she doubted that she would ever marry and settle down. In the early part of her analysis, she frequently presented herself as a humdrum person, and she desperately fought off any temptation to become "too involved" with me. Later events in the analysis showed the Oedipal guilt which forced her to keep her distance in the analytic consulting room but at the time to be described below there had been only occasional hints of this guilt.

As she described her flirtations, it became apparent that they were anything but spontaneous. She would meet a young man and it would occur to her that she might "fall in love" with him. She would then reject this possibility because it had the ring of promiscuity to her—after all, she had just been "in love" with another man. She would think about the possibility over and over again until, ultimately, she could convince herself that the flirtation would just be a game, a pretense. Then she could flirt. "When I say to Tom, 'I love you,'" she told me, "I'm lying. I don't really love him; it's just for fun, so it doesn't count."

The patient had had an active imagination during her latency period. She had thought of herself as a fairy princess, a naive and pure "lady" who would be courted (not sexually, of course) by a knight in shining armor. Now, as a much less naive young adult, she still sought to re-enact this childhood dream which contained both the sexual impulse and its prohibition. By flirting, she could get men to be attracted to her, and indeed she had many suitors. But she had first to protect her purity by negating the derivative of her sexual impulse and then offering this derivative to the other person. The forbidden Oedipal impulses produced the ideation of being seriously in love. She worked on this ideation until she could convince herself that she was only pretending; "I'm actively thinking of being in love, so it really isn't so: that is, I really do not have Oedipal impulses." Then, with the conscious ideation, "I'm *not* in love," she would lie: that is, say "I love you." This lie expressed the Oedipal wish and simultaneously served to help keep it repressed. She "knew" it wasn't true and the fact that the young men responded made it all a game. "If it were real," she told me, "I couldn't say it."

The existence of at least two identities was also shown by this patient. She was one person in the analysis and quite another when she was flirting. Even when she was flirting, however, she never lost sight of her humdrum "loveless" personality; the flirting was a "pretense" and expression of a "make-believe" identity, not "really" her.

Now, with such a detailed discussion of various aspects of the lie, it is easy to lose sight of the obvious: a lie is a social maneuver designed usually to allow the liar to gain satisfactions which would be denied him if he told the truth. Or it is designed to avoid dangers which might arise if the truth were known. These adaptive functions are well known to all of us and need little elaboration here. The task of the clinician is to be aware of the immediate and obvious goals of the liar, the social situation, and, if possible, simultaneously to look beyond the obvious to learn as much about the inner life of the patient as possible. By looking at, but also beyond, the obvious purpose of the lie, by going beyond the *intention* of the lie, we may learn some things about the patient which are much less obvious, farther from his consciousness; and which may, at times, have more stable and far-reaching effects on his personality and behavior.

At first glance, this discussion might seem to run counter to my discussion of intentionality where I emphasized the restriction of that term to the relatively conscious sphere of mental activity. There is no real contradiction, however. The aspect of the lie which should be considered manipulative is that aspect which was intended; we need not and should not ignore the other aspects of the lie, however. In our discussion with the patient, we may choose to focus on the fact of the manipulation or on the goal of manipulation; to interpret deeper and unintended aspects immediately and directly will probably be incomprehensible and may increase the resistance. Nonetheless, with our knowledge of the economic function of lying, we must also be aware that limiting our inquiry to the intended aspect of the lie may aid the patient's attempts to repress the underlying aspects. For, if we accept the lie as "only a lie," we help the patient avoid the truths underlying the lie.

Earlier in this chapter, we came across instances where the expression of untruth was not considered to be lying because there was no attempt to deceive the other person. Let us return now to some of these situations. The simplest one, of course, is where the patient does not know the truth. Rumors, for example, may be started by someone who intends to deceive, but are often carried by people who have no access to the facts. On the other hand, there are those who so much wish to believe the rumor that they insulate themselves from the facts. Often (but not always) our patients who transmitted misinformation to us did have access to the correct information but unwittingly avoided it or pushed it out of consciousness. The economic situation here is different from that of the lie, which involves the conscious realization of the facts and the intent to deceive. And, of course, there is a "grey area" where the facts may be readily accessible to consciousness but are temporarily "overlooked." As with intentionality, I am talking about relative degrees of accessibility to consciousness; in some cases, lying is obvious, in some cases it is apparent that the facts are so unavailable to consciousness that it would be incorrect to say that the patient intended to deceive, and in some cases we just cannot make an adequate judgment.

It is not difficult to apply the thoughts developed here in reference to lying to other forms of deception. Even when the person deceives by telling the truth, as in the story with which I opened this chapter, the psychological principles elaborated here are pertinent. Empathy, in terms of what the other person wants and how he will react to the information (true or false), is required. At least two sets of thought (the real and the distorted) must appear in consciousness with all the economic and dynamic considerations this implies. The configuration of identities must be present, although perhaps not readily observable. And, as we shall see in chapter 7, considerations of morality are always present to act as determinants of whether the deception will be tried.

CHAPTER 6

PUTTING SOMETHING OVER

While the preceding chapters have dealt with some of the psychological mechanisms underlying the formation, act, and content of the manipulation, we have yet to consider the attitude of the manipulator toward the other person. How does he feel about the one whom he manipulates, and from what do these feelings derive?

We may start with a distinction I introduced in the last chapter. In the discussion of empathy, I noted (following Fliess) that all "practical psychologists" utilize empathy, and, that in this respect, psychoanalysts and manipulators have a common skill. An essential difference, however, lies in the fact that the psychoanalyst has a basic respect for his patient as an individual, a respect which is lacking in the manipulator. Schafer (1959, pp. 270 f.), writing about the psychoanalyst, noted that "generative empathy is a sublimative, creative act in personal relationships which combines the gratifications of intimate union with the recognition and enhancement of separateness and personal development of both persons involved. . . . In the end it enhances rather than replaces and impoverishes object relations." Other analysts (Stone, 1961; Greenson, 1967) have also stressed the attitude of respect for the other person and for his integrity as a separate person as essential for psychoanalytic work. Psychoanalysts share this attitude with mature teachers, parents, and others whose intention to influence has a predominantly generative[1] cast.

We may contrast this attitude with that of the liar and the manipulator. The manipulation, arising out of a conflict of goals, is in part a power struggle. It is differentiated from some other forms of influence by the fact that the manipulator has little or no real interest in the other person except as he can be used in the

1. The words "intimacy" and "generativity" are used in the sense described by Erikson (1968).

pursuit of the manipulator's own needs. To use Eck's (1965) word, there is no *loyalty* to the other person.

The manipulator uses the other person as a means to an end rather than as a fellow human being; he devalues the other person as a person in his own right and sees him as a tool. In that respect, the other person becomes an extension of the manipulator's own self, much as a man uses a machine in order to accomplish work he could not otherwise do. However, often there may be a kind of admiration for and loyalty to the machine; we take pride in our automobiles and we are impressed by industrial technology. Not so with the person we manipulate. He is frequently an object of contempt, a disposable item to be used and discarded or to be kept around for convenience and pleasure but not for friendship. It is true that people can manipulate their friends at times, but while they are engaged in the manipulation, the quality of the friendship is significantly altered. And, in contrast to the person with the generative attitude, the manipulator not only derives pleasure from the success of the interaction, he also experiences a sense of power and exhilaration. It is these attitudes which I subsume under the phrase "putting something over."

Now, there are many attitudes we can have toward another person besides a generative one or a feeling of putting something over on him. We can have feelings of admiration or envy; feelings of distance, estrangement, or intimacy; a host of neurotic feelings; fear or dread, etc. Of particular importance in the clinical situation is the distinction between the feeling of putting something over on the other person and the attitude that the other person may be available to gratify one's needs. We often hear clinicians refer to the dependency needs of their patients. The interpersonal frame of reference, in particular, tends to direct focus on the unwillingness of patients to assume responsibility and their need to use other people to gratify their demands.

There is a difference between a dependent or other neurotic relationship wherein the person uses another person for need gratification, and a manipulative relationship. As we have already seen in chapter 2, often the person is unaware of his use of other people for need gratification whereas in a manipulative transaction, the person is necessarily conscious of his desire to influence another person by deception. In addition, in a dependent relationship, for example, the dependent person does not experience contempt for the other person, and when the need is gratified, he usually experiences satisfaction or perhaps even feelings of friendship or love for the other person. Not so the manipulator; he tops off his contempt for the other person with a feeling of exhilaration.

Of course, nothing exists in pure culture; many manipulative acts also gratify dependency and other neurotic needs. For example, a man may intentionally employ deception in order to win the affection of a woman whom he seeks as an Oedipal object and a maternal caretaker. Several themes may be interwoven in the behavior. However, the manipulative aspect is a theme in its own right, and the feeling of putting something over has its own dynamics.

We may begin to explore these dynamics by returning to the businessman described in chapter 4. He had come to analysis because of marital problems. Instead of being an intimate relationship, his marriage was an endless series of confrontations. The analysis, too, was marked by provocative "games" in which he would try to put something over on me by baiting me into giving him an interpretation which he had already figured out. It was important for him to see the analysis as an absurdity and to demonstrate how gullible I was.

After several months of analysis, we had the opportunity to examine one of his manipulative attempts to put something over on me. This attempt was ushered in during a period when some important business negotiations were not going at all smoothly. Ordinarily a skilled negotiator, he apparently had met his match and he was in danger of coming out second best in this particular deal. For the first time, he began to express an interest in my other patients, and it became clear that he felt a sense of rivalry with them for my attention. Underlying this interest was his complaint that the analysis had not made him a better negotiator and that I was not taking care of him and giving him some of my potency.

One day, he pondered aloud the question of whether he could ask me to start five minutes earlier on the following day because he had to catch a bus. He decided that he "didn't want any favors" from me, and he never asked; instead he said that he could really make the bus anyhow if he hurried.

The next day he said he had decided not to take the bus. Then he launched into a vehement discussion of the way the "establishment" reacts against the hippies. He pointed out the hypocrisy of the complacent middle class (although he himself was a rather successful businessman, he tended to identify with rebellious youth rather than with the bourgeoisie). After a pause, he said, "Do you know why I don't want to go on the bus? I've figured it out. The bus is a long, tunnel-like vehicle. Tunnels and corridors frighten me; they're too much like vaginas sucking me up. Women are a bunch of fascists and their vaginas are dangerous. You know, Freud was absolutely right about that."

While I was even more convinced of his fear of vaginas than he was, I was quite certain that he was not afraid of buses or corridors. "Are you afraid of buses?" I asked.

He became angry. "You're confusing the issue," he shouted. "Every time I talk to you I get all mixed up; no, it's not you who's confusing the issue, it's me. Oh, shit!" And with a sigh his anger gave out.

I then told him that his reference to tunnels and sucking vaginas, just like the ones in Freud's writings, was really a kind of bait to get me to take seriously what he put forth as a joke.

"Yes, I know that," he replied. "I'm really angry at you for not offering to change the time. But, damn it, you won't fall for it—you never do. And if you don't fall for it, you're catching me at it and it makes me feel stupid. Why do I feel caught? This whole damn thing is like a game and we're competing for points." It was now apparent that taking the bus had not been important; making me feel the bus was important and influencing me to change the time was his prime issue.

That night, he had a dream which was reported during the next session. He was in an operating room and there was the smell of "Airwick." It was as if there were some terrible smell in the room which had been covered over with the "Airwick." He saw himself on the operating table with his stomach opened up and "they" were cleaning it up. They were taking out "shit and coins."

He readily associated the operation with the analysis, and in reference to his feeling stupid yesterday, he expressed the conviction that I would find him "full of shit" and not worth much. His association of the coins with something else was most interesting: "They were nickels," he said. "Wait! Not just nickels, they were *buffalo* nickels. Maybe the shit was buffalo dung. Hah! That's me trying to buffalo you, yesterday.[2] You come looking for coins and all you get is shit!" His low mood about being stupid and found full of shit had now turned to delight in buffaloing me.

The dream, then, pictured an invitation to be penetrated and exposed. But the exposure, rather than revealing a penis, was a kind of castration, creating a cavity in front containing feces. In all probability, this combined his desire to receive the penis vaginally and anally. At the same time, his masculine strivings were hidden. "Look at me," he was saying, "and you'll find a cloaca—not worth much—full of shit." With this, he tended to remove the focus from the phallic to the anal sphere, but at a severe loss to his vanity. He was ashamed. However, he could recoup his losses by turning the shame into secret but conscious pride. His shit had become a weapon, as had his intellect, to buffalo, baffle, and defeat the other person. And his pleasure in putting something over on the other person helped him cover over (the "Airwick") the deep sense of shame that he felt.

Not long afterward, one of his dreams revealed a sentimental side to him. His sentimentality embarrassed him severely. It made him feel weak, vulnerable, and unmasculine. He became very concerned about his "image." His clothes became very important to him. Should he get a hat? It would make him look more dignified; he would be taken more seriously in the business world, and he would look like a real man. Finally, he decided to buy a hat, and the next day he told me about the purchase. On the following day, when I came out to get him in the waiting room, I saw a loud, sportsman's hat hanging on the coat rack. It was the kind of hat one might wear to a football game (or even to go fishing, for that matter); it was not what the well-dressed man on Wall Street would wear. I wasn't even certain it was my patient's hat but it surprised me; it was not what he had led me to believe he was going to buy.

During the hour, he asked me how I liked his hat. He laughed because he knew I must have been surprised; he was sure he had fooled me. I traced for him some of his struggles about masculinity.

---

2. While he did not say it, buffalo dung is very similar to bullshit.

I pointed out how ashamed he had been about his sentimentality and the idea that he might be projecting a sloppy and weak image. He tried to counteract this with a masculine hat, but he became anxious; thus he arrived at a compromise; he did get a hat, but it was really a joke. And while his fears about masculinity compelled him to make a joke of himself (like the cloaca full of shit), he again fought off his shame by playing the joke on me.

After a thoughtful pause, the patient suddenly remembered an incident when he was seven. He had fallen into a puddle while playing outside and had run home. His mother had been entertaining some women, and when he appeared on the porch, she made him remove his dirty outer clothes and "parade through the house in my underwear in front of all those damn women." This led to our discussion of his embarrassment about his "small" penis and how women made him feel particularly small. He began to see more clearly the interplay between the fear of his phallic pride, his phallic shame, and the anal regression with its defense —the contemptuous shitting on the other person. These, then, were some of the ingredients of his feeling of putting something over on the other person. And they were, of course, aspects of the same conflicts which determined his intentionality.

Thus, we see that this man's need to put something over on me was bound up with his feelings of pride and shame. At a time when his pride was threatened partly by his difficult business negotiations and partly by his feeling that he was not favored enough by me to receive some of my potency, he attempted to restore his self-esteem by putting something over on me. If he could best me, his shame could be masked and his pride restored. If he could not, his sense of shame with its anal referents became apparent.

These dynamics are intimately tied in with the feelings of contempt and exhilaration which comprise the feeling of putting something over; however, we must look more deeply into the underlying dynamics to understand the relationships. Several theoretical formulations can help us with our task.

A. Reich (1960) has described the regulation of self-esteem in narcissistically oriented men. According to her formulation, these men live in constant fear that their penises will be lost. Any depreciation of self or loss of an object is experienced as a kind of castration. The narcissistically oriented man reacts to this loss with magical denial. He repairs his wounded self-image by unconsciously thinking that he has the greatest phallus possible. The conscious derivative of this denial is the pride and boastfulness of the narcissistic man. His reality-testing has become attenuated to accommodate his megalomanic image and he will often undertake tasks which others would feel were too risky or foolish. In this stage of magical denial, he has regressed to an early level of development where the differentiation between self and object is not so clear. Reich has postulated that it is the fantasy father—that is, the psychic representation of the father—which is the giant phallus, and the restoration of self-esteem is accomplished by the unconscious fusion of the narcissistically wounded self with this phallus-father.

In his work on depression-prone patients, Rado (1928) developed a theoretical understanding which has considerable similarity to Reich's formulations. He felt that with the loss of an object, the depression-prone person suffered a severe narcissistic wound. The object was introjected and split, with the good aspects of the object introjected into the superego and the hated qualities of the object introjected into the ego. Thus the ego, or self, becomes hated (depreciated) while the good qualities of the superego become enhanced. The only possible resolution is for the internalized bad object to be destroyed so that the self can be reunited with the introjected good object in the superego.[3]

While these condensed versions do not do justice to Reich's and Rado's theories, they do suffice to provide us with certain guidelines. Both theories imply that when a person's pride is attacked, he has a depreciated self-image, and that he seeks to restore his self-esteem by a fusion or reunion with an introjected good object. In Reich's formulation this fusion is with the all-powerful phallus-father; Rado maintained that the reunion recapitulates the unity of the baby with the nursing breast. The similarities between these two types of reunion are more outstanding than their differences. The crucial feature of the mechanism whereby self-esteem is restored is the unconscious reunion of the self with a nourishing, powerful, internalized object: that is, a return to the

3. The psychic situation Rado described is quite different from that postulated by Bonime (chapter 2) where the appeal is to an external object.

earliest narcissistic conditions. This early narcissistic state of fusion with the source of power and nourishment underlies the affect of elation according to both Rado (1926; 1933) and Lewin (1950). Thus, I postulate that the sense of exhilaration which accompanies the feeling of putting something over on someone is a derivative of the elation which accompanies the restoration of self-esteem by the reunion of the self with the introjected good object.

Now, while Rado and Lewin speak of this reunion as between the ego and the superego, most authors agree that self-esteem and shame have to do with the relationship between the ego and the ego-ideal. In psychoanalytic circles, the question of whether the ego-ideal is a substructure of the ego or of the superego is a matter of debate. I believe that Rado and Lewin included the ego-ideal in the superego so that there need be no inconsistency between their view and that of others. However, I choose to avoid this theoretical question of structure here, because it is not crucial for our discussion. Basically, it is not the reunification of *psychic structures* which produces the exhilaration; it is the reunification of the representation of the self with the representation of the good, nourishing, and powerful parent which is important. The restoration of self-esteem rests on a regression to a state which antedated the formation of superego and ego-ideal.

When we reviewed Rado's formulation, I mentioned that the introjected bad object had to be destroyed in order to make the ego sufficiently acceptable for a reunion with the superego to take place. How can this bad object be destroyed? Abraham (1924) laid the groundwork for understanding this mechanism; unconsciously it is expelled through defecation[4] or, as Lewin (1950) and Jacobson (1946) have suggested, the internalized bad object is spit out. As in the case of the object of the reunion (breast or phallus), the distinction between defecation and spitting out the bad object is not so important as is the common element that the process is unconsciously seen as one where the ego purges and cleanses itself of a bad internalized object. Having rid itself of the

---

4. Actually, the example Abraham gave was of defecating expulsion of the object leading to depression (object loss). It is quite reasonable, however, that bad introjects can also be purged in this (psychic) manner, leading to a "purification" of the ego, as Rado suggested.

shameful introject, the purified self is now more acceptable and the reunion can occur. And it is this process of purging which underlies the feeling of contempt. We saw this quite graphically in the dream of the businessman. When his pride was attacked, he portrayed himself as stupid, worthless, and with a stomach full of a bad substance—feces. With his contemptuous mocking of Freud and me he was ridding himself of the feces by giving it to me: "You come looking for coins and all you get is shit." Had he been able to shit on me more successfully, he would have been rid of the shame, and his pride would have been restored.

This purging with its affect of contempt is also a projection in a very literal sense. The person unconsciously is saying, "I am shameful—no, I am not shameful, you are shameful." This projection of the bad introject is also illustrated by another of the businessman's deceptions which he employed to restore his wounded narcissism. He went to a picnic and took part in a baseball game. During the warm-up period he was very concerned about whether he would be placed high or low in the batting order—that is, whether he would be judged a good or poor hitter. He hit the first two practice pitches well, but as he missed the next few pitches, he was mortified. "I was furious at myself. It was like I was *possessed by something* which wouldn't allow me to hit. *I was so angry at myself I could have killed everyone.* Then I thought to myself, 'I'll tell them that's all the practice I need. I'll fool them and they'll put me high in the batting order. As soon as I had the idea I felt better; I was still cleverer than they were.'"

The entire sequence of the purging and the reunion was illustrated at a much later point in his analysis. He heard of a schoolteacher in another state who had been accused of immorality in her private life and was threatened with dismissal. He became incensed at this and he readily identified with the teacher. He felt that she was a victim of establishment prying. On the one hand, he reasoned that her private life was her own affair as long as she taught competently; on the other hand, through her, he felt that the authorities had discovered the dirty and shameful hidden part of him. During the analytic session just prior to the time when the teacher would be having her hearing, the patient again described how dirty he felt. He recalled his feeling of worthlessness as a child when he had been sent off to school while his younger brother was allowed to stay with mother. He became angry at his mother and he began to mock her with bitter contempt. He then recalled a neighbor, Mr. Johnson. "I used to play with his son. Mr. Johnson would come out to say, 'Don't you have to go home now for supper?' He just wanted to get rid of me. He had beautiful flowers. I should have shit all over his flowers." After a pause, he continued, "Shit! Shit is the subject of the hearing—both hearings, the teacher's hearing and this hearing. Can you see how dirty and angry and shitty I am—really unappealing. Cleanliness is appealing. They want me to be a clean, unaggressive little thing with no sex at all." Another pause. "The problem, I guess, is how to get rid of all that shit without letting on. That's what I do! I play tricks on them and they never really know they got shit on."

A few days later, the patient read in the newspaper that the teacher had been cleared of her charges and that she would be allowed to teach. He discussed the whole situation with some of his friends including some attorneys. He was exuberant as he told me that the teacher had won her case. "I knew she would win," he said. "The school officials are such idiots. They really got bombed at the hearings. Before the decision, one of my lawyer friends asked me how I thought it would turn out. Can you imagine that? He is a lawyer and he asked me—like I was the mastermind. I was so excited I couldn't get to sleep last night. When I was a kid I used to have that trouble sometimes. My brother would be in the crib across the room and I would lie there kind of in a panic, like the sky would open up." I asked him about the sky opening up and he replied, "It's like some old Jewish story or other—the sky would open up and God would take me!" He became excited. "I'm the ONE," he shouted, "the brains, the best!"

A few weeks later he returned to the reunion theme. He was feeling particularly inept and stupid as his self-assertiveness was increasingly inhibited by his sense of guilt. He recalled the nighttime episodes in these terms: "I used to lie there panicky waiting for the sky to open up and God would take me. No! Wait a minute —I wasn't panicky; it was more excitement and reassurance. That's what it was, excitement and reassurance. God would take me. I wasn't shitty and stupid; I was better than my parents. They were shitty and stupid." He paused reflectively, and then said, "I came in here feeling so stupid, and all of a sudden I feel great."

Let us now recapitulate the formulation of the dynamics underlying the feeling of putting something over. Essentially, it is a maneuver used to repair a narcissistic wound. The wound, actual or imagined, opens up feelings of shame and a depreciated self-image which is the reflection of an unconsciously held bad introject. The bad introject must be purged and this is accomplished through a projection. The conscious reflection of this process is the feeling of contempt for the other person. When this is accomplished, the person has been purified and the reunion with the good, powerful, and nourishing object can occur. The conscious reflection of this is the restoration of pride and the feeling of exhilaration.

While these dynamics underlie the feeling of putting something over, they do not fully account for the manipulation itself. Rather it is these themes, blending with the dynamics underlying the other three components of manipulation—conflict of goals, intention to influence, and deception—which determine that the narcissistic wound will be repaired by a manipulation. In this regard, we should note that a perceived conflict of goals in itself may be sufficient to stir the feelings of a narcissistic person and initiate the repair process, for a person with strong unconscious feelings of worthlessness may see the conflict as heralding a mortifying defeat for him unless he takes action.

The opportunity to analyze people with strong manipulative tendencies does not arise very often. With their fragile narcissism and their need to look contemptuously to the outside as the source of whatever troubles they may experience, and with their propensity toward alloplastic rather than autoplastic reactions, they do not often come to analysis. An unusual opportunity to glimpse the unconscious mind of one such chronic manipulator recently presented itself from a nonclinical source (Tomalin and Hall, 1970).

Donald Crowhurst had entered a race sponsored by the London *Sunday Times*. The task was to sail solo around the world without putting into port, a feat far beyond Crowhurst's ability. Not long after he embarked from England, it became apparent to him that he would not win the race—perhaps not even complete the trip. Feigning electric-power difficulties, he broke radio contact and remained in the Atlantic Ocean. He kept two sets of records: one with his true positions and one with a false record indicating his "rapid progress" around the world. His intention was to re-appear in time to win the race. However, as one of his logbooks shows, he became psychotic, and when his boat was found, he was no longer aboard. To judge by the log and by the appearance of the boat, it is probable that he went overboard voluntarily rather than that he was a victim of some external disaster.

All his life, Crowhurst had struggled for self-esteem. As a boy, although he had done adequately in school, he had berated him-self for not doing better. He was well known for his bravery, and he laughed at the other boys who were afraid to follow his lead. The youthful Crowhurst was described as a charmer when he wanted to be; he was clever but easily aroused to anger when thwarted.

In the Royal Air Force he was known for his daredevilry; some of the risks he took led to rather serious accidents and to repri-mands. His pranks and practical jokes made him the life of the party, and he had a wide circle of admirers.

One particular part of Tomalin and Hall's description of Crow-hurst is especially pertinent to our consideration of the role of contempt and pride in putting something over. "A part of this impressive public personality was a set of basic ideas about life, which he would often expound to his friends. He thought, for a start, that life was best looked upon as a game played in friendly fashion against society, authority, and God (if God existed, which he doubted). This was life's tortuous game. . . . He also thought cleverness was the most important virtue, and stupid people were not particularly worth taking trouble with."

Crowhurst's narcissism was well summarized by one of his friends (quoted by Tomalin and Hall): "The thing about Donald was that he thought himself God. Everything in his life revolved about his belief in himself, and he was always so quick and clever he could make others believe in him too. He thought he was so wonderful—and he was, a smashing bloke, a genius. But he wasn't God, and that's why all his troubles were his own fault."

In addition to his exploits, the "charmer" Crowhurst was able to manipulate people to support his efforts or to fall for his pranks. At times, as in the *Sunday Times* race, the manipulation served some clearly observable goal, such as the prize money and fame; often the advantages were not so apparent and the need to manipulate was so tied in with his prevailing narcissistic character that the advantages to be gained were not at all clear and he seemed to manipulate just for the sake of manipulating.

The themes underlying narcissism and putting something over emerge in some Christmas poetry he wrote while at sea. It was late in December when he really had to confront himself with the fact that his heroic voyage was impossible. This led to an outburst of exuberant but inaccurate radio messages. Alone at sea at Christmas time, he struggled with his nostalgia and wounded narcissism. His poetry was a mixture of romantic heroism and quests for peace and love.

Flanders Fields[5]

There where the greenest grass is found
Our most valiant deeds were done
For the stupid (for the) Earth's can't distinguish
The noble blood of the English
From the hateful blood of the Hun.

Or was it the other way around
Anyway—to the glory of the Nation
We killed a lot of the Swines
So let's all join in the laughter
Let peace reign hereafter
No man waging war in our times.

Here is the noble Briton, Crowhurst, killing off the swine. The contempt is not only for the hateful-blooded Hun (we shall learn more about his feeling for bodily fluids) but also for the stupid . . . who cannot tell whose blood is good and whose evil. Then, in a line which reveals the blurring of boundaries he asks, "Is it the other way around?" Thus, perhaps, he is in part the "stupid . . . who can't distinguish." It is not now clear who is to be killed (purged) but it is clear that after the purging there will be laughter (exhilaration), peace, and love.

5. The poem is reprinted here as it appears in the logbook.

The unconscious fantasies were made even plainer six months later when he began a lengthy and psychotic elaboration of his "philosophy." This was a pretentious combination of philosophy, mathematics, science, and religion wherein pure intelligence and scientific reasoning became fused with Truth, Love, and God. The ultimate goal was "cosmic integration" and while the "cosmic mind" was abstract pure intelligence (love, truth, etc.), it was also the mental representation of the phallic father. One passage in which he contemplated the bodily limitations of integrating within the "system," was rent by an agonized, "Alas, I shall not see my dead father again."

Another poignant section started, "Once upon a different sort of time, a boy fell out with his father." The "perfect father," God, and his "favorite son" had argued about the value of apes (physical body with all its imperfections). The story was quickly broken off and the need for reunion was elevated to the level of the intellect. "The Masses are Critical Masses. They Can Come Together in Love or Hate. IT IS THE MYSTERY OF FREE-WILL."

God was a very powerful being, and Crowhurst's goal was to reunite with Him, to become like Him and to become Him. As he felt himself achieving this goal, his sense of magical omnipotence increased. "I could play the game better than the cosmic beings (God's intelligence, etc.)," he wrote. "I can make myself a cosmic being by my own efforts." He felt that his "powers of abstraction are powerful enough to do tremendous damage."

The mental representations of the mother which contributed to the reunion are more obscure. It may be significant that he commenced the writing of his philosophy (a real yielding of himself to psychotic thinking) on the day following his mother's birthday. That he was aware of her birthday is evident from his tape recordings. On June 22, he said, "It's my mother's birthday tomorrow and I'm glad that I've been able to establish contact (radio contact) because it means she will get some little greeting." Was the philosophy the greeting and the contact? Mother, not father, was the religious one in the family, and, after a lifetime of scorn, Crowhurst returned to God in his philosophy.

Alluding to one of his own earlier essays, he referred to himself as the "Misfit"—painfully, heroically, alone and rejected by society as a bird who has left the nest. Now, the misfit had a new task: "We will be ready to begin another painful adventure. We will be your gods, and will have to learn how to live with our parents in a new system. We are in the womb of the universe."

Thus we see the underlying striving for reunion described by Reich, Rado, Lewin, and others. And how was this reunion to be achieved? He must free himself from the ape-like physical body to become pure intelligence. The last tape recording, made on his mother's birthday, gives a striking example of the narcissism and the purging. "I feel tremendously fit . . . as though I could realize all those ambitions I nurtured as a boy. . . . My reflexes amaze me, they're so fast, you know I catch things almost before they've started falling." After a scornful reference to fat and flabby men, he turns his attention to unhealthy ways of living. "I'm sure we're in terrible danger from it and there's absolutely nothing like going to sea for getting rid of all the poisons, you know, harping back to Strangelove's—the sort of Strangelove's Colonel . . . the poisons in your body, you must get rid of them. I don't know what they are but they've got to go." (Remember the "hateful blood of the Hun—or was it the other way around.") And, as the psychotic system developed in the following days, not only poisons but the whole physical body had to be purged. Obviously, when he said he was "tremendously fit" he was unrealistically attempting to deny his underlying sense of bodily inadequacy and wickedness. Unfortunately, his pride had been mortally wounded, and in the next few days his whole physical body became an object of disdain; it had to be purged before the reunion could take place.

Thus, the features underlying the sense of putting something over are seen here as the unconscious underpinnings of the type of narcissistic character structure which impels some people to manipulate repetitively in what often seems like a meaningless fashion.[6]

Now while some people like Crowhurst are driven to manipulate, and others may be inhibited in their ability to do so,

6. We will return to the subject of this type of chronic manipulator in chapter 10.

there are people for whom manipulation or its inhibition is not an issue. I refer to those relatively mature individuals who are able to develop intimate and generative relationships, relationships based on a genuine love and concern for other people. It is not that these people will never manipulate; indeed reality may dictate circumstances in such a way that manipulation may be entirely appropriate and adaptive. In that case, these people are able to draw on their pride and shame, purging and reunion, and they will derive pleasure from the manipulation. However, the shame, contempt, and pleasure sequence will be in the service of the adaptation; it will not be an overriding determinant of the behavior. In other words, while able to manipulate in these infrequent situations which may demand it, these people do not prefer to relate to people manipulatively.

Intimate and generative relationships are heirs to the consolidation of the sense of identity gained in adolescence. An essential part of this consolidation, which is a main task of the adolescent period, is the building of self-esteem. The adolescent's struggles in this area are well documented by Deutsch (1944) and Jacobson (1961) who have shown how the vacillations between intense pride and intense inferiority feelings represent serious narcissistic vulnerability. Many adolescents respond to this vulnerability by becoming manipulative. Indeed, as some of our mental hospitals have been turning their attention to younger and younger patients, manipulation has become an ever more prevalent phenomenon on the wards. And it is often the patients who never seem to grow out of their adolescence who are among the most manipulative. I believe that in addition to the intensification of the id impulses and reshuffling of the defensive patterns, in addition to the shifting identifications and the casting about for new love objects, much of the provocative and manipulative activity of the adolescent follows the sequence outlined above—narcissistic wound, shame, contempt, and restored pride with the exhilaration of reunion. Indeed, the process of devaluing the parents, a hallmark of adolescence (Blos, 1962), does not seem to be a mere withdrawing of libido from the parent (internal or external). Often, with manipulative adolescents, we do not see a lack of interest in the parent; we find, instead, an intense but contemptuous involvement.

It seems to me that these adolescents are purging themselves of internalized bad parents partly in order to support their narcissism. With these considerations in mind we can see that manipulative behavior, like so much of the adolescent's behavior which may distress us, is appropriate to the tasks of his age.

In an often more charming way, manipulation may appear as an age-appropriate maneuver in the Oedipal child as well. What makes it more charming is the fact that the young child is not equipped to lie as well as the adolescent is. However, Woolf (1949) relates the story of the five-year-old boy who came from a family in comfortable economic circumstances. One day, he went out on the street and begged for coins. He claimed that his family was in financial trouble. That evening, while eating strawberries and cream for dessert, he laughed and wondered aloud what the donors would think if they could see him now. Woolf describes his feeling of triumph and strength and his satisfaction at having proved his superiority. Here we have all the elements of putting something over by manipulation. The identity he chose in his pretense reveals his inner portrayal of poor (bad, worthless) parents. He then proved (regained) his superiority by devaluing the donors, thus getting rid of the worthless introject; and he had a sense of triumph and well-being ("I can eat delicious food"). This process is necessary to the child who is at such a competitive disadvantage in the Oedipal period.

We must now confront the question of whether the process described as "putting something over" applies to all manipulations. One way of answering this question is to follow the course charted in chapter 1; this is an answer by definition. If I choose to call an act "manipulation" only if it contains the four components, then, it follows (circularly) that the feeling of putting something over on the other person is present in all manipulations. However, this leaves us with two further considerations: does the sense of putting something over always involve the process described here, and to what extent does this process determine the manipulation?

In considering the first question, we must ask ourselves which parts of the process are conscious, and hence relatively discernible, and which parts are unconscious. The conscious elements of putting something over are the devaluation of the other person and the pleasure at having actually become superior to him. As I explained in chapter 1, these feelings are a part of the manipulative process, but it may take some probing on our part to get the manipulator to acknowledge them. After all, these feelings are not prized in our society. Competition and winning do have high value in our culture, but the winner is supposed to be a "good sport"; he is supposed to compliment his opponent, not disparage him. We think ill of the victor who ridicules the loser.

When we come to the unconscious underpinnings of these feelings, I cannot say whether they are the same for all manipulators. I believe that they are, but as I noted, psychoanalytic study of manipulators is not easy to come by. We can only speak about those few manipulators whom we can study; the rest is generalization.

Now, what about all the more obvious motives, both conscious and unconscious, which impel people to manipulate? What about the sense of power, the thinly masked sadism, the need to control other people—perhaps to counteract the fear of being controlled? What about Oedipal competition and sibling rivalry being reenacted in the social or treatment situation?

I do not imply that these themes should be overlooked; indeed some of these themes have been touched upon explicitly or implicitly already and have been discussed by St. Clair (1966). These motives can be seen to be related to the processes I have emphasized in this chapter. And as one or another motive is more prominent in any particular patient, the manipulation will take on that patient's particular coloring. However, the underlying process, basic and common to all manipulation, is, I believe, as I have outlined.

I have already referred to the question to what extent this process determines the manipulation. In some patients and at certain phases in development the defense of narcissism seems to provide the major force behind the manipulation. In other patients, gratification of certain other needs may impel the manipulation, with the pleasure of putting something over as an added benefit. This was illustrated in chapter 3 by my discussion of the acting-out masochistic woman. In still other people, those who have achieved a more mature way of relating to people, manipulation may be used only occasionally—and perhaps even with some reluctance—when the situation offers no alternative. Even in these instances, however, while the need to put something over may have played a very minor role in initiating the manipulation, the satisfaction from this process provides some exhilaration when the manipulation "works." And why shouldn't it? In all of us, no matter how mature, the infantile narcissism lives on.

CHAPTER 7

CONSIDERATIONS OF MORALITY

The preceding two chapters have dealt with components of manipulation which violate our generally accepted social values. We frown on deception and we think little of the exploiter who enjoys putting something over on another person. These activities are not in tune with conventional morality and it behooves us to consider, from a psychological point of view, the impact of morality on manipulation.

Piaget (1932) has shown how the development of moral values proceeds as the child grows up. A morality dependent on the presence of others who are authorities is the first type of morality to appear. This is a morality based on rules and laws. From this authority-dependent position, the child progresses to a position where he has a primary concern for other people in his peer group rather than for rules. Rules are considered changeable under certain social conditions, and cooperation with his peers at times takes precedence over parental rules. The important issue is that rules be the same for all members of the group. In late childhood, the child begins to develop the concept of what Piaget refers to as "equity," where moral judgment takes into account not only the rules and the peer values, but also the various psychological and social conditions surrounding an action. The child begins to have an interest not only in what is done, but also in why it is being done. Consideration of the other person looms large in this type of morality. The trend, then, is away from the domination of authority's rules toward a relative autonomy with its emphasis on the various reality factors. There are mixtures of all these positions in all of us, and, depending on the stress and the situation, one or another of these morality-determining conditions will become prominent.

The conscience of the adult is a blend of the internalized punitive figures of the infantile period and the modifying effects of the socialization process as the child moves out into the wider community. This latter process, with its diminution of egocentricity and its balancing of absolute dicta with social circumstances, is implicit in Piaget's formulation. Freud (1930) has pointed out that the internalized component may become particularly severe if the infant has had very strong aggressive feelings of his own—feelings which, through fear of retaliation, he has been forced to turn inward. These people, especially, will have difficulty in progressing along Piaget's developmental line; socialization may do little to lead them toward the position of a morality based on equity. Their consciences tend to be quite severe; moral rules are moral rules, and, as a first approximation, we would surmise that such people would probably manipulate very little.

The person functioning primarily on the level of peer-cooperation may engage in manupulative activity if his social milieu endorses such activity. Thus, as I noted in chapter 1, despite our rules of honesty, our society condones and encourages all sorts of deceptive activity—"it's the way we do things around here." And, in times of social stress and strong group cohesiveness (for example, political activity), we often see people who might not ordinarily manipulate—either because of honesty or out of consideration for other people—become freed from a sense of guilt as they join their colleagues in manipulation.

The person functioning primarily on the level of equity is least likely to manipulate. With a focus on consideration for others, he may be tactful and distort or omit the truth, but not for the pleasure of putting something over on the other person. Manipulation seems quite contrary to the concept of equity. However, as in all attempts at systematic understanding, we must avoid too rigid a categorization. For example, Mr. A. may see that Mr. B. is about to be victimized in a most unjust fashion by Mr. C. Mr. A. may choose to lie and put something over on Mr. C. in order to prevent the victimization. Mr. A. is moved by strong considerations for the situation and feelings of Mr. B., and he has to put aside his sympathy for Mr. C. I could present many such examples which serve to show that the outline of moral development, while helpful to our understanding, is by no means clear-cut.

Let us take a closer look at our first approximation which led us to suggest that people with overly severe consciences may be unlikely to manipulate. This would be true if the conscience had only an inhibiting function. However, a strong conscience may assert itself after the fact as well as before. Certain circumstances may cause the conscience and the moral considerations to be swept aside until after the manipulation has been enacted. Two such circumstances can serve to illustrate this point. As we shall see in chapter 8, certain features of the hospital ward milieu may offer some patients the opportunity to stand up before the whole community and shout, "Mea culpa! I have manipulated." An exhibitionist and masochistically oriented patient may suspend his moral considerations in order to manipulate and then be punished and make public atonement. We might say that in this situation the conscience sacrifices its opportunity for a small anticipatory chiding in order to gain a much larger chiding and atonement through punishment after the forbidden act has been committed.

In the second illustration, we have the situation where the severe conscience is swept aside by the demands of the need to put something over. Recalling the dynamics of this need (chapter 6), we come to the consideration that narcissistic repair may take precedence over conscience. A person who feels narcissistically vulnerable may defend himself against his shame by manipulating someone, and during this time his guilt may be suspended. The phallic-narcissistic student described in chapter 5 had reached a point in his analysis where his self-image was crumbling. He had begun to realize that his pseudomasculine pride was both superficial and a defense against intense longings to be cared for and loved as a dependent "womanish" child. He was mortified by these newly discovered (or actually rediscovered) feelings, and he was driven to make increasingly frantic attempts to restore his sense of pride. One night, at a social gathering, he felt that another man was the center of attention. He quickly drew the conversation around to summer employment and he told the group that he had earned $2,000 during the past summer. They were quite impressed and the spotlight was turned on him as they asked him how he had done it. Since the whole story was a fabrication, he had to invent a quick series of lies to cover his announcement. All that evening after he had gone home, and again the next day, he was bothered with the obsessive thought, "What did I do a thing like that for? Why did I have to lie to them?" In his analytic hour he was quite well aware of the function of the lie; indeed, shame had been the major theme of his dreams on the previous night. However, the knowledge that he had had to defend himself against this shame by a lie calculated to draw admiration to himself did not suffice to stop the obsessional ruminations. These were products of his guilt—guilt which had been held in abeyance until after the manipulation had been employed in an attempt to restore his self-esteem.

What we have come upon is the interplay between shame and guilt. Both affects are stimulated by hostile introjected objects as well as the rules and expectations of those in the person's current milieu. While guilt is primarily concerned with punishment for moral transgressions, shame is concerned with a felt deficiency, a failure to live up to the demands of the ego-ideal. While there may be some question whether shame is a precursor to guilt and is thus reflective of conflicts belonging to an earlier stage of development (Piers and Singer, 1953) or whether both affects reflect "equally advanced although different superego functions" (Lewis, 1971), there can be no doubt that either affect can mask the other and thus help defend against the dangers of the particular conflicts underlying the masked affect. Further, as Lewis has noted, different people have different superego styles, both in the way they react to internal shame or guilt situations and in terms of the question whether they react predominately to shame or guilt situations. I believe that narcissistically oriented people are more aware of shame issues while people who are oriented more toward objects as other people[1] may be more guilt-oriented. However, the relationships between shame and guilt are so complex, particularly when we consider that these affects may be largely unconscious, that no simple correlations between morality and manipulativeness can be meaningful. Another example can illustrate the complexity of the problem.

The businessman described in the preceding chapters had agreed to be the guest speaker at a businessmen's dinner. He thought very little of his audience, and he did not prepare his remarks. Consequently, his speech was dull and poorly received. After the meeting, one of his friends commented to him about his flat perform-

1. See chapter 10.

ance. He recounted this experience to me in his next analytic hour, and he noted that he still felt upset about it. He then went on to discuss how his father had always put a premium on his cleverness. "He just wanted me to be clever so he would look good; he never cared about my conduct, just so I looked good so he would look good. That's how he runs his life—protecting his image."

Later in the hour I pointed out that the patient himself had put a high premium on cleverness, and, like his father, was concerned with his own appearance. I suggested that he examine his feelings about the events of last night.

"You're right!" he exclaimed. "I don't have any guilt. I don't think I did anything wrong from the audience's point of view—I couldn't care less about them. It just made me look bad. All I was interested in was looking better. When my friend came up to me I was furious with him. I wanted to say, "Fuck you. If you hadn't stuffed yourself so much at dinner, you could have stayed awake better during my talk. I didn't say exactly that. What I said was, 'Everyone gets tired at evening meetings and after you have had a good dinner it's hard to settle down to listen to a speech.'"

Here, as so often with this chronic manipulator, we see that the guiding forces of his behavior lie in the realm of pride and shame; his public image is more important than the issue of "doing right by" the other person. Yet, as the analysis revealed, much of his life was governed by an unconscious sense of guilt. Because of his unconscious sadism towards women, he was driven constantly to try to make amends. He treated women badly in the long run, but if they asked favors of him he felt that he had to grant them. He resented this sense of obligation, but he was powerless to refuse. It was clear that granting these favors was felt as a sense of obligation, not as a chance to prove his potency. Indeed, as was seen in chapter 4, whenever he began to express his masculinity, his Oedipal guilt would inhibit his assertiveness so much that his intentionality was abridged. In these periods, he could not manipulate effectively, not because of moral scruples about manipulating, but because he was apathetic and anergic.

Since, in both this chapter and the preceding one, I have emphasized the role of shame and narcissistic repair as a driving force behind manipulation, it is reasonable to ask if people who are more prone to shame are more prone to manipulate. No such simple relationship occurs. For, as Lewis has pointed out, there are many possible ways of dealing with shame, only one of which is what she describes as "turning the tables"—the projection of the shameful introject, the purging which may be manipulative. Other shame-prone persons may have other, nonmanipulative reactions; indeed their guilt may prevent them from expressing the hostility of "turning the tables." For example, these people may resort to fantasied revenge or dreams of glory.

If there is any general guiding principle concerning the role of one's personal morality in the processes of manipulative behavior, it is this: The manipulative behavior itself is impelled by a morality of shame and the need to resolve the shame; if there is guilt about the manipulative action, this guilt may be suspended to allow the manipulation to take place. The function of shame is probably always directly involved in the manipulative process itself; guilt may inhibit the manipulation directly, it may inhibit it indirectly by undercutting the processes of intentionality in general, or it may help shape the character and style of the manipulation.

Thus far we have been considering the role of morality from the standpoint of the internal mental processes; the assumption has been that the values of the environment condemn deception and putting something over. Of course, the concept of a uniform set of standards and values in our society is an illusion. There are significant explicit and implicit differences in the values held by various segments of our society. The subculture from which the patient comes may openly or covertly encourage manipulative behavior. In this case, while the patient's manipulations may violate the standards of the larger society, they may reflect the standards of his own subculture, and the need for his inner mental processes to deal with moral questions may be minimized.

The patient who comes to our attention from a subculture which places a high value on the ability to deceive and manipulate will, of course, have a greater tendency to act manipulatively than a patient coming from other subcultures (Miller, 1958; Hollingshead and Redlich, 1958). I would speculate that there are roughly two kinds of subcultures placing a high value on manipulation. One is a society which openly condones manipulation and sees nothing wrong with it. Deception is taken as a matter of course and little concern. The other is a society which professes the values of honesty and truth but which actually encourages manipulation and deception (e.g. in business dealings). In the first society, the patient will rarely come to us because of manipulative behavior as such, although the results of certain manipulations, such as those which draw him into conflict with the law, may bring him to our clinical attention. During the course of our clinical contact with this patient, we may observe his tendency to manipulate, but if we consider this behavior pathological and attempt to treat it, we may be missing the point. Neither the patient nor his family and friends see the tendency to manipulate as deviant.

In the second type of milieu, the situation is somewhat different. Although manipulation may secretly be highly valued and practiced by family and friends alike, there is a tacit agreement not to acknowledge it as a valued behavior; instead, the members of this group profess the opposite values of honesty and straightforwardness. True, they may talk and laugh about successful manipulations (in business, for example) but these are isolated from the manifest value-system—they are rationalized and justified as exceptions. Johnson and Szurek (1952) have described parents who preach morality and good conduct to their children (and who probably think that they place high value on conforming behavior) but who, through subtle hints, invite their children to misbehave. The children themselves may be consciously unaware of the real priority of values which their parents have, but the message has gotten through and the value systems of these children have become indelibly engraved with the hidden value system of their parents.

Not infrequently one member of the family or group—often an adolescent—manipulates in such an open and consistent manner that, although he may be enacting the actual hidden values of the group, he is violating the manifest value system and perhaps causing some painful self-scrutiny on the part of others in the group. Here, the manipulating individual is seen as a deviant, and the request for clinical help may involve in part a request to help (or make) him stop manipulating. In situations such as these, it may be necessary to work with the family to help explore the mythical value-system. Otherwise the patient's internalized propensity to manipulate, together with its adaptive value in terms of his social realities, may make change impossible. And such change is not possible precisely because the patient sees no conflict between his actions and the values of his milieu—no moral problem presents itself to him.

Now this does not mean that such patients are without guilt feelings or feelings of shame. It means only that in such situations the deception and the feeling of putting something over on someone are not major areas of conflict. As we have seen, other aspects of behavior may involve severe crises of conscience while manipulative activities per se may not.

As we have considered the role of morality, we have once again come upon the interplay of the internal psychological regulating forces with some of the forces of the patient's environment. The moral stance which a patient takes vis-à-vis manipulative behavior reflects both the conscience which he developed while growing up and the values of his current milieu. We must now turn to this current milieu to look more closely at some of the reality factors which influence manipulative behavior.

CHAPTER 8

REALITY FACTORS

While the discussion of the four components has considered manipulation primarily from the point of view of the internal psychological processes of the manipulator, from time to time we have had to consider the realities of the situation in which the manipulator finds himself. For example, we considered the conflict of goals arising from what may have been an unjust or inappropriate hospital confinement. We saw how the desire to influence can have an alloplastic outcome (intentionality) if the object of the influence is known to be compliant, or an autoplastic outcome (e.g. fantasy) if the object has the reputation of being immovable. Deception is shaped by the realities of what the object will believe. The shame which impels the manipulator to put something over on someone may be triggered by an embarrassing social situation. And the values and standards of the individual will reflect in great part the values and standards of his subculture.

In this chapter, we shall examine in more detail a variety of reality factors which relate to manipulative behavior. Although these processes may operate in a wide variety of social contexts, we shall focus our attention on the psychiatric treatment situation. For it is this situation with which we are most familiar and which we can observe most easily.

Now it was in the discussion of the conflict of goals that we first encountered considerations of the real situation in which the patient finds himself. In that chapter, however, I emphasized the importance of understanding the *perceived* reality—the situation as the patient understands (or misunderstands) it. When we now examine the reality factors, we must step outside of the patient to consider reality irrespective of the patient's distortions or of his awareness. For manipulation, like all behavior, is influenced not only by inner forces but also by the situation in which the patient is immersed. This is the reality as defined by Erikson (1962, p.

463): "Reality . . . is the world of phenomenal experience perceived with a minimum of idiosyncratic distortion and with a maximum of joint validation." It is a reality which is in part obvious and in part very subtle. The patient (and staff) is influenced both by the aspects of the situation which he notices and about which he makes conscious judgments, and by aspects of the situation, such as values and standards, which escape his notice.

Many psychiatrists emphasizing the "here and now" focus mainly on this reality and on the transactions which occur within the social system where the patient finds himself. Minimizing the importance of the unconscious internal regulating processes, they may adopt the approach suggested by von Bertalanffy (1966, p. 716): "If the psychophysical organism is an active system, occupational and adjunctive therapies are an obvious consequence . . . more important than 'digging the past' will be insight into present conflicts, attempts at re-integration and orientation toward goals and the future." Unfortunately, this active desire not to "dig into the past" often serves as an excuse for ignoring the patient as a human, feeling individual and disregards the particular internal psychic equipment which gives him his individuality and in part determines the specific manner in which he will act within the system.

Psychoanalysts, on the other hand, have frequently been so absorbed with the genetic underpinnings of their patients' internalized psychic processes, that, with some notable exceptions, they have tended to understress the importance of the current realities. This is not to say that the conception of psychoanalysis as an enterprise dealing only with the past is correct. Nonetheless, the dimension of obvious and subtle current realities which has been added by many contemporary psychiatrists and social scientists is an immensely important one. It derives its importance and its usefulness not as a replacement of the individual point of view of psychoanalysis but as an expansion of this point of view. In terms of psychoanalytic metapsychology, we are here considering predominately the adaptive point of view. As Rapaport and Gill (1959) have stated: "Adaptation relationships are mutual; man and environment adapt to each other . . . Man adapts to his society—both to the physical and human environments which are its products" (p. 160).

It would take a far more knowledgeable social scientist than I to detail a comprehensive description of all the realities surrounding the manipulator in the clinical situation to which he must adapt. The historian, economist, anthropologist, sociologist, and political scientist could all contribute to our understanding of the social forces which comprise the patient's milieu. What I shall do in this chapter is to pick out certain features of the treatment environment which have impressed me; these will serve both as specific illustrations and as examples of some kinds of social forces which are active.

Not all patients come from subcultures which have the same styles as those found in mental hospitals. The clash between the style of a patient's subculture and the ward environment may be so great that the patient may feel isolated, misunderstood, and mistrustful. Often, this lack of trust is misdiagnosed as "paranoid." This diagnosis is incorrect; it is not a mistrust based on projective mechanisms but a mistrust of the unfamiliar or a mistrust of one cultural style because it is different from another. In his own culture, the patient might be very trusting. In unfamiliar circumstances, the patient, feeling trapped, may resort to manipulation, either to define himself or to show his contempt for the other culture and his superiority over it, or to escape the threatening culture altogether.

Within the cultural realities of the hospital ward itself, we can observe other external forces impinging on the patient and playing a role in determining whether he will manipulate. In his article describing the influence of the "standard operating procedures" of a ward on a patient's behavior, Stern (1970, pp. 744 f.) wrote: "Institutional messages are expressed through the most highly stable and formalized operations of institutions. . . . An institution speaks through its formalities, its rituals; these formalities take many forms—architecture, dress, the way people are grouped, the standard operating procedures, etc. Not only value systems but expected modes of behavior are signaled through these channels. These formalized operations occur automatically and, since they involve things and behavior, we rarely consider either that they communicate or what they communicate. . . .

"This capacity of institutions to determine human behavior, to set the value system, to force individuals into certain types of interaction is perhaps best demonstrated by Standard Operating Procedures (S.O.P.'s). These pieces of quasi-ritual institutional behavior not only define, in operation, the character of the institution, but also implicitly state, define, and determine the limits of behavior and the relationships of individuals."

The older mental hospital of several decades ago, by its architecture, staffing patterns, and virtually every other aspect of the milieu, tended to push many of its patients toward apathy or despair. Stripped of their own clothes and many of their freedoms, they became nameless, faceless members of a large crowd. The schizophrenic patient, already suffering from a wounded and blurred sense of self and seeking retreat from a frightening world, was encouraged to retreat even further and to allow his sense of self to continue to crumble on his slow course toward death (Arieti, 1955). Several years ago, I was a junior psychiatrist in one such hospital. My job was primarily to interview each of the almost two hundred "chronic" patients under my "care" at least once in a three-month period in order to write the required "progress" note in the chart. In addition, I attended the physically sick and answered the inquiries of relatives. There were no nurses on the ward. The aides made certain that patients went to meals, to the movies and "dances," and to various simple occupational assignments. The occasional disruptions of the routine were handled by physical restraint (seclusion or wet packs) and by a telephone call from the aide to the clinical director, who, over the phone, would adjust the medication. There were also unofficial methods of handling disruptive patients, such as secretly administered social and physical abuse. It was a lulling routine which worked smoothly and gave no one much trouble. All members were more or less locked into their places in the system and there was little possibility of a patient's shifting from an apathetic role to that of "person in his own right." I do not recall that patients on this ward manipulated to any significant degree. It may be that with such a large number of patients and so few staff, many manipulations went unnoticed. However, I believe that the atmosphere of the ward tended to foster psychological processes which made manipulation unlikely. Interpersonal interaction among the patients was generally not encouraged; the good patient was the quiet patient. The sense of self, so necessary for the intentionality which is required for manipulation, was continually undercut as the patient was treated as an impersonal being. There probably were relatively few goal conflicts because the patients' apathetic retreat was quite adaptive to the requirements of this ward.

Not all patients in hospitals such as I have just described were chronic schizophrenics, of course. Antisocial people, with their high internally driven propensity to manipulate and the strong clash between their personal style and that of the hospital, sometimes became patients in these institutions, although rarely on the "chronic" wards (Cleckley, 1955). There were indeed goal conflicts and these patients did manipulate, but the overall incidence of manipulation was kept down by occasional severe unofficial punishment and by extrusion from the hospital. These people, not fitting into the institution's concept of "sick" and being a source of actual or potential disruption of the peace-and-quiet routine, tended to be quickly discharged from the hospital.

A remarkable change has occurred in many hospital wards with the development of the concept of the therapeutic community (Jones, 1953). Attention has shifted from the treatment given *to* patients or the custodial care provided *for* them to the possibility of working *with* them and having them participate as a community in the treatment process.[1] Instead of fostering a further dissolution of the sense of self, these wards generally bolster the sense of self by emphasis on the responsibility of the patient, attention to his clothing and individual expression in his room arrangement, and focus on his role in the patient and family community. The concept of the patient as a decision-maker (Rubenstein and Lasswell, 1966) rather than a passive follower of a prescribed routine further enhances the patients' initiative and sense of activity.

Prominent among the new values introduced with the development of the therapeutic community is that of sharing one's feelings and problems with the whole community. Jones (1957, p. 215) made this very explicit: "It is one of the characteristics of the Unit [his therapeutic community] that it is considered desirable to talk about one's feelings and to share these confidences with

---

1. I remember one psychiatrist in a large, custody-oriented hospital who began to experiment with "group therapy." She invariably referred to her sessions with thirty or more patients by saying, "I'm doing group therapy on them."

everyone. Privileged communication, even between patients and staff, are discouraged, the preference being for communication to the group."

In practice, the application of therapeutic community concepts varies widely from ward to ward. The availability of sufficient numbers of ward personnel, the variety of disciplines represented on the staff, the degree of training and emotional maturity of staff personnel, the patient composition of the ward, and the actual commitment of the various members of the staff to the values of the therapeutic community all play a part in determining the social realities to which the patient must adapt. Nonetheless, most modern hospital wards which attempt to implement the processes of a therapeutic community share the values of patient participation, patient activity, and sharing within the community. I believe that these values tend to increase the incidence of manipulation by making its conscious and unconscious psychological underpinnings more adaptive.

In contrast to the older-style institutions, many modern hospitals tend not to extrude the nonpsychotic disruptive patients. There is a greater emphasis on attempting to treat a variety of personality disorders. Goal conflicts are apt to be more prominent on these wards. Wards oriented toward activity, progress, and behavioral movement of patients tend to emphasize the importance of goals, and the individual's response to this emphasis is often likely to be his seeking a goal which conflicts with the acceptable goals of the community. In addition, there is frequently a built-in conflict of messages given to the patient which may be reflected in a conflict of goals. On the one hand, the patient is told that he is a responsible person and is to be held responsible for his actions; at the same time he often has to prove his "responsibility" by conforming to the mores and routines of the community. In effect, we often say to the patient, "I expect you to be a socially responsible person, but you'll have to prove it and, at least in the beginning, I'll treat you like a socially irresponsible person."

Many hospitals employ a "step system" where patients progress up a graduated scale of freedom. Starting from a position of restriction to the ward, the patient may next be allowed to visit other wards in the company of staff or a group of patients. Later, he may be allowed to go out of the hospital in groups or with a "buddy," and ultimately he may be allowed to come and go by himself as he pleases. This freedom of movement, which outside of the hospital would be called a "right," is termed a "privilege" within the hospital. The patient must earn his privileges by demonstrating to the staff and patient group that he is able to handle them. This requires that he show competence and reliability by adapting to the values of the hospital—that is, cooperating and discussing troublesome problems with others in order that they will be less likely to erupt into undesirable action when he is off the ward. Often this becomes a conflict situation with the patient wanting more "privileges" (rights) and the patient-staff group being reluctant to grant them. The resourceful patient may employ a variety of manipulative measures to press his claim. He may attempt to make his doctor feel guilt for the restrictions; he may go through the motions of revealing some painful problem in order to prove that he has a "good relationship" with his therapist and can now be relied on. He may attempt to split the staff into opposing factions; the "good" staff members now press his claim with the "bad." In community meetings, he may trade off approval of another patient's request for that patient's approval of his.

Other realities of the hospital situation also create conflicts of goals which impel manipulative activity in order to overcome an oppressive environment. You will recall the case of the lawyer, which I described in chapter 3. Here was a man who had come to the hospital in a depressed state. Now, his depression had lifted and he was anxious to leave the hospital and resume his practice. He saw the need for further psychotherapy, and he intended to pursue it on an outpatient basis. His doctor probably had a variety of interests in keeping him in the hospital. Some of these interests might have had to do with the low hospital census and the doctor's therapeutic zeal. The doctor brought considerable pressure to bear on the patient by telling him that no reputable psychiatrist would treat him if he left the hospital against medical advice. The lawyer-patient responded by attempting a manipulation (secretly getting an outside consultant) to bring pressure on the doctor to alter his stand and to give him an "honorable discharge." I considered this man's manipulation an actualizing and adaptive maneuver designed to cope with a hospital which was probably imprisoning him rather than treating him.

Our professional orientation toward pathology often tends to make us overlook the adaptive value of behavior. But worse, it sometimes gives us a "holier-than-thou" attitude when a patient's goals conflict with our own. Thus, when we see the occasional manipulation, especially when enacted by a generally nonmanipulative patient, we must ask ourselves if the manipulation is something to be treated or if it is the patient's way of adapting to an unjust and oppressive environment. For if it is the latter, certainly a major portion of the treatment must be aimed not toward the patient but toward the hospital milieu. It may be that some of our rules and procedures force patients to manipulate in order to achieve entirely reasonable objectives. It is striking how often psychiatrists are easily able to see to oppressiveness in society at large while they remain blind to the oppressiveness of the hospital systems they devise.

Why do hospital wards have these oppressive influences? Any society tends to resist change and the self-examination which may lead to it. This dynamic is analogous to the forces of repression within the mind of an individual which leads him on the one hand to the avoidance of "dangerous" self-observation and on the other to the erection of certain defenses which help maintain his "order of things." Despite the teachings of Jones (1952) and Rapaport (1959) that all participants in the ward community must be considered parts of a dynamic system, in times of social disturbance (usually disturbance which threatens the status quo), the ward community, like society at large, chooses its scapegoats (Stanton and Schwartz, 1954). Since those in power have the greatest stake in preserving the existing social systems, hospital communities most often turn the patients into scapegoats. Indeed, a searching analysis of most hospital ward systems will reveal that the design of the ward is as much for the morale of the staff as for the treatment of the patients. And when trouble arises, the sensitivities and reputations of the staff are usually much more carefully considered than those of the patients. It is an unfortunate feature of institutional life that if significant numbers of staff people become unhappy and leave, the institution will break down. Patients are much more expendable.

Intentionality is enhanced in the therapeutic community by the fortification of the sense of self and the value placed on activity.

Whereas on the older ward it was adaptive not to intend, not to plan, not to initiate anything, the more modern psychiatric wards encourage these activities. In addition, a high but subtle value is often placed on the intention to influence others in order to gain satisfactions (in spite of the manifest stand of some staff members that such influence is undesirable). The whole process of gaining "privileges" and requiring staff and patient acquiescence in order to be allowed to implement personal decisions involves "proving" oneself and influencing others. This is one consequence of the value placed on sharing and communicating.

Sharing and communicating within the community have implications for the psychological processes underlying deception also. The empathy of the "practical psychologist" [2] is a very useful skill on such a ward. It is well to know the ward values, standards, and expectations so that one can temper one's public utterances to fit the desires of the listening public. On such a ward, one's public image is important.

Often there is another subtle complex of messages conveyed to the patients, messages like those to which I referred earlier in this chapter in discussing the impact of family values. Some wards, stressing patient responsibility, assume strong manifest positions against what they call "acting out," but what, within the highly moralistic context of the ward, might better be called "disruption" or "misbehavior." Despite this manifest position, some of the staff members may thrive on the crises caused by misbehavior. Such crises may appeal to their voyeurism or provide a vicarious outlet for their own inhibited impulses. The "good" patient-staff meeting may be the one in which some patient's manipulation comes to light and is the focus of a lively discussion, perhaps culminating in a confession, the imposition of some sanctions, and an aura of repentance and resolution. In the absence of such crises, staff morale may sag and some staff members may feel useless. Oriented as they are around the treatment of misbehavior, if there is no misbehavior, they may feel they have nothing to treat.[3] The patient, alert to the subtle as well as to the overt messages of the ward, may adapt to this value hierarchy with an increased tendency to

2. See chapter 5.
3. The need of some people for the deviant actions of others is illustrated in the nonhospital situation by R. Eissler (1949) and Seidenberg (1970).

deceive and manipulate and subsequently to be detected and to confess.

It is a hallmark of many contemporary hospital wards that they set definitive standards of behavior for their patients, standards which at times exceed those set for the staff. On one occasion, for example, my staff was quite upset that certain patients were not prompt in keeping their therapy appointments and would occasionally leave the ward without telling the nursing staff where they were going. (These were patients who were allowed off the ward at will; the concern was not that they would get into trouble off the ward, but that by neglecting to inform the staff, they were breaking a ward rule.) I pointed out that our resident physicians frequently were late to ward meetings (and, for all I knew, to their therapy appointments with their patients), and I drew an outburst of embarrassed laughter from them when I inquired how strictly they followed the policy of informing the nursing staff and the hospital telephone operator whenever they left the ward or the hospital. Such discrepancies in standards can easily lend themselves to contempt on the part of the patients which is a part of the feeling of putting something over.

Another way in which some hospital communities encourage the desire of the patient to put something over on the staff by manipulating is in their reaction to the manipulation. A patient with an internal psychological propensity to seek the narcissistic gratifications of putting something over on the staff may be amply rewarded by a staff which makes a large public display of the manipulation and which, through overt or covert messages, shows the patient how much it cares about good behavior and how much it has been hurt by the manipulation.

Now, those who harbor a pejorative view of manipulation might defensively interpret the foregoing analysis as a devaluation of the concept of the therapeutic community. Such a conclusion is neither accurate nor helpful to our scientific understanding. Every type of social organization has its effects on the thought and behavior of its members. Our focus in this book is on the thought and behavior which comprise manipulation; the analysis of the effects of some of the values and practices of certain therapeutic communities is restricted to those having a bearing on this particular psychological phenomenon. Any attempt to evaluate a therapeutic community would have to be enormously broadened to include a discussion of a wide range of psychological phenomena, and some value judgments would have to be rendered about these phenomena.

As I mentioned earlier in this chapter, wards vary considerably in their adherence to the values and practices of the therapeutic community. In addition to the factors I have already enumerated, there are those which I might refer to as ideological variations.[4] Some wards place a great emphasis on individual psychotherapy, particularly psychotherapy with a psychoanalytic orientation. Such wards tend to value privacy of therapeutic communication. There is less concern with overt behavior and less attempt to control it (except in clearly dangerous situations). Stress tends to be placed on individuality rather than on conformity. There may be a long-term outlook; what the patient does today is less important than the gradual reordering of the inner psychological processes in the hope that this reordering will eventually lead the patient to be free of his crippling inner conflicts. Group and community meetings tend to be seen as preserving the atmosphere in which the psychotherapy can take place.

Another type of ideology, although it is rarely acknowledged as such, places the maintenance of the particular type of community in the foreground. The investment here in the welfare or the progress of the patient is diluted by the investment in the maintenance of the stability of the ward organization. There tends to be a set of overt or covert rules which ensure that the valued group processes are perpetuated. A ward staff valuing this ideology will be quite moralistic in its outlook, viewing deviation from the rules and standards as a threat to the continued stability of the group.

A third type of ideology is organized around activity and the actions of the patients. The emphasis, here, tends to be on what a particular patient does and how he behaves here and now. There are acceptable and unacceptable modes of behavior, and the aim is to keep the patient active while channeling his activity in the "right" direction.

I believe that the realities conveyed to patients by these differing ideologies tend to evoke varying amounts of manipulation accord-

4. The groupings and ideas expressed in this section on "ideologies" are strongly based on the theoretical presentations of Parsons (1951b) and Edelson (1970).

ing to the degree to which they convey the manipulation-enhancing values outlined on pages 127–31. As a tentative hypothesis, I suggest that the individual therapy-oriented ward minimizes manipulation, the community-maintenance ward with its emphasis on rules and morality invites more manipulation, and the action-oriented ward, with its stress on "acceptable" activity and results, encourages a still greater incidence of manipulation.

At first glance, it might seem that we have here a hypothesis which can be tested in an easy, straightforward manner. Unfortunately this is not so. While ideologies differ on different wards, in actual practice there are ideological mixtures on all wards. Indeed, it is not always an easy task to identify the ideology of a ward; the clinical director may define it in one way while the staff may practice it in another.

Further, psychiatrists with different ideologies will not always agree on which behavior should be reported as manipulative. Observers who eschew the intrapsychic approach tend to view a greater range of behavior as if it were consciously intended (Parsons, 1951; K. Erikson, 1957). Yet another difficulty in testing the hypothesis arises from the fact that wards with differing ideologies will tend to treat different types of patients.

The hospital community provides a convenient society in which to observe and study the various forces and procedures comprising the realities to which the patient must adapt. Part of the community—the patients at least—is relatively captive, the composition of the community is reasonably stable, and the openness of the culture lends itself to this kind of observation and study. However, there is a wide variety of settings in which clinical psychiatry is practiced, and these different settings could each be subjected to an analysis of the interplay of their values and procedures with the psychological processes involved in manipulation. And even in any one of these types of setting (day hospital, crisis intervention center, private psychotherapy, community-oriented storefront clinic etc.), there will be variation depending on the ideology and commitments of the staff.

Many crisis-intervention centers, such as emergency inpatient or outpatient brief treatment units, probably draw from a population which employs a relatively high degree of manipulation. Some, but by no means all, suicide gestures are manipulative, just as are other types of strikingly deviant behavior which might be intentionally and deceptively employed to influence others. Where crisis-intervention centers are available, the people involved are appropriately seen there for diagnosis and at least initial treatment. The existence of these centers and their easy availability may sometimes set the stage for their incorporation into this type of manipulative behavior. On the other hand, those centers with a firm policy of a limited period of treatment tend to provide relatively little ongoing reward for "sick" behavior, and the approach to the problem which often includes work in a family-oriented setting may reduce the patient's need to manipulate and may help the family avoid reinforcing the manipulation. One effect of a firm time limit is that if the manipulation is concealing some real distress, the patient knows that he has a limited amount of time in which to change the focus of attention to the distress itself.

Some community-oriented clinical settings have mixed agendas which, at times, may tend to encourage patients' manipulation. While maintaining an interest in the individual patient, clinicians in this setting often adopt the position of the patient's advocate against an environment which is seen as oppressive and productive of mental illness. (Riessman and Miller, 1966; Thursz, 1966). In such a setting, the patient, knowing the clinician's intense interest in changing the social and sometimes the political system, may exploit this interest for his own personal gain by manipulative behavior toward the clinician. Or, sometimes the clinician and patient collaborate in planning and executing some manipulation designed to "beat the system." While the behavior here may be manipulative, in the ideology of that particular setting it is not necessarily pathological; it is seen as constructively adaptive.

The situation with mixed agendas which may create more fertile soil for manipulation is by no means confined to community-oriented psychiatrists. Clinicians practicing in educational and industrial settings often find themselves serving both the patient and the institution. Even in the practice of outpatient psychotherapy, the clinician's considerations of the need to make a living, to encourage referrals, and to enhance his reputation in the community may be communicated to the patient and set the stage for manipulation.[5]

5. These situations will be discussed more fully in chapter 11.

With the wide variation in styles, ideologies, and methods among psychiatrists practicing individual psychotherapy in an outpatient setting, it is difficult to generalize about the effect of this setting on manipulation. It may be that, especially where the clinician does not practice brief time-limited therapy, some patients are encouraged to employ the sick role over a prolonged period in order to influence and control others in their environment; the psychiatrist, not seeing the patient interacting with these others in a group setting, may be less aware of the manipulative aspects of the prolonged consultation. Furthermore, there are some workers who feel that the professional isolation of the individual psychotherapist renders him particularly prone to be manipulated. Indeed, some writers (Dreikurs et al., 1952) have suggested that one of the advantages of cotherapists is that it makes it more difficult for the patient to be manipulative in therapy. Whether this is so will depend to some extent on the ideologies and expectations of the cotherapists. If there is a high expectation that the patient will manipulate and a delight on the part of one therapist in exposing the manipulative attempts made against the other, the patient may be encouraged to liven up the sessions by manipulating. This situation is similar to that described in my discussion of some therapeutic communities. On the other hand, whether the individual psychotherapist will be prone to overlook and go along with patients' manipulations will depend on his ideology, his ability to look into his own motivations and reactions, and his clinical acumen.

The discussion of the individual psychotherapist raises for examination another area of the realities surrounding the manipulator. Whether in the individual or group, outpatient or hospital setting, the patient is influenced not only by the values and the messages of the particular setting, but also by the reactions and responses of various individuals within the setting. The responses of these individuals will also be influenced by the social system in which they are immersed; in addition, however, they will be governed by their various personal psychological styles.

There are many intrapsychic factors which determine how a staff member will respond to manipulation or even how he may invite manipulation. For convenience, we may divide these factors into two groups: those which tend to make the staff member overly prone to go along with the manipulation, and those which tend to make him overly concerned with and oppositional to being manipulated.

We have already encountered one of the psychological factors which may tend to make a staff member go along with a manipulation. In the discussion of empathy (chapter 5), I pointed out that the question of whether a person will manipulate or be manipulated depends partly on the ease with which he can relinquish his empathic identification. The manipulator is successful because, through a trial identification, he can intuit what the other person wants or will respond to. Likewise, the staff member empathically identifies with the patient to understand his position. The competent staff member, having sampled his patient's thinking, will then relinquish the identification in order that, as himself, he can make use of the information he has gained. Some people, however, find it difficult to relinquish this identification and they lose sight of their own selves and their roles as they become immersed in their identification with the patient. They then become rather easy objects of the patient's manipulation, and the patient will seek them out when he wants to manipulate. A striking example of this came to my attention several years ago when a colleague attempted to treat a gambler with an antisocial personality at the insistence of the patient's family. Before long, the colleague was introduced to gambling while rationalizing that he was going to the casinos with the patient merely to establish rapport.

Closely related to the difficulty of relinquishing identification is the need for complicity for vicarious enjoyment. One of the forces which attracts some people to the mental health field is the need to share in the excitement of other people's lives. By being the "professional," these staff members can rationalize their curiosity and excitement by calling it "work."

A sociopathic young woman whose long history of promiscuity disturbed her parents and the hospital staff alike had succeeded in convincing the staff that the relationship with her current boy friend was different. There was very little evidence to support her contention. The relationship had started when the boy had picked her up at a rock concert which she had secretly attended while telling the staff she was going elsewhere. Despite the fact that the staff of this hospital normally screened the new boyfriends of its patients very carefully, they knew surprisingly little about this young man—except for the fact that one of the nurses had met him one evening and said he was very handsome and polite. The patient, sensing the staff's interest in the "romance," kept various staff members "informed" about the respectable progress of the "deepening mutual attachment." Some staff members even speculated whether marriage might be in the offing, a marriage which might straighten out this young woman's life.

There were other staff members, however, who were impressed with how little was known about the man or the relationship, and despite the pleas that it was important to trust this patient, they began asking her enough questions to reveal that she had woven a fabric of lies and deceptions. At this point, the staff reacted in anger and forbade the patient to see her boyfriend. The young woman appeared quite repentant and agreed, but she said that the romance could not be broken off abruptly. She would like to meet the man in a quiet, intimate restaurant setting and break the news to him gently. Despite the skepticism of some, others on the staff, impelled either by their vicarious enjoyment of the fairy-tale romance or by their vicarious excitement from the secret, illicit affair, persuaded the group that her proposal was reasonable, proper, and courteous. This "good-bye" was parlayed into at least three more dates that the staff knew about.

The enjoyment of the manipulation is sometimes based on the staff member's relationship to other staff members and to authority in general. In the discussion of putting something over, I described the component of contempt which represents part of the purification processes supporting the manipulator's narcissistic image of himself. These dynamics, particularly prominent in chronic manipulators, are, of course, not confined to patients. At times staff members harbor the same contempt for authority and the same grandiose image of themselves. They may overtly or covertly encourage patients to manipulate the staff as an expression of their own need to depreciate the hospital's capabilities.[6]

There may also be collusion between staff member and patient to manipulate for some mutual gain. It is not unheard of, for example, to discover that a staff member and a patient have been having a secret sexual liaison, and that the staff member has

6. See chapter 11.

actively colluded in the deceptions and manipulations which made these trysts possible.

The relationships among staff personnel may lead one staff member to invite manipulation in yet another way. Workers with strong masochistic trends may be unconsciously driven to incur the wrath of their co-workers. When the manipulative patient approaches this person with his request or proposal, the worker may feel that the proposition is reasonable. He may be aware that others on the staff will disagree strongly with his decision to grant the request and he may experience considerable turmoil in attempting to reach a decision. What he does not realize is that often the deciding factor in his mind is his unconscious need to reach a conclusion which will place him in a position of public condemnation by his colleagues. He has encouraged the manipulation, then, as a vehicle for obtaining the masochistic gratification of having his colleagues say, "How could you let the patient manipulate you like that?"

Not infrequently, staff members, troubled by their own aggressive impulses, are overly afraid of harming their patients. This sometimes leads to an exaggerated concern for fairness. These workers are prime targets for the manipulator who plays on people's guilt. Every request carries with it the explicit or implicit question, "Don't you trust me?" or "Are you calling me a liar?" Every contact between patient and staff member becomes a trial rather than a therapeutic encounter. "How do you know I'll do it?" and "Can you really prove that I did it?" become the issues of discussion rather than the question of what is going on with the patient. The guilt-ridden staff member withers under such an attack, and rather than risk an unjust accusation, he may yield to the request or overlook the manipulative behavior.

Another appeal which causes turmoil in the person who is afraid to do harm is, "You're standing in the way of my one chance to change." For example, a patient with a strong need to view himself as a favored exception among patients had been unable to commit himself emotionally to the therapeutic group activities of the hospital. Despite the fact that he had never persevered in constructive projects in the past, when he asked to be excused from ward activities in order to pursue special training during the day, some staff members found themselves in rather severe conflict. They agreed that there had been no change in this patient which would indicate that his new project had a better chance of success than his previous undertakings; however, when he confronted them with, "How can you tell if you don't let me try?" and, "Here I'm trying to make something out of my life, to prepare for the future, and you're standing in my way!" they began to back down. They did not want to be responsible for ruining this boy's future. The whole issue of his need to be the favored exception—a characteristic which had been lifelong—tended to fade into the background.

Another, sometimes quite subtle, set of inner psychological mechanisms may make some workers prone to be manipulated. These mechanisms have to do with activity and passivity. Staff members with strong passive needs may be inclined to invite manipulative requests. As I suggested in chapters 4 and 5, the need to abandon the sense of activity is related both to the firmness of the sense of self and the difficulty of relinquishing the empathic sampling of the other person's viewpoint. The passively oriented person then becomes susceptible to the suggestions of the other person. This susceptibility may express masochistic and submissive traits and/or the unconscious sexual desire to be seduced.

These, then, are some of the intrapsychic factors which tend to make staff members encourage manipulative behavior on the part of their patients; other workers are guided by inner forces which make them overly concerned with and oppositional to manipulation. Some of these, of course, represent the converse of the forces just described. Staff members who need a very strong sense of activity, perhaps as a defense against their own passive longings, may insist on "calling the shots." They tend to see every interaction as a struggle for control. Either the patient wins or the staff wins. Nobody, but nobody, will put anything over on this staff member. This attitude can express a variety of unconscious dynamic themes, such as Oedipal competitiveness and the fear of being overwhelmed and rendered impotent, sadistic wishes, an exaggerated need for autonomy, stubbornness, etc. Paradoxically, at times this attitude encourages manipulative attempts on the part of the patient because the staff member may convey his intense interest (and secret excitement) in the battle for control, and the patient responds to the worker's interest and expectations.

I believe that some of the dynamics underlying the over-concern about being manipulated are revealed in one of the unfortunate current trends in psychiatry. As I noted in chapter 2, many contemporary psychiatrists suggest that most patient behavior represents manipulation in the service of obtaining dependency gratification. This activity in the service of passive needs (Freud, 1932) is seen as a power-struggle between patient and staff, a struggle for control. The concern over allowing the patient dependency gratification and the fear of allowing him to regress do have a rational basis in clinical experience; earlier in this chapter, I referred to hospital situations which fostered a kind of dependency and regression that rendered many patients incurable. However, nowadays from time to time we encounter a staff member whose fear of patient dependency and regression is so strong that it suggests an inner neurotic conflict, perhaps a conflict over his own dependency longings which is aggravated by the feeling that the patient, by manipulating, has rendered him passive. Sometimes the result of this attitude is that the patient is not admitted to the hospital when he should be or is pushed out of treatment or out of the hospital prematurely. While the doctor may be focusing on the prevention of regression or dependency gratification, he may overlook the inability of the patient to exercise reasonable control of his impulses or the effect of the premature discharge on others in the patient's environment.[7]

When we consider that each staff member brings to the group which comprises the hospital system his own internal dynamics and regulating mechanisms, we can easily see that embedded in the values, ideologies, and procedures of the system as a whole are a variety of often divergent individual tendencies. These differences may burst into clear focus when the patient is manipulating. The staff may be divided between those who fail to see the behavior as manipulation or who wish, for many of the reasons enumerated above, to encourage the behavior and those who feel that the behavior interferes with therapeutic progress or who resent the prospect of being manipulated. Burnham (1966) has pointed out that the patient often plays a major role in engineering such disagreements as a means of splitting ambivalence. However, the pre-existing tendencies of the various staff members provide

7. Some possible effects of premature discharge are enumerated by Lustman (1969).

fertile soil for such a maneuver. In addition, as Stanton and Schwartz (1954) have described it, staff dissension is often reflected in disruptive patient behavior.

The realities which the environment presents to the patient are composed not only of the thoughts and actions of staff members but of the other patients as well. The degree to which manipulation will become a part of the atmosphere of the ward will depend partly on its patients. During the last two decades, as many hospital units expanded their interest from the care and treatment of schizophrenic patients to a focus which included the hospital treatment of adolescents with impulsive behavior problems and of antisocial patients, the staffs were confronted by a variety of new problems. Among these was the realization that, in some wards at least, treating more than a few antisocial personalities at one time led to a kind of contagion which produced havoc in the unit.[8]

Patients, just like staff members, have a variety of reactions to manipulation by other patients, and these reactions also reflect both the social setting and their own inner dynamics. When the staff is being manipulated, there may be collusions and deals by some in the patient group. One parent's manipulation may have rewards for all, and the manipulative patient may receive considerable support in group meetings. Even when the reward is not so widespread, one patient may support the activities of another in the expectation that the favor will eventually be returned. Many patients hesitate to refuse the requests of their fellow patients.

The degree to which patients will knowingly and purposefully support their fellows' attempts to manipulate the staff depends in part on how well the sense of community is developed at that particular time. Where an atmosphere of strong commitment to the therapeutic community exists, there will be less tendency to collude in manipulations aimed at the staff. However, even in the most "democratically" organized ward there is always some patient-staff differential which can create a we-against-them atmosphere.

When the patients feel themselves to be the objects of the manipulation, they react with the same gamut of attitudes and

8. Other wards with different ideologies have not experienced such havoc even with large numbers of antisocial patients; in some cases, the manipulative atmosphere on these wards is high but it is not considered "havoc."

responses which we encountered earlier in the discussion of staff reactions. These reactions may be more easily detected in patients because they are defined as "patients" and thus are legitimate objects for our observation and study.

Among various types of patients, I have found that those with strong phallic narcissistic character traits often tend to get involved in the manipulative activity of other patients. A striking example of this occurred when an elderly man was admitted to the ward. Although he carried a medical diagnosis of osteoarthritis, one could never be certain how much this accounted for his behavior. He appeared quite helpless and requested to have his meals served; others had to move his chair and, at times, even open doors for him. While he seemed depressed, one wondered whether his lack of energy was in the service of maintaining the sick role and being waited on. Several patients with phallic-narcissistic orientations objected to his behavior and complained that they were being manipulated by him. Strikingly, it was not the staff who had ordered the patient to be so catered to but the patients—especially those who were complaining the loudest—who had spontaneously complied with his requests. It was only when staff raised the question of why these patients were waiting on him that they were able to stop. Their complaints subsided, and the "helpless" patient proved not to be so helpless after all. His spirits picked up, and he was soon discharged.

While I do not have sufficient data to be certain of this formulation, I would speculate that some of the complainers had adopted their phallic-narcissistic style as a defense against their own dependency longings, longings which they saw as unmasculine. The arrival of this patient provided them with the opportunity to express two dynamic themes. By unconsciously identifying with the helpless patient, they could help him and thus gratify their own needs for help. Simultaneously, by complaining about his "manipulative" behavior they could publicly repudiate their dependency needs and fortify their sense of masculinity. Along with this, on a more nearly conscious level, their masculinity was threatened by their feeling of being taken advantage of.

This sampling of forces operating on many levels within the social system in which the manipulating patient is immersed gives some idea of the variety of reality factors to which the patient adapts and which adapt to the patient. Thus, with any given patient, it is not only the complex of internal psychic processes which determine whether he will manipulate; forces within his milieu will serve to enhance or to inhibit the expression of these psychic processes.

CHAPTER 9

SYNTHESIS

As we have examined in detail the four components of manipulation and considered the role of morality and reality factors, we have treated them as relatively separate processes. This division has been a convenience to aid us in our thinking and our study; however, such separations are artificial and do not reflect the realities of psychological life. The manipulator thinks and behaves as a whole person. These "separate" processes overlap, contain common psychological elements, merge and blend with one another. Let us look at a clinical example with a view to illustrating this synthesis of processes.

Beatrice, an adolescent girl, had been hospitalized for many months. Her severe phobic symptoms and her fluctuating sense of reality had led some staff to regard her with a diagnosis of "borderline schizophrenia" while others labeled her "adolescent turmoil." Turmoil certainly had characterized her hospital stay. Extremely clever and charmingly appealing when not in the grip of some phobic terror, she constantly posed a challenge to the maintenance of ward rules. Her phobias impelled her to avoid many activities at which attendance was required. This led to restrictions of her "privileges," and she constantly sought ways of regaining them. The staff was particularly alert to her manipulations and while it did not consider manipulativeness to be a major problem of her life-style, there was a concern that the ward rules and sanctions be firmly and uniformly upheld.

Early in her hospitalization, Beatrice found visits with her family extremely trying. Her parents, quite intimidated by the glimpses of the violence which they saw behind her symptoms, were unable to interact with her in any reasonable fashion; their own conscious fears, as well as their unconscious fears of their own aggression, led them to give Beatrice a variety of mixed messages which only served to excite her and aggravate her symptoms. The visits were so disorganizing for Beatrice that the hospital had severed all contact between her and her family.

Partly because of her phobias (she would not go outside) and partly because of shame and low self-esteem, Beatrice had cut herself off from all her friendships. Behind this were intense fears of annihilation and strong upsurges of sexual feelings in any sort of sustained friendship. At the time of this particular manipulation, she had just been able to discuss some of these fears with me, her therapist, and it looked as if she might be able to begin to reach out for friendships. At first, she had asked to be allowed to have a pet dog in the ward, but this request was turned down. Then she began to worry that her bird at home had died. Shortly thereafter she said she would like to get in touch with some of her friends in her home town in an adjacent state. She was given permission to use the telephone for this purpose. During the first telephone call another patient overheard her saying, "Hello, Mom! How is my bird?" This was reported to the nurse who immediately cut off the telephone call. Beatrice was enormously pleased with herself and boasted to other patients about how she had outwitted the staff and how she could get in touch with her parents despite the staff's regulations; indeed, she would get her parents to take her out of "this crummy hospital."

It would be impossible (and a tour de force) to attempt to delineate all the processes which went into this manipulation. However, I shall describe some of them in order to illustrate two points: the relation between conscious and unconscious processes and the interrelations among the processes (synthesis). The material I draw on is partly observation (i.e., what she exhibited in her behavior and talked about in her therapy with me at the time of the manipulation) and partly reconstruction (i.e., what I learned from knowing her parents and what I learned during the course of several years of intensive therapeutic work with her). Of course, there is no possible way of being certain that the reconstructed points actually had bearing on the manipulation; often our illustrations must rest on the reasonable rather than the certain.

There were at least three conscious conflicts of goals: (1) she wanted to telephone her mother to find out about the bird and she knew the hospital staff would not allow this; (2) she wanted to outwit the staff and she knew the staff would try to prevent this; (3) she wanted to bring pressure on her parents to take her out of the hospital and she knew the staff would disapprove of both the pressure and the desire to leave. All of her assessments of the staff's positions in these conflicts were reasonably accurate reflections of the realities with which she was confronted. This third goal was most ambivalently held. It was not at all clear that she really wanted to leave the hospital; in part, she wanted to be told she had to stay. Thus, any guilt she felt about enjoying the hospital (and, as we shall see, there was considerable guilt) would be assuaged because she was being "forced" into staying. In all probability, this third goal would not have been sufficient impetus for the manipulation without the other two goals.

Looking at her three goals, we can see how the manipulation combined both satisfaction-gaining and danger-avoiding elements. The staff saw Beatrice's behavior entirely as an attempt at satisfaction. She wanted a "privilege" she did not have—the right to call her mother—and she wanted to have the satisfaction of putting something over on them. They were unaware of her guilt or any possible dangers which she saw in continuing to stay in the hospital. Indeed, at the time, I, as her therapist, was not clear about her need to avoid these dangers either. I was aware that she had begun to draw closer to me, and after a long initial struggle, we did occasionally have a working alliance. I sensed that this beginning of harmony was difficult for her, but I did not immediately relate the manipulation to an attempt to avoid the danger of involvement with me.[1]

While the goal of leaving the hospital was probably less clear in her mind, she was well aware of the goals of reaching her mother and outwitting the staff. Thus, she formulated a plan; she would say that she wished to call friends. The plan was quite clear to her and she knew it would work because she was aware that the staff had been concerned about her isolation. She also knew all along that she would be lying. She could well distinguish between what she would be telling the staff and what she planned to do. And she was sufficiently pulled together so that she knew who she was and who the staff was and which of the two ideas (call mother

---

1. Had I asked myself, "Why the manipulation at this time?" I might have been more sensitive to her conflict in therapy (see chapter 3).

or call her friends) belonged to whom. She also had a strong sense of activity about the manipulation. She had planned the lie, she knew she was executing the manipulation, and this sense of activity made her proud. *She* (with a reasonably firm sense of self) would best the staff; they were no match for her cleverness (contempt) and even though she was ultimately caught she felt the exhilaration of having tricked them.

Thus, we can see that all of the conscious components of the manipulation relate to one another and that our separation of components has more to do with our analysis than with psychological reality. The content of the lie, for example, is part of the deception, part of the anticipatory plan, part of the conflict of goals in that her empathy enabled her to understand which goals the staff approved of and which they disapproved of; the fact that she lied had to do with intention to solve the conflict of goals in an alloplastic manner and her need to put something over on the staff.

More of these interrelations can be seen when we examine some of the less conscious components of the manipulation. Let us start with the manifest content of the lie: "I want to call my friends." Up to around the age of puberty, Beatrice had been a reasonably popular girl, but contacts with her friends had dropped off markedly after she reached the age of 12. To her, friends were disgustingly sexual. They were interested in boys while she was not. She had engaged in some sexual play with girls in her prepubertal years, and memories of these activities now filled her with guilt. Her closest friend, in particular, had a father who was outwardly a civic leader, but who secretly kept a hoard of "dirty" books and magazines which she and her friend used to look at. And one of her most vividly embarrassing memories of activities with friends was the time she and two friends (a girl and a boy) had gone into a bathroom together. The boy went behind the shower curtain and pressed his erect penis up against it. While the girls could not see the penis itself, Beatrice had traced its outline on the outside of the curtain.

This complex of attitudes and memories must have been threatening to emerge into consciousness as she drew closer to me. Not long after the time of this manipulation, she was able to tell me that she had to keep her distance from me or she would be tempted to look for the outline of my penis in my trousers. She tended, at that time, to see me as she saw her father.

Her father, a college professor, was an easy-going, friendly person (or, in Beatrice's words, "a good-natured slob"). He was quite obviously seductive with his daughter, and, prior to her hospitalization, one of the ways they both expressed and defended themselves against their sexual attraction was to get into violent arguments which would end by Beatrice's going out of the room and slamming the door.

She also saw her father as weak and under her mother's domination. Like her mother she tended to devalue his intellectual achievements; she was "not interested" in what he accomplished at college. At home, he was boorish, sexual, dirty, and a "nothing."

Beatrice was quite certain that when she was young, she and her father took showers together. Her father also tended to urinate with the bathroom door ajar. Thus, being with her father was sexually stimulating and particularly revived her interest in seeing the penis. And as she became less distant from me (stopped slamming the door), these impulses pressed for expression and gave rise to the content of the lie. "I want to call my friends" in part meant, "I want to participate in sexual activities and look at the penis." This meaning, however, was not at all readily available to her consciousness.

At the same time, by saying she wanted to call her friends and knowing it was a lie, and by getting others to believe this lie, she was aided in her disavowal of these sexual impulses. "I don't *really* want to call my friends" meant "I don't really want to do these dirty things."

In the context of the foregoing, we can already discern some of the components of the reality-based idea, "I want to call my mother." What better protection against the sexual impulses vis-à-vis the father—or the therapist-father—than to call mother with the hope that she may get Beatrice out of this "crummy (dirty?) hospital." And this mother in particular!

Mother was seen as a tight, domineering, opinionated prude. Where father was dirty, mother was neat. The entire upstairs of the house had been carpeted with white carpet and everyone had to remove his shoes before going up to the second floor. Mother was clever; as a result of her business acumen she had made several wise investments and had accumulated a sizable amount of money for the family. True, at times she tended to be ruthless in her business dealings. She was contemptuous of those whose business ventures turned out poorly, and was equally contemptuous of her husband and his profession. He may have been the intellectual in the family but she was the clever one.

Consciously, Beatrice saw her mother as the powerful and dominant parent in contrast to the weak father. Unconsciously (and these fantasies emerged only much later in therapy), she felt that her mother had a secret phallus. A childhood fantasy of hers had been that dogs had two penises and she surprised herself during one therapy session by a sudden conviction that this indeed was the case. This had associations with her mother's two breasts—perhaps these were the female penises. In addition, however, she had the conviction that her mother's penis was hidden in her vagina and if she (Beatrice) were ever to masturbate, she would find "something in there." Thus her mother had a penis, but it was a hidden penis—a penis under control and not disgustingly obvious (remember her mother's prudishness in contrast to her father's obvious sexuality).

Mother's cleverness and father's sexuality provided a morality which made Beatrice's manipulation not only feasible but desirable. Both parents actively colluded in arranging secret contacts with her,[2] contacts which contained both the pleasure of outwitting an opponent and the excitement of engaging in an illicit activity.

Now we can return to one of Beatrice's conscious goals which was not only to call her mother but to call her in order to ask if her bird were still alive. She had proceeded from her desire to have a dog (two penises?) to worry about her bird. In part the bird represented her fantasied phallus (Krauss, 1913) and the question of whether it was alive or dead related to fears of her castration. If she still had the bird, it was a hidden phallus or a phallus in disguise.

Let us consider now some of the identifications involved in the manipulation. Although these must have been exceedingly complex, we can discern at least two aspects of identification which

2. This aspect of the family's involvement will be discussed further in chapter 12.

were prominent. The distortion, "I want to call my friends," expressed the partial identification with her father—sexual, dirty, and at the same time good-natured and friendly. The ideas of her real intention, "I want to call mother" and "I want to fool the staff," embodied elements of identification with mother checking on the hidden female penis (bird) and cleverness in besting people. Like her mother, Beatrice could also express contempt for those she defeated, thus proclaiming her own power and devaluing others who were "stupid" and more openly sexual. In addition there was both a compliance and an identification with staff members who liked the excitement of "disturbances" in the ward.

Another aspect of her sense of identity should be mentioned here: her identity as an adolescent. It was around the age of puberty that Beatrice had developed severe psychological trouble, and it was not without good reason that some staff members gave her the diagnosis of "adolescent turmoil." She had difficulty in acknowledging her adolescence and she dressed in much younger styles and wore no make-up. Her difficulty here was, of course, partly a repudiation of her sexual development and urges and partly an expression of her identification with her mother—prudish and with hidden sexual parts. The staff, on the other hand, was quite anxious to lead her into adolescence. Older nurses offered her advice on grooming and styles of clothes, and she was constantly encouraged to "act your age." While she steadfastly refused these offers, she could allow herself empathically to know what would please the staff—the request to call friends as an adolescent should wish to do; that is, she could understand this clearly and placidly as long as she knew it was a lie as far as she was concerned.

Being clever like her mother helped provide Beatrice with the sense of self necessary for her sense of activity. Were she more desirous of being like her sexual father, or if she were more capable of realizing this desire, she might have been torn between the two identifications and her activity might have been paralyzed (Schecter, 1968). However, the whole object of the deception lent itself to her purging the representation of her father, her disavowal of any tendency to identify with him, and her repudiation of his sexuality. It also rid her of having to look at his penis and to feel ashamed of her own body. This sense of activity and its link with the hidden penis was echoed by another practice of hers during that period. Beatrice was a fairly accomplished pool-player, and she took considerable pride in beating several of the boys on the ward. Secretly she enjoyed pressing her crotch against the table while taking a shot and feeling the something (table) between her legs. The sense of power gained by this secret feeling and the contempt of her male opponents fortified her.

The economics of the lie and her sense of activity reinforced each other. "If *I* lie (actively), the latent contents of the lie (sexual urges) are not true, and conversely, if the contents of the lie are not true, I am purged of guilt-ridden sexuality and the shameful exposure of my dirty self, and I am free to act unhampered by guilt and shame."

Thus far, I have discussed the underpinnings of Beatrice's manipulation from the point of view of phallic and Oedipal conflicts, and indeed these were quite prominent. There were other elements as well, but I am unable easily to relate the prephallic libidinal conflicts to the manipulation. The purging of the dirty-sexual material undoubtedly had anal as well as phallic referents, and the two penises-breasts equation supplies us with a hint that reaching her mother had strong oral elements. The whole concept of the bird, not only as a penis, but also as a transitional object (Winnicott, 1953) is pertinent here also. Beatrice did, at times, have difficulty in distinguishing between herself and others, although this was not a prominent problem for her. Indeed, I have already indicated that her boundaries were sufficiently firm for her to feel active and plan alloplastically. It is quite possible that the desire to check on the bird represented the conscious manifestation of her difficulty in maintaining ego-boundaries. We can speculate that, given her need to "slam the door in my face" and to purge me, her unconscious feelings of having annihilated me (and all objects) may have been stirred. Then, in part, checking on the bird may have represented a transitional state towards the restitution of objects. At other times in her therapy, these fantasies were quite vividly conscious, and indeed she was unable to intend, act, or manipulate at all. At this time, however, the threat of loss of object-relatedness was probably not conscious and was only represented in the manipulation; thus, she was able to feel like a self who could act on objects.

These, then, are some of the probable processes which entered into the manipulation. What we have conveniently separated for our analysis and our understanding all comes together in the mind of the manipulator.

CHAPTER 10

THE MANIPULATIVE PERSONALITY

We can conveniently distinguish three rough groupings of manipulative situations. In the first group, we see the maneuvers of those people who do not ordinarily employ manipulation, but who, under certain social circumstances, use manipulation as a strategy to achieve particular ends, as a means of attaining satisfaction and pleasure. Prominent among such situations are attempts by patients to be charged lower fees or to get preferred time schedules, manipulations to gain certain "privileges" or a certain "status" in the hospital, manipulations to gain permission to do something which might otherwise be forbidden by staff, sexually seductive manipulations, and manipulations serving the need to draw attention to themselves.

The second group contains the manipulations brought into play as a means of avoiding perceived danger and discomfort. Examples of this type of situation are the attempt to avoid an unpleasant task, such as examinations or work assignments; manipulation in the service of a phobia; manipulation in the service of repairing crumbling ego boundaries; manipulation to avoid anticipated punishment; and manipulation to avoid unpleasant or anxiety-producing encounters (such as with one's therapist, at times).

The third group of manipulative situations is distinguished from the first two groups in terms of the life style of the manipulator. The patients involved in the situations of the first two groups do not manipulate chronically and repeatedly. They manipulate for a reason which often becomes obvious in the course of the interaction. The patients involved in the third group manipulate for reasons that may be less obvious. Often they seem to manipulate for the sake of manipulating; this is a life style of predominant trait of their characters. The manipulations in this group

Parts of this chapter have been previously published (Bursten, 1972).

frequently seem downright silly—nothing more than pranks. They may lead the manipulator to be punished repeatedly; there seems to be no advantage gained by their behavior. "The psychopath," wrote Cleckley (1959), "often makes little or no use of what he attains as a result of deeds that eventually bring him to disaster." Unlike the advantages brought about by the first two groups of manipulations, fewer of the advantages of the third group are accessible to the consciousness of either patient or staff, and thus the behavior seems less reasonable and more impulsive. In terms of our four components, we will be well advised to seek the instigation of manipulations of the first two groups primarily in the conflict of goals while manipulations of the third group are more prominently impelled by the need to put something over on someone than by the manifest goal conflict. Thus, the third group is driven more from within the individual while the first two groups are affected to a greater degree by the circumstances in which they find themselves.

The situation is roughly analogous to that of other personality patterns. For example, all of us employ compulsive behavior at times. Some people, corresponding to our third grouping, have a major portion of their lives guided by the need to undo their forbidden impulses and the need to express their reaction-formations. They are the compulsive personalities and their compulsive behavior is driven chiefly from within, with little regard for the social circumstances. Others, with predominately different personality structures, will employ compulsive mechanisms under certain psychosocial stresses; their compulsive behavior, while traceable to the same underlying psychic processes as those active in the people with compulsive personalities, is triggered more immediately from external rather than internal forces.

Who are these patients whose manipulations fall into the third grouping? Until recently, they were referred to diagnostically as "sociopaths," and before that, they were labeled "psychopaths," "psychopathic personalities," "constitutional psychopathic inferiors," etc.

The diagnosis of "sociopathy" was a mixed bag containing a variety of behavior deviations. A wastebasket of the nomenclature, it might well have been called, "He doesn't fit anywhere else and his behavior is offensive." This conglomerate diagnostic category included an array of conditions which had little in common with each other except that society found these behaviors particularly offensive (Cleckley, 1959; Robins, 1967). In part, the category was "bitterly condemned . . . as providing a psychiatric diagnosis whereby criminal and psychiatric cases might be mixed" (Brill, 1966).

Recognizing this situation, the authors of the *Diagnostic and Statistical Manual of Mental Disorders* (1968) eliminated the category of sociopathy and distributed the collection of disorders previously subsumed under this category throughout the nomenclature. In clinical use, however, the term "sociopath" remains and usually refers to the antisocial personality. In the newest nomenclature, the antisocial personality is described thus:

> This term is reserved for individuals who are basically unsocialized and whose behavior pattern brings them repeatedly into conflict with society. They are incapable of significant loyalty to individuals, groups or social values. They are grossly selfish, callous, irresponsible, impulsive and unable to feel guilt or learn from experience and punishment. Frustration tolerance is low. They tend to blame others or offer plausible rationalizations for their behavior. A mere history of repeated legal or social offenses is not sufficient to justify this diagnosis.

This description clearly demonstrates the blending of the criminal and the psychiatric viewpoints. We tend to diagnose these individuals both on the basis of certain mental processes (inability to learn from experience, callousness, rationalization) and in terms of social deviance (antisocial, conflict with society, offenses). Furthermore, the social deviance aspect of this particular diagnosis often carries with it an explicit or implicit pejorative.

To some extent, of course, all characterological diagnoses have their social deviance aspects. However, the other personality disorders are defined primarily in terms of certain personality organizations (mental processes) which are felt to be relatively stable, internalized regulating mechanisms. These may help the individual to adapt to his milieu, depending in great part on the nature of the milieu. Again, we may take obsessive compulsive personality as an example. A person with this type of personality has a particular organization (and characterological diagnosis) whether he is contentedly placed in a milieu which lends itself to his compulsivity and in which he is not deviant, or whether he finds himself in an unstructured and uncertain milieu which causes him anxiety and points him up as deviant. It should be possible to describe a type of personality organization of the chronic manipulator which can serve as a diagnostic guideline even when the patient is not particularly socially deviant or criminal. I propose that we abandon those diagnostic labels which imply the mixture of psychological and sociological factors, and that we look for a set of common psychological characteristics which will enable us to make a truly characterological diagnosis.

On the surface these individuals are said to have little sense of responsibility, conscience, or guilt. They are unable to learn from experience; they form superficial relationships with considerable callousness and little loyalty; they show marked egocentricity, have little regard for the truth, and glibly justify their behavior when confronted. How can we understand these qualities in terms of a dynamic characterological formulation?

I believe that much of what we see in the behavior of the "antisocial personality" reflects a peremptory need to manipulate. The psychodynamic constellation governing this type of character is that described in chapter 6. These are intensely narcissistic people, but people whose narcissism is quite fragile. Their lives are governed and regulated by the repeated need to repair narcissistic wounds through the mechanisms of purging the shameful introject and reunion. Again and again, they are driven to put something over on someone and to manipulate. I refer to these people as "manipulative personalities"; they constitute our third grouping. While others may manipulate primarily on the basis of the situations in which they find themselves, the manipulative personality is driven to manipulate primarily by his inner dynamic position—his character structure. At times, he, too, will manipulate for obvious personal gain or to avoid danger, but beyond this, he will manipulate for the sake of manipulating—as an expression of his personality—even if he has to provoke goal conflicts to set the stage for the manipulation.

The fiction that the "antisocial personality" does not learn from experience stems from our focus on the obvious rewards and punishments. The manipulation itself is the primary goal of the manipulative personality, and the fact that a manipulation may not work or may lead to punishment may have no more effect on his need to manipulate than the inconvenience of promptness may have on the needs of the obsessive compulsive personality.

To understand the superficiality of relationships, the egocentricity, callousness, and lack of loyalty which characterize persons with manipulative personalities, it is necessary to understand the psychology of people with narcissistic types of object relationships.[1] Freud (1914) described two types of relationship that an individual may have with others; narcissistic and anaclitic. In the narcissistic relationship, the person is so involved with himself that he seeks objects who represent some aspect of himself and with whom he can easily identify. The object may be attractive because the person sees in it what he himself is or was in whole or in part, or what he would like to be. Thus, loving the object is really a form of loving oneself. The other type of object choice requires a more clearly differentiated object; someone who is not the person himself but rather a separate individual who is capable of gratifying him. Eisnitz (1969) has pointed out that the term "anaclitic," based as it was on an early type of instinct theory which is no longer used, is not appropriate; he has suggested the term "attachment" to describe object relationships where the interest is primarily in the other person *as* another person. While I hesitate to introduce my own special brand of terms in our field—a field which is already overcrowded with special terminology—I feel that "attachment" is ambiguous because a narcissistic person might become quite attached to someone who is as he himself would like to be. I suggest the term "complementary object choice" to indicate that the object choice is not primarily based on an extension of the self and that it gratifies the needs of the individual or otherwise interacts with him.

Now, Eisnitz has made the important point that relationships comprise varying admixtures of narcissistic and complementary components. When we say that a person seeks (say) a narcis-

1. Kohut's (1971) book on the psychoanalysis of narcissism appeared too late to be integrated into the text of this book. It is an important addition to our understanding of narcissistic personalities and is particularly relevant to the discussions in this chapter and chapter 14.

sistic type of object choice we are talking about the predominant features rather than necessarily the exclusive features of the relationship.

There are some important differences between these two types of relationships. The complementary type implies a relatively separate object who is seen as having value in his own right; he can gratify the patient's needs. A person forming complementary relationships might have feelings of respect, concern, love, pity, sadness, etc.—all qualities which are not prominently evident in the attitudes of narcissistic persons. The narcissistic person places great value on himself and tends to devalue others. As Kernberg (1967) has indicated, the basic need is to identify with (to be) an all-good, all-powerful person and thus be protected from the hostile, persecutory, outside world. This basic need is expressed by a magical sense of omnipotence and the need to seek out objects who reflect this omnipotence and can be seen as extensions of the self. "There is no real 'dependency' in the sense of love for the ideal object and concern for it. On a deeper level, the idealized object is treated ruthlessly, possessively, and as an extension of the patient himself. . . . The need to *control* the idealized objects, to use them in attempts to manipulate and exploit the environment and to 'destroy potential enemies,' is linked with inordinate pride in the 'possession' of these perfect objects totally dedicated to the patient" (italics his).

Rosenfeld (1964) has stated that this omnipotent narcissistic stance has been adopted because the patient would find a complementary object relationship[2] too dangerous. Having a separate object on which one has to depend for gratification raises the prospect of frustration, anger, envy, and pain. The experiences of infancy have taught these people to avoid the risk of separate objects and complementary relationships; safety is to be found only in omnipotence and relationships with those who are like themselves and can be seen as extensions of themselves.

It is these early experiences of pain and frustration which have led the narcissistic person to devalue all but the most powerful giving figures, according to Kernberg. Objects which cannot immediately provide satisfaction are seen as worthless; objects

---

2. Rosenfeld, of course, did not refer to "complementary object relationships"; I adapt his concepts to my terminology.

who frustrate must be vengefully destroyed. And objects must be defensively devalued "in order to prevent them from becoming feared and hated 'persecutors.' "

Since the manipulative personality is a type of narcissistic person, we now gain some insight into the superficiality of his relationships, his callousness, lack of loyalty, and egocentricity. He must be omnipotent; he cannot invest in or depend on others because at best they will frustrate him and at worst they will persecute and destroy him.

Now, there is a gamut of narcissistic personality types and all of these types probably have the same broad underlying dynamics pushing them away from complementary relationships and making them egocentric, superficial, and callous. For example, there is the pouting, chronically resentful person who presents himself to the world as disappointed. There is the paranoid character whose suspiciousness and rage can be stirred at a moment's notice and who lives in constant (and probably conscious) expectation of betrayal. The phallic narcissist is exhibitionistic and full of pride, and often achieves considerable success. The manipulative personality is driven to put something over on other people. What are some of the factors determining that a person with the infantile underpinnings of narcissistic relationships will turn into a manipulative personality? While I cannot be very specific about the genetic origins of the factors determining that a particular narcissistic personality will be manipulative in type, there are three areas in which we have some clues—the degree of self-object differentiation, the mode of narcissistic repair, and the value system.

The manipulative personality develops a better sense of self-object differentiation than the paranoid personality. The paranoid personality is so beset by ideas of reference and projections of his own rage that he often must wall himself off from relationships with others in order to maintain any sense of integrity at all. The manipulative personality, while predominantly narcissistic in his relationships, is much more at ease with other people and he is not in much danger of losing his boundaries in his relationships. The phallic narcissist probably differentiates even better between self and object, and he has the capacity for a greater mixture of complementary relationships with the predominantly narcissistic ones (W. Reich, 1949). While the basis for these differentiations must lie in the vicissitudes of infantile orality, the strength of the sucking and biting impulses, and the reaction of the mother, as well as in the ability of the mother to allow and to foster the child's differentiation from her during infancy, the details of these features of infancy must yet be worked out.

The degree of self-object differentiation is tied in with the mode of narcissistic repair. The manipulative personality repairs his narcissism by the dynamics of putting something over, as described in chapter 6. That is, he does something to the other person. The paranoid personality and the chronic complainer have what seems to me to be a less sophisticated method of handling their wounded narcissism: they bellow with rage or cry with frustration much in the same manner as the little infant who knows only *his* needs and who cannot well tune in to the existence of other people. They desperately *demand* things from the world; they do not seem to be clear enough about the world to *use* it in any subtle fashion.

Putting something over, then, is the mode of narcissistic repair of the manipulative personality, and contempt is its vehicle. By purging the shameful introject in this manner, the patient is able to restore his sense of omnipotence and thus he is probably spared the need to regress to the more primitive rage of the paranoid personality. As I have shown in chapter 6, the purging with its feeling of contempt has strong libidinal roots in anality and defecation. Thus, in addition to the state of individuation of the infant, there must be some strong contributions from the anal period of development which help mold the narcissistic personality into the manipulative type.

The role of anality in the formation of the manipulative personality has not been sufficiently emphasized, perhaps because the role of the oral and phallic conflicts have been so apparent (Wittels, 1938, Bergler, 1944). The contemptuous purging has strong anal features. We see other suggestions of strong anal influence in the manipulative personality; there is the emphasis on shame, the need to please (or to appear to please), and the dramatic quality of speech coupled with dramatic action, which Greenacre (1950) has related to the anal phase of development.

A striking example of the anal use of words and its role in contempt was given by a hospitalized patient with a manipulative personality. This patient, with very few obvious predominantly anal traits, was fond of writing notes and letters to the staff. One such letter started with the "plea": "Please excuse my noise this morning." The letter was signed, "Cassius Windemuss I." I might speculate on the similarity between "Cassius" and "gaseous," but no such speculation is needed to see the wind in "Windemuss." Another of his letters was even more explicit: "There are styles and there is wind. There is probably more wind than style in writing as in life. Long warm wind translated as hot air. Once I thought that if I could sound like the King James version of the Bible, I could, I would have achieved style. I never use one word where two or three will do. The more the merrier. I was particularly fond of words over one inch. The longer the better. The Merriam-Webster people should give me a bonus or something. You had to have a dictionary handy to figure out just what the H— I was getting at. After looking up the words of eight cylinders, you would arrive at the happy conclusion that I had not really said anything at all. Lots of gas." The blend here of the anal use of words with the phallic image of the length (the pseudomagnificence of his vocabulary) reflects both his narcissism and his feelings of expulsion of bits. We are reminded of the taunt of the businessman described in chapter 6: "You come looking for coins and all you get is shit."

The third area of factors differentiating the manipulative personality from other narcissistic personalities is the area of the value system, particularly with regard to deception. Lying has been studied from two vantage points—the development of reality-testing (differentiating reality from fantasy) and morality.

It is generally agreed that there is a period in infantile life when the child cannot lie. As we have seen, lying requires a degree of differentiation between reality and fantasy which the very young child does not reliably possess. Woolf (1949) maintained that a child cannot lie before four years of age because of the blending of fantasy and reality. It is of interest that Gesell and Ilg (1946) in their growth gradient of "truth and property" considered the question of honesty to be first relevant at age four, and age five was described as the age that "fanciful stories and exaggerations continue, but the child begins to distinguish real from make-believe and may know when he is "fooling."

Greenacre (1945) has written about the "psychopath's" reality sense. "The degradation of the sense of reality by the opportunistic need to be pleasing," and the attitude that "what *seems to be* is more valued than what *is*" (italics hers) is traced in part to defective development of reality-testing. In general, the parents of her patients placed great emphasis on having a good public image and on concealing things which might damage that image. This, together with the mother's need to delay the infant's separation from her, impairs his ability to distinguish reality from illusion.

The position I have taken in this book is that we can speak of lying only when reality-testing is sufficient for the patient to have the conscious information available for him to assess the truth. If he is so much under the sway of his impulses, and his reality-testing is so impaired that he is not able to assess the truth (or, more accurately, only minimally able to assess the truth), we do not describe him as lying; likewise, if he is so repressed that he keeps himself ignorant of the truth, the question of lying is also irrelevant.

Manipulative personalities I have seen were, indeed, more interested in illusion and public image than in truth, but I have not found it profitable to view this as primarily an impairment of reality-testing. While their lies have the elements of magical thinking and negative omnipotence,[3] I have felt that they were usually quite aware of the truth. You will recall that in my discussion of various ways in which distortions reach consciousness, I pointed out how reality-testing may be compromised in a wide variety (if not all) of psychological conditions. I believe that the manipulator, like other liars, probably has less "impairment" of reality-testing than many neurotic patients.

For example, a college student[4] handed in a term paper which

3. "If I say it, it really isn't so." See chapter 5.
4. I did not meet the student, so therefore I cannot certify that he has a manipulative personality. However, this behavior is so typical of manipulative personalities when they are caught that it can be used here illustratively. The story was told to me by the professor, an academic colleague of mine.

looked vaguely familiar to his professor. The professor did some research and found the article from which the term paper had been plagiarized almost word for word. He reported the matter to the dean who informed him that the student had been caught previously in a similar offense. The professor was advised to have a talk with the student.

"I called him," the professor told me, "and asked him to come to my office. I told him to bring the book from which he had copied the paper. 'What book?' he asked me. He denied any knowledge of an article similar to his paper. I told him that I would bring the book.

"When he came to my office, I showed him his paper and the book. He admitted that they were similar—similar?! They were word for word! Then he offered to write another paper, and when I said I wouldn't accept another paper he said, 'Why don't we forget the whole thing!' "

This student was more interested in his image and its consequences in terms of his being expelled from college than in the truth or reality of the situation. We may postulate that, in part, one of his identities believed in the excellence of "his own" paper. But the predominant part of his self was well aware of the deception and had minimal restriction of reality-testing.

Let us return to Greenacre's statement, "What *seems to be* (appearance) is more valued than what *is*," for herein lies a key. I believe that it is the *values* rather than the reality-testing that deserve emphasis. And it is in this area of values—the guiding morality—that we come to another difference between manipulative personalities and other narcissistic personality types.[5] Our student, like most manipulative personalities, has an adequate knowledge of reality, but the truth is not relevant to him. Public appearances are important, and if these are likely to become tarnished, he becomes threatened, and he will do his best to preserve a good image. Telling the truth has a very low priority for him. He is not usually embarrassed if he is caught in a lie; if worse comes to worst and he cannot preserve the image of

5. Kernberg (1970b) has written, "The antisocial personality may be considered a subgroup of the narcissistic personality . . . (with the) same general constellation of traits . . . in combination with additional superego pathology.'

honesty, he will resort to the image of contrition. He does not *feel* contrite but he knows that his public expects contrition and thus, with still another deception, his "good image" is restored. Honesty and lying have little pertinence.

The pseudologies of the impostor—whom I consider a type of manipulative personality—have also been described by some authors (Linn, 1967) as defective reality-testing. Again, I feel that the emphasis on this factor is misplaced. Certainly the impostor has a strong infusion of fantasy in his real life; however, those few impostors I have seen clinically did know truth from fantasy, but the question of honesty and integrity was not important to them. What I believe happens with impostors and, in general, with manipulative personalities, is that they may lose themselves temporarily in their assumed identities. This is a situation which is common with professional actors and others who tend to dramatize themselves. So, to this degree, reality-testing is compromised, but we may say that it is comprised in the service of putting on a good performance. The ability to test reality is readily available and can be called back easily, in contrast to (say) a psychotic person or person with amnesia or multiple personality. In the service of a good performance, reality-testing may have little value—it may even be a hindrance; therefore, it is temporarily suspended. But a moment or two later, the patient easily knows that he has been lying, and that the lie was important in order to support a good image.

In my view, then, the manipulative personality has a sufficiently firm sense of reality to lie; his deceptions depend more on considerations of morality than on reality-testing. As we have seen in chapter 7, the style and the interplay of shame and guilt form the moral framework for the manipulation. The need to protect and repair his narcissism places the emphasis of morality on shame. The enhancement of his own self-esteem meshes perfectly with the values taught him by his parents, as described by Greenacre (1945): "It matters far less what you do than what you look like to others." His parents teach him a morality of pride and shame and to go along with his internal dynamic position. While he is aware of reality, truth (and guilt) are not the crucial issues.

Johnson and Szurek (1952) have pointed out yet another parental contribution to the morality of the manipulative personality. Speaking of the formation of "superego lacunae" in the child, they described the parents as preaching morality while at the same time giving the child every subtle encouragement to violate the rules. Thus the child learns that rules and guilt can be suspended and devalued. The parents' enjoyment of his exploits, which he undoubtedly perceives, must reinforce his self-esteem at a time when rules and guilt have been pushed into the background.

Now, in my discussion of lying and deception, I de-emphasized the role of the loss of reality-testing in favor of the role of values. There is another area, however, where the attenuation of reality testing is often strikingly apparent. Many manipulative personalities are risk-takers.[6] Often they undertake schemes with so little chance of success that they have been thought either to lack the foresight to see the consequences of their actions, or to be driven by unconscious guilt to engage in activities which will lead to punishment. I do not think that either of these explanations grasps the essential features of the manipulative personality. I believe that the judgment of these people is often limited by their narcissism. As A. Reich (1960) has pointed out, there is a disavowal of the limiting reality when the narcissistic person must repair his wounds. His feelings of omnipotence take over, bolstered perhaps by a sense of oneness with a benevolent universe, and he thinks he can accomplish the impossible. He is not realistic, and in this sense his reality-testing is limited. However, the attenuation is in his appreciation of the dangers and of his own limitations; this is quite different from the questions of reality which we discussed in considering his deceptiveness.

To recapitulate: The manipulative personality is a type of narcissistic personality. His object choices are generally seen as extensions of himself; he cannot relate to others as separate individuals worthy of respect in their own right. He differs from other types of narcissistic personalities in at least three respects. He has sufficient self-object differentiation to be able generally to maintain ego boundaries and to use other people for his own ends. His major role of narcissistic repair consists of purging his

6. Greenacre (1945) has pointed out that these patients feel they will be miraculously saved. My discussion is consistent with her formulation.

shameful introject through contempt; in large measure this reflects anal mechanisms. His value system is such that truth is subordinated to image-building in his priorities.

These, then, are some of the factors which play a part in separating the manipulative personality from the broader class of narcissistic personalities. Many people whom we currently diagnose as antisocial personalities are impelled largely by these factors and should be called "manipulative personalities." True, it is often possible to see what advantage is gained by their particular manipulations, but it is the hallmark of manipulative personalities that they will attain their goals by manipulation rather than by other means because they are constantly engaged in the unconscious struggle to shore up their narcissistic self-image.

Even among the class of manipulative personalities, we encounter a wide variety of types. There are differences in the types of identities assumed by various persons and differences in the degree of impulse control. These two features are intimately related developmentally. As Jacobson (1964) and Erikson (1968) have shown, the ego's mastery of impulses and its knowledge of and adaptation to reality depends in great measure on the consolidation of the various identifications and their values into a sense of identity. Drawing heavily on the identifications of infancy, this consolidation provides much of the work of adolescence.

I can illustrate some factors guiding the development of different styles (identities) among manipulative personalities only in a most sketchy manner. Let us contrast the manipulations of the businessman with those of Donald Crowhurst (chapters 4 and 6). Let us assume that the earliest years gave both men the propensity for a persistent and peremptory need to manipulate. The businessman had severe conflicts about the expression of his masculinity and he had to conceal his ambition protectively behind either trickery or inertia. In his analysis, it became quite evident that he protected his penis from attack by pretending that he did not have one, or if he did, that it was only a joking one anyway. In this, he emulated his image of his father whom he saw as ineffectual. He was Jewish, and he saw the historic role of the Jew as being liable to persecution and having to hide his ambitions and resort to trickery. Thus he lived by his wits, pretending to be a joke—no threat to anyone—while cleverly manipulating in subtle ways.

His family put a high value on scholastic achievement and in part his choice of a business career was a fulfillment of and a rebellion against their wishes. In adolescence, he decided that he would not conform to their plans for him; indeed to succeed as the family's prize scholar was too threatening. Hence he embarked on a business career, but one where he used his wits. He "had a good head" and used it in his career, but the career was deflected from the central values of his parents.

Crowhurst, on the other hand, grew up as part of the British ruling class in India. His father, a railway superintendent, was taciturn and competent when sober, but after drinking he would return home potentially violent. These were exciting and dangerous times when young Donald would be spirited out of the house to the safety of neighbors. While at the neighbors' house, Donald reflected the excitement by entertaining them with "vivid stories, imitations, and jokes." [7] In this way, he learned to master the anxiety of the situation through a kind of playful identification with the aggressor.

Crowhurst's mother was very religious and there is a suggestion that she lived in a kind of unreal world. This was her second marriage and her first husband had "made my life a misery with drink and chasing after women." She tended to deny that Mr. Crowhurst had these tendencies and she idealized him as kind and with great "intelligence, capability, honesty, sincerity of purpose, powers of organization, and love of humanity, and the gift of handling men—used to having hundreds of men under him." She was indignant at the thought that her husband might have to be in a subservient position and she was determined that—even at the price of her own martyrdom—Donald should have every opportunity.

From these very fragmentary data we may speculate that Crowhurst's infancy and latency situation was sharply different from the businessman's. The successful resolution of the Oedipal anxiety here was not to be secretly clever under an assuming

7. While the data about these stories come from people who knew the Crowhursts when Donald was ten years old, there are suggestions that this kind of drama may have been a recurrent theme throughout his childhood.

shield, but rather to become playfully grand and a leader. This was coupled with a family situation which put a high value on excitement. His mother's fanatical religiosity must have promoted Donald's sense of being special and protected, and his omnipotent tendency to deny his own limitations found support in his mother's practice of denial. Thus, the stage he chose for his manipulations was one of excited, active, and risk-taking bravery.[8]

Variations in the types of manipulative personalities also rest on differences in impulse control. In 1939, Henderson characterized three types of "psychopaths"—aggressive, inadequate, and creative. While his characterizations have not been uniformly accepted (McCord and McCord, 1964) they do suggest that there are differences in the ability of manipulative personalities to harness their impulses. As we shift from the use of the term "antisocial personality" with its implications of deviance and offenses against society to the term "manipulative personality," we begin to realize that there are those who are internally driven to manipulate but who do not get into serious conflict with society. Some of these people adapt quite well; they seek and find places in our culture which provide them with an outlet for their manipulativeness, or even put a premium on it. This type of manipulative personality includes some successful businessmen, politicians, administrators, and probably people in almost every walk of life. These people have found an environment which is receptive to their manipulative personalities, but, in addition, they are sufficiently well integrated to pursue an adaptive course without the severe disruptions of impulsive outbursts which characterize those manipulative personalities who repeatedly get into trouble.

Kernberg's (1970a) detailed description of the levels of character development provides a framework for conceptualizing these variations. He has placed "antisocial personalities" on the low level of character development—a level characterized by minimally integrated identifications, instinctual impulsivity, and little capacity for stable object relationships. While some "antisocial personalities" may be organized on this relatively primitive level, other manipulative personalities seem better placed on his inter-

---

8. Another manipulative style, imposture, also leans heavily on the configuration of identifications. This is described in chapter 5 and chapter 12.

mediate level. Here, the capacity for guilt is still somewhat impaired, identifications are still not smoothly integrated, and magical ego ideals impel a need for self-glorification. Object relations may be somewhat more stable and there is less tendency for instincts to erupt. On this level, there is a greater use of repressive mechanisms, rather than the sole use of splitting—a kind of dissociation of parts of the personality—which characterizes the lower level.

Now, Kernberg (1970b) has made the point that many narcissistic personalities are distinguished from the more usual types of borderline personality by "their relatively good social functioning, their better impulse control, and what may be described as a 'pseudosublimitory potential,' namely, the capacity for active, consistent work in some areas which permits them partially to fulfill their ambitions of greatness and of obtaining admiration from others." What occurs in these people—and this includes many manipulative personalities who have successful careers—is that there is sufficient integration of their identifications to provide a check on their impulsivity and to give them direction and adaptation; nonetheless, the peremptory quality of their need to put something over in order to protect their narcissism makes their relationships, and often their work, shallow. Under particular stress, usually involving threats to their narcissism, they may indeed become eruptive; this may be written off as their idiosyncrasy or their temperamentality, but it is evidence of the lack of real firmness of integration; their consolidation is very brittle.

One such stress is adolescence. During this period, under the sway of intensified instinctual urges and the need to break away from the parents, a remodeling of psychic structures takes place, a remodeling which should lead to a consolidated sense of identity and life-purpose in the adult. This is a time of comparative brittleness of ego-integration. In addition, as I have described in chapter 6, the issues of self-esteem come into such prominence during adolescence that a certain amount of putting something over as a means of narcissistic repair might be considered age-appropriate. Thus, we might expect adolescence to be a particularly active time in the life of some manipulative personalities, when they might operate on a somewhat lower level of integrative function in Kernberg's scheme, while the postadolescent period might show a better integrated and less impulsive level of functioning. Indeed, some workers (Henderson and Batchelor, 1962) have had the impression that "psychopaths burn themselves out as they get older," although we might say that their period of "adolescence" is quite prolonged. While this "burning out" concept has been called into question (Maddocks, 1970) there are some people with manipulative personalities whose impulsivity becomes sufficiently eruptive during adolescence for them to be termed "antisocial personalities," but who settle down in such a fashion after adolescence that they escape clinical attention altogether.

For example, James was the favored firstborn son in his family. Even during his latency period, he managed to get into what was then considered mischief by his doting parents. He would often lie with no apparent gain; occasionally he would be truant from school; and there were some stealing episodes. James's father was a very prominent man in the community, but at home his mother tended to ridicule and diminish his stature. Public image was very important in this family, and James quickly learned the importance of reputation. Through the period of his puberty and adolescence, his behavior became so unmanageable that, for a while, the family considered sending him away to a military school in the hope that he would "control himself." In his early twenties, following two years in the army, he married his childhood girl friend and settled down to the serious business of studying to go into his father's profession. Being exceedingly bright, he did well in school and had a meteoric rise in his profession. His father's prominence in the community was matched by his own; he was generally admired and his advice and counsel were frequently sought. His antisocial activities ceased. Nonetheless, signs of his manipulative personality remained. He had a series of divorces and remarriages which testified to his inability to form stable relationships of any depth. He remained a braggart, and he continued to contrive fantastic, if relatively harmless, lies. He was a most clever contender in his profession and was known for his ability to outmaneuver and outsmart his opponents. The regulating dynamics of his personality remained those of the manipulator, but with the consolidation of his defenses and his identity, the impulsive antisocial features were subdued.

Thus, I have described some of the dynamic features of the manipulative personality—a class defined by psychological features, and resting on the peremptory need to express the dynamics of putting something over. Some, but not all, of these people are antisocial. In some cases, the consolidating work of adolescence succeeds in providing sufficient control over the impulses for these people to be productive and quite adaptive. In other cases, there is less consolidation and they remain impulsive and continue their pattern of eruptive offenses against society.

CHAPTER 11

THE PSYCHIATRIST AS MANIPULATOR

While the behavior and thought of patients have provided us with a convenient avenue for the study of manipulation, I have pointed out from the outset that this type of behavior can be found in many walks of life. Psychiatrists, too, manipulate. In fact, when I first embarked on this book, I mentioned to several colleagues that I was writing about manipulation and many of them initially thought that I was writing about deceptive practices employed by psychiatrists. While this is not the case, there are some good reasons for including at least this brief chapter on psychiatrists as manipulators.

As I mentioned in chapter 8, we often demand from patients standards of behavior which we ourselves are unwilling or unable to uphold. And, unlike some of the parents I have referred to, we tend to preach a nonmanipulative morality to our patients while rationalizing and justifying our own manipulations. Adding to this the fact that some workers tend to view all patient manipulation as evidence of pathology and to adopt a pejorative attitude toward this type of behavior, it may broaden our perspective to see how we ourselves manipulate.

There is yet another reason for including this discussion in a book dealing with manipulation in clinical psychiatry. As we shall see, the manipulations in which we engage on several levels have their repercussions on the clinical scene. The targets of these manipulations may be as broad as society itself, or as narrow as a coworker or a patient.

Manipulation as a tool of the psychiatrist in an administrative position is common and very possibly necessary. As this chapter is being written (late 1970 and early 1971), money for funding programs has become extremely tight in the United States. While the administrative heads of clinical units always needed to be concerned with their financial sources, in many cases at this time the concern has become almost a panic.

Money is rarely given as an outright gift to be used as the administrator's clinical judgment dictates. Legislators and the National Institute of Mental Health respond to demands from many parts of society. The wise administrator tailors his program to whatever may be currently valued by his funding source. In a very real sense, this financial stimulus has given impetus to the use of a variety of new and promising directions and techniques in psychiatry. As Klerman (1969, p. 819) has noted, the urban crisis "is accelerating the trend toward social psychiatry and community mental health. It is accelerating trends toward brief therapy, consultation, family and group therapy, and community action. It is shifting the balance of training programs. More significantly, it promises to force major changes in mental health practices and go against current concepts of professional activities and aims." Certainly, one of the mediating mechanisms between the urban crisis and these trends is the need to go where the money is.

It is not our purpose here to evaluate these trends. What commands our attention is the way in which the financial needs in this system (or probably in any system) evoke manipulative activity on the part of the psychiatrist-administrator—an activity which has its effect on the kinds of clinical services offered. At a recent meeting which I attended, a psychiatric administrator made his dilemma very plain: "We can't afford to be idealistic any more. If we want to have the money to operate the programs we think are sound, we have to design programs which will be funded and ask for enough so that we can have money to run our old programs too." This psychiatrist, interested in direct services, felt that his funding sources would not finance them. Knowing of the interest of the funding source in community consultation and the training of paraprofessionals, he would submit his requests in terms of those types of programs and pad the requests to help finance his direct services. This, in turn, would lead him to embark on programs which he might not have undertaken at this time if he had not needed the money.

A psychiatric agency unexpectedly ran into a large deficit which would have proven to be very embarrassing. The situation was discussed with a potential government funding source. This source knew that the legislature would never allow it to make up the deficit. However, the government source was interested in setting up a new type of service, and the agency, although woefully unprepared to implement the service at the time, agreed to undertake the project in return for which the funding source padded the first year's budget to include the deficit. The service, having been hastily thrown together, may have been as much a disservice as a service to its clinical clientele during its turbulent first few months; however, the funding source had established its pet project and the agency had acquired the funds to make up its deficit in a manner which aroused neither the ire nor even the curiosity of the legislature.

Are these and similar activities by psychiatrist-administrators manipulations in terms of the definition we employ in this book? We might be inclined to deny that these are manipulative activities; they are good administrative practice and may well be necessary for survival. "Everyone does it and everyone takes it for granted that it is done." Particularly if one adopts a pejorative attitude toward manipulation or if one considers as manipulative only that behavior which is deviant (a covert pejorative attitude, perhaps), one might be hard-pressed to call these administrators "manipulative." Indeed, often the administrators label those who express concern about these maneuvers with psychiatric pejoratives, accusing them of hysterical naïveté about the way the world works or of having obsessionally strict and rigid superegos. Nonetheless, these maneuvers are manipulations. There are conflict of goals, intentionality, and deception involved in these activities. The administrator's sense of putting something over on the funding source (or the legislature) is harder to demonstrate; in committee meetings the attitude of the administrator is often sober and full of thoughtful concern for the agency. However, at cocktail parties or in private conversations it is frequently possible to observe the administrator's pleasure and glee in having "pulled the deal off." Then the pride in his cleverness and the thinly veiled contempt for the other party may become apparent.

Manipulation by psychiatrist-administrators is not confined to fund raising, of course. Often these administrators are responsible to various groups—boards, superiors, funding sources, subordinate

staff, consumers and would-be consumers of the service, etc.—
and these groups pull in opposite directions. Little wonder that it
requires a juggling act to keep things running, and that manipulation is often part of this juggling act.

Beyond these types of manipulation where the repercussions
usually reach the patient indirectly (for example, by determining
which clinical services will be available), there are manipulations
by psychiatrists which more directly involve the patients themselves. One type of such activity might be called "collaborative
manipulation." Here, the psychiatrist and the patient either explicitly or implicitly join to put something over on a third party.
We have encountered an example of this activity in chapter 8
where I described collusion between staff member and patient to
deceive and put something over on other members of the staff.
This situation differs from those where a manipulative patient di-
vides the staff by playing on the guilt, masochism, or vicarious
interest of his doctor. The situation to which I refer here is one
in which both patient and doctor share a common goal and are
aware of the manipulative means employed to achieve it.

Doctor C found himself in a strong ideological disagreement
with the prevailing atmosphere of the ward to which he was assigned. As the ward chief, I emphasized the use of individual psychotherapy based on psychoanalytic understanding within the context of a ward community where patients were encouraged to discuss their interactions and group problems with the community
and where it was understood that therapeutic plans for individual
patients formulated by their primary doctor would be discussed,
shared with, and sometimes modified by other staff members in
group discussions. This doctor, with a strong background in behavior therapy, was clearly incorrectly placed on this ward. Indeed
even his assignment to my ward had its manipulative aspects;
he had come to our city to work in another clinical setting, one
more appropriate to his interests and skills. However, that clinic
did not have the financial resources to pay him, whereas our hospital had a paid opening available.

Doctor C acknowledged that he saw his role on the ward as
"gadfly." His comments and questions often provided us with a
fresh viewpoint, and his challenges to our institutionalized methods
sometimes led to profitable rethinking of the issues. However, he

challenged so persistently (and sometimes even when it was clear that he had not thought an issue through at all) that it became rather hard to work with him; it often seemed that he challenged for the sake of challenging and more in the service of maintaining his "gadfly" role than in presenting and thinking through an issue. Not uncommonly, he would encourage patients to challenge ward procedures and values, both in thought and action. For example, in a meeting where an effort was being made to encourage communication among members of the ward community, he might turn to a patient who had just been asked a question and say, "Mr. So and So, you don't have to answer any questions if you don't want to. What's important is that you make up your own mind whether you want to answer or not."

At one point, a patient with manipulative character structure who had a long history of antisocial activity came to the ward. Having been charged by the police with disorderly conduct, he was released on his own recognizance pending his trial. He promptly came to the hospital where he complained of depression and was admitted to our ward. Once he came to the ward, his depressive features were not prominent; he was pleasant and often helpful, but it was generally agreed that he was intensely narcissistic, deceptive, and manipulative. The chief resident assigned him to a doctor on another ward for individual psychotherapy (off-ward therapist) while administrative matters were to be handled by Dr. C. It soon became clear to the staff that the patient, although given a pass to go to court, had gone elsewhere; nonetheless, Dr. C persistently declined to involve himself with this question even though he had approved the pass for this purpose. Only through a circuitous route did we learn that on several occasions Dr. C had entertained the patient at his home. When I asked Dr. C about this, he readily acknowledged it, explaining the invitations by saying that they could "rap" better in the home atmosphere and he was really developing a good working relationship with the patient. When other staff members pointed out that Dr. C was not the patient's therapist and that he might be undercutting the therapeutic efforts of the off-ward therapist, he denied any such intention. He maintained that the therapy could go on; he was engaged in a relationship from which the patient could learn and there was no conflict between this and the patient's "formal" therapy. The off-ward therapist began to report to us that the patient did not come to the sessions and at times was not even on the ward during the therapy hours. As his administrator, Dr. C was supposed to take up issues such as this (and the court appearances) with the patient. Instead, he ignored these problems and continued to give the patient freedom to come and go as he wished and to encourage the relationship with him.

At a somewhat later time, Dr. C made it very plain to me that he had considerable contempt for the "establishment"—the police, the law, our ward values, and my therapeutic ideology. "Of course I hid things from you, Dr. Bursten; I had to—otherwise you would not have let me do them. It's really too bad that you were defined as ward chief and I as your subordinate. This has prevented you from learning from me as much as I could have taught you."

Again, I must point out that there is an element of truth in his narcissistic "lament"; also, it is not our purpose here to examine the merits or the errors involved in the treatment approach to the patient. This case illustrates very clearly the collaborative manipulative effort on the part of patient and doctor to put something over on those elements of the "establishment" which, in common, they held in contempt—both in the milieu of the law and the courts and the milieu of the ward.

The opportunity for collaborative manipulation frequently arises in clinical settings other than the hospital ward. With our increasing awareness of the manner in which certain social and political forces lock large segments of our population into positions where their potentials are unfulfilled and their aspirations are frustrated, the whole concept of mental health services has been called into question. The mental health worker has been urged to shift from his traditional stance of disciplined non-involvement to a role where he becomes passionately involved in the alleviation of social ills (Riessman and Miller, 1966; Thursz, 1966; Tullipan and Feldman, 1969). Whatever the clinical merits of the simultaneous mixture of clinical treatment of an individual with the attempt to alleviate social ills (Marmor, 1970), a passionate involvement with the latter may make the psychiatrist more likely to join the patient in a manipulation aimed at the offending segment of the society.

Two areas in which this type of collaboration occurs with some frequency are evaluations for draft deferment and for therapeutic abortions. There are psychiatrists who are disillusioned with the current war in Southeast Asia and are committed to the idea that a change in our country's priorities is essential. They feel, along with many of our youth, that the military draft is wrong. When requested to write a letter supporting a young man's exemption from military service on psychiatric grounds, some of them are prone to a convenient confusion of the disaffected and the mentally ill (Ollendorff and Adams, 1971). They express their own distaste and contempt for selective service by diagnosing as mentally ill young men who are reasonably intact psychologically but who are trying to evade or avoid conscription because of their disenchantment with the values of American life. In many cases there is a conscious attempt to deceive as the psychiatrist carefully weighs the words he writes so that, in their ambiguity, they will not actually lie, but will convey a degree of psychiatric disability which will impress the draft board.

I can illustrate this process in terms of the evaluation for therapeutic abortion where the issues regarding collaborative manipulation are similar. At the time of this writing, Connecticut law stipulated that therapeutic abortions could be performed only to save the life of the mother "or that of her unborn child" (sic). Thus, to impress the abortion committee of a hospital, a psychiatrist had either to imply that the patient, if not aborted, was a serious suicide risk, or that she was so unreliable that she might induce a septic abortion by herself and thus seriously endanger her life.

A middleaged divorced woman had had a very unsuccessful marriage. She had become pregnant before the marriage, and in her characteristic masochistic manner, she married the father of the child knowing that he was an alcoholic and irresponsible. She had two more unplanned pregnancies, both of which occurred because of her miscalculations; no contraceptives were used. As the marriage deteriorated, she developed interests in other men, never really enjoying the sexual aspects of these relationships, but drawn to the men because they were weak and she could "help" them. And, indeed she had many strengths. She was bright, efficient, responsible to her children, and hardworking.

I had occasion to talk with this woman shortly after her divorce, and it was apparent to me that there was little essential change in her life. She was providing for the children as she had always done, she was still dramatically overemotional, and she still sought out the company of men who would lean on her.

Shortly after our conversation, she became pregnant by one such man, and, in her usual efficient manner, she learned the route to a psychiatrically-based therapeutic abortion. The psychiatrist who evaluated her forwarded to me a copy of the letter he sent to the abortion committee of the hospital. It was several pages long, an impressive-looking document portraying her life history in detail. I shall excerpt some parts of the letter.

> During her marriage, Mrs. L. has experienced extreme and acute anxiety attacks which have required medical attention. She has also experienced brief periods of despair and despondency which have increased in duration during the last year. Her constant anxiety and depression are aggravated by financial stresses. . . .
>
> Recently, her loneliness and frustration have driven Mrs. L. to submit to the advances of an older man. . . . [She became pregnant by him and] the previous despair and despondency have returned, accompanied by suicidal ideation. She now feels trapped.
>
> Recently, there has been a breakdown in her defenses so that she is unable to ward off the anxiety, depression, and anger. She has strong feelings of inadequacy and worthlessness. She has become increasingly self-destructive as shown by her pregnancy. She sees for herself, and I agree, no other recourse but an abortion by any means whatsoever—or suicide.

I saw this woman again after the evaluation but before her abortion, and the picture she presented to me was not at all as dangerous as the letter implied. She seemed no more suicidal now than at other times, and while she knew she was in a predicament, she was quite capable of handling herself. She knew that if an abortion were denied in Connecticut, she could go elsewhere, and although this involved expense and inconvenience, she could manage it. This kind of efficiency was quite consistent with her characterological make-up. She was always the efficient provider; indeed, this managerial tendency had played a significant part in her selection of helpless men. There was no doubt that the pregnancy was a problem and that she was not happy about it. She did worry some and had some anxiety. However, I failed to detect the "breakdown of her defenses" or the degree of anxiety and depression indicated in the letter. As for the self-destructiveness, to the extent that masochistic (or more generally, even, neurotic) patients are self-destructive, so was she. But it seemed to me that the context of the letter also conveyed the probability of *imminent* self-destruction—suicide—and this I failed to see in her.

I also saw the patient following her abortion in Connecticut. She was quite pleased that she had "gotten through" the abortion committee, and, of course, was relieved that this ordeal was over. Other than that, she was substantially the same woman I had seen on previous occasions.

What could account for the disparity between the letter and my observations? Two minor hypotheses (which I never really believed) occurred to me. Perhaps, in order to get the evaluation she wanted, the patient dramatized and willfully exaggerated her distress; that is, she may have manipulated the psychiatrist who would write the letter. Alternatively, perhaps she felt so relieved and encouraged by the response of the evaluator that by the time I next saw her, she felt that her crisis had passed. My major speculation, however, was that there was collaborative manipulation on the part of the psychiatrist.

With the patient's permission, I discussed the report with the psychiatrist who sent it to me. He readily acknowledged with a knowing smile that he had "emphasized" certain features. Actually, his appraisal of the woman was about the same as mine, "but," he said, "you can't write that in an abortion letter. The fact that she's in a tough spot is not enough; it's got to add up to suicide or she'll never get the abortion." When I suggested that if she failed to have the abortion in Connecticut she could go elsewhere, he became somewhat indignant and asked why she should have to go elsewhere. He felt (as I do) that a woman should have the right to determine whether she wants to go through with the pregnancy. He was quite contemptuous of those "bastards" who had prevented abortion reform in the last session of the legislature. "If I can screw them and perform a humanitarian service at the same time, so much the better."

The manipulation speaks for itself, and the fact that it may be done in the service of humanitarian goals makes it no less a manipulation.

In this regard, I find one report in the literature quite interesting. Platt et al. (1969) did a follow-up study on 26 women who had had therapeutic abortions on psychiatric grounds in a state where they could be performed on such grounds when there was a risk of suicide or of psychosis if the pregnancy were not terminated. In their restrospective interviews, five women acknowledged that they had exaggerated their symptoms to the examining psychiatrist. Three women had actually concealed genuine suicidal ideation. Four of the women cited their physicians (obstetricians and psychiatrists) as the source of their knowledge of the acceptable criteria. Two more women readily inferred the acceptable criteria from the questions asked by the psychiatrist.

The authors discovered that one third of the women had not truly met the legal criteria for therapeutic abortion. Nevertheless, they had been granted the abortions. The authors postulate that the interviews of the examining psychiatrist may have tended to emphasize psychopathology in contrast to the interviews of the research team which may have encouraged the denial of pathology. While this may have been so, it suggests that at the very least, the examining psychiatrists were trying to "emphasize psychopathology." However, I believe that to this we must add the probability that some of the examining psychiatrists exaggerated the pathology in their reports in the manner I have illustrated above.

In addition to this collaborative type of manipulation, there are situations where the patient himself is the target of the psychiatrist's manipulation. These situations may arise whenever there are strong conflicting and competing goals within the delivery system. For example, all hospitals, public and private, must keep their censuses up. Maintaining a full ward may sometimes conflict with the needs of particular patients. Under the threat of financial cut-backs, hospital personnel sometimes admit patients who might be treated as outpatients. They also sometimes postpone the date of discharge, deceptively citing clinical reasons for the delay.

The need to have patients cuts across every type of practice. Therapy groups need certain numbers of participants; private practitioners need a certain number of paying patients. Specially funded clinical programs usually need a record of a large number of patient-contacts in order to justify their continuance, and the amount of time spent with any one individual may be decided less on clinical grounds than on the need of that particular delivery system for a rapid turnover.

Delivery systems which also have teaching and/or research aims also have competing interests. Procedures may be performed for other than clinical purposes, and the patient is often led to believe that the procedure is part of his therapeutic program.[1] A patient may be told that he is being given a *new* rather than an *experimental* drug. Not infrequently, a consent form is worded with the same deceptive care as the abortion evaluation letter cited above. The following is one such form.

> As a routine part of your treatment in this hospital, you are asked to participate in our investigation of family relations. Our social worker will interview you and one or more members of your family. The results of these interviews will be kept strictly confidential by our research team except for communication with your doctor when the information we obtain will be helpful to your treatment.
>
> By studying the relationships among family members, we will gain further knowledge about mental illness. We would appreciate your cooperation in signing this consent form.
>
> I, ———, agree to participate in the family relations study at **XXX** hospital.

This form strongly suggests that there is a significant treatment component to the study and that the patient himself will benefit by participating. The study had been going on for over a year when I discussed it with the researcher. I asked him how many times interview results had been discussed with the patient's doctor. He

1. A classic medical hospital instance of manipulation in the service of teaching material is in the pursuit of autopsies. In a large number of hospital deaths, there is little clinical need for an autopsy. Yet a hospital is rated, in part, by the number of autopsies performed, and pathology residents need autopsy experience. It sometimes becomes a badge of honor for an intern to boast that he "got" a large number of autopsies. A common deception is to tell the family that the cause of death is uncertain and that there may be some familial disease which can be revealed by autopsy— information which could be helpful or reassuring to the family.

replied that they had never been discussed; everyone in the hospital was too busy. I then suggested that his consent form did not make it at all clear that participation was voluntary and that the patient could receive treatment in the hospital even if he declined to participate in the research. The investigator looked at me as if he could not believe his ears. "If they knew it was voluntary, we'd have a hard time getting subjects," he said.

Now when these multiple interests occur they are not always competing or conflicting, and they do not always result in manipulation of the patient. For example, the therapist who needs to fill a group may also believe that the recommendation of group therapy for a particular patient is reasonable and psychiatrically sound. The state of our knowledge is such that we have no definitive and generally agreed-upon criteria for determining the optimal form of treatment in most cases. Members of our profession differ widely in their therapeutic ideologies and talents. It makes a great deal of sense for a psychiatrist to recommend a therapeutic approach with which he is familiar and in which he is skilled. Likewise, the teaching or research interest may not conflict with good clinical practice. In any particular case, it might be difficult to determine whether the psychiatrist has really manipulated the patient—whether, indeed, he has the (secret) gleeful feeling of having put something over on the patient. But I have no doubt that this type of manipulation does occur.

In institutions such as universities, hospitals, and large clinics, the goals which may compete with optimal clinical practice are often imposed from above—that is, not by the treating psychiatrist, but by his superiors who must attend to the needs of the institution. As a rough rule of thumb, I have found that the further removed one is from actually treating patients (administrators, teachers, researchers), the less do the clinical needs or rights of individual patients occupy center stage. I do not feel that these "removed personnel" have contempt for patients; when they demand that the ward be filled they are not manipulating. These people have less *concern* for individual patients, not contempt for them. Their vision is focused on institutional needs. It is the subordinate—the treating psychiatrist—who is sometimes caught in the middle. With his primary focus on the patient, he is often forced to manipulate—that is, to tell the patient a lie and to put something over on him in order to follow the directives of his superiors.

There are other types of situations in which the psychiatrist manipulates the patient. The conflicts of goals in this group of situations has less to do with treatment or another institutional goal, such as research, finances, etc. Here the manipulation is instituted for more personal reasons. In the last chapter, for example, I enumerated several types of psychological factors which might lead staff members to invite or to oppose a patient's manipulation. Some of these factors may also induce the psychiatrist to manipulate his patient.

The most obvious group of factors are those which have occupied our attention for most of this book. Psychiatrists are not immune from the forces which cause people to manipulate. Further, some psychiatrists are manipulative personalities as described in chapter 10, and are so driven by internal forces to manipulate that they may repeatedly take advantage of their patients (Cleckley, 1955). Others, with other personality structures, may have conflicts over activity-passivity and may be driven to make the therapy into a contest to see who can outwit the other.

Young and relatively inexperienced doctors are often confronted with still other problems which impel them to manipulate their patients. They may make mistakes or feel that they have made mistakes. At times, they may manipulate in order to cover up the mistake and avoid embarrassment. They may feel vulnerable because they are still in training and may try to create the impression that they are not. At one psychoanalytic institute, this "problem" was discussed with the candidates still in training. They were advised that if they were asked if they were "regular" analysts or "just students," they should reply that they were graduate psychiatrists or board-certified psychiatrists rather than acknowledge their student status. I do not know if this deception is a prevalent practice; I do believe, however, that candidates generally are happier if the question never comes up.

We have all heard of instances where a patient's family, anxious and bewildered by his psychotic behavior, have tried to "humor" him by pretending to believe his delusions. I recall a phone call from a distressed woman whose mother had, once again, become quite paranoid. In this condition, the mother would heap abuse

on various relatives and would turn to her daughter for confirmation. The daughter, fearful of rousing her mother to even greater
anger, would agree that the relatives had wronged her mother.
In that way she hoped to "get on the good side of her mother"
even though she did not share the mother's views of the relatives.
She hoped to influence the mother to calm down, and she enjoyed
the feeling of being able to fool her. Now, while it is generally
agreed among psychiatrists that we should not fool or "humor"
paranoid patients—they are already mistrustful and they are
acutely sensitive to deceit—I have, on several occasions, super-
vised residents who have acted toward their paranoid patients as
this daughter did toward her mother. One resident spelled out the
manipulation clearly. "What I did," he said, "was to gain the
patient's confidence. He feels that his boss has it in for him and
I agree with him. Then, when he knows I'm on his side, he'll open
up more." I pointed out to the resident that he was deceiving the
patient at the very time when he was asking for the patient's
trust. The resident insisted that the patient would never catch on.
"He's kind of out of it anyway, and I can sound very convincing."

In several of the examples enumerated above, we must ask
whether the actions of the doctor were really manipulations or
whether they were deceptions but not manipulations. Here it is
useful to recall the discussion in chapter 1 about the social psychologist. I believe that novice psychiatrists may have greater
tendencies to manipulate their patients precisely because their
sense of their professional status is so vulnerable. They may need
to differentiate themselves from their patients or to put themselves
at a distance from them by deceiving with the feeling that they are
putting something over on them. As one grows more certain of his
position, he has less need to prove himself superior to others. The
more experienced doctor may, for other reasons, actually believe
that deception is a necessary part of treatment but he may derive
less pleasure from the fact that he has put something over on the
patient and more satisfaction from the course of the treatment.
While I do not employ deception as a therapeutic technique, I do
not take the position that psychiatrists holding a different view
are all manipulators.

The question of what does constitute manipulation on the part
of the psychiatrist comes up rather frequently. In his book on

psychoanalytic technique, Greenson (1967) has discussed several types of "manipulations" used by psychoanalysts and by those who have modified or deviated from standard psychoanalytic procedure. "Manipulation," he wrote (p. 50), "refers to an evocative activity undertaken by the therapist without the knowledge of the patient." As examples of manipulation in psychoanalysis, he cited the use of silence in order to allow the patient's affect to intensify and the bringing up of material which the patient is avoiding. Antianalytic (but, at times therapeutically useful) manipulations include the adoption of a kind of relationship with the patient which he finds gratifying, determination of the frequency of interviews as a means of avoiding regressive dependency on the therapist, and (I would add) the various techniques used in the "ward management" of hospitalized patients, and the environmental management of all patients (Alexander et al., 1946; Levine, 1952; Novey, 1959).

While these various technical measures are manipulations in the common usage of the word, in the clinical—in the psychological—sense which I discussed in chapter 1, they usually are not. These measures are applied by the psychiatrist with the intention of influencing the patient, but they are not usually deceptive nor are they accompanied by a feeling of having put something over on the patient. True, they may become manipulations if, for example, the psychiatrist adjusts the frequency of visits in the name of avoiding regressive dependency when in reality he had a speaking engagement in another city, and he takes pleasure in fooling his patient. However, in the majority of cases, I prefer to call these measures "therapeutic maneuvers" or "techniques" and to reserve the word "manipulation" for the psychological activity described in this book.

Patients themselves occasionally feel they are being manipulated by the therapist's maneuver. Sometimes a patient will say to me, "You know why I act this way but you're not telling me. You're manipulating me. You're not being honest with me."

It may be true that I have a good idea of what underlies the patient's actions and that I am withholding the interpretation. I might feel, for example, that to interpret the action at this time would lead to an increase in resistance either by raising the patient's level of anxiety or by giving him an intellectualized formula which has no real meaning to him (Glover, 1931). However, if we look at the therapeutic contract, we can see that this is not a manipulation. I have never implied to the patient that I would tell him everything that occurs to me. Rather, I have agreed to see the patient with the implicit understanding that I would use my talents and my judgment in the furtherance of the psychotherapeutic enterprise—and if that enterprise, in my judgment, requires the withholding of an interpretation, it would be a "breach of contract" to be goaded into interpreting prematurely. More often than not, when a patient accuses me of manipulating in this manner, he has other things on his mind. He may be acting seductively, he may be complaining about parental secrets and this may be an expression of voyeuristic urges, he may be asking to be fed, or he may projectively be defending himself against his own narcissistic desire to put something over on me by announcing that he feels I am putting something over on him.

CHAPTER 12

SOME PARTICULAR SITUATIONS

It should be apparent by this time that manipulation is widespread and that it takes many forms. In this chapter, I shall describe certain particular situations which a psychiatrist may encounter in the course of his clinical work. These situations are chosen primarily because they have caught my interest and challenged my curiosity. They are not meant to represent a complete list of special situations nor are they necessarily the most common.

MUNCHAUSEN'S SYNDROME[1]

Munchausen's syndrome has simultaneously fascinated and vexed general hospital physicians for many years. First described in 1951 by Asher, it gets its name from Baron Munchausen (1720–91) who had a reputation as a teller of tall tales about wartime adventures (Small, 1955; Chapman, 1957).

Patients with this syndrome wander from hospital to hospital presenting dramatic symptoms and lurid medical histories. The initial fascination of the medical resident soon turns to vexation as he realizes that the patient who was admitted as an acute medical emergency with an intriguing diagnostic problem has perpetrated a hoax. When confronted with his fraud, the patient is not contrite or apologetic; instead he invents further cover-up stories or becomes indignant and signs out of the hospital just when the physician had planned to present him as a case of Munchausen's syndrome at grand rounds. The hostility generated by these patients in the staffs they have manipulated is frequently so intense that some authors (Williams, 1951; Gatenby, 1955; Irvine, 1955) have suggested setting up a "rogues gallery" in order to keep them from being admitted to hospitals and using up valuable time and services.

By the time the psychiatrist is called in, the medical staff has

1. This section is a modification of a previous publication (Bursten, 1965b).

usually discovered the hoax and the patient is already indignant and ready to leave the hospital. These are far from optimal conditions under which to study a patient. However, some years ago, I was fortunate in being able to conduct two interviews with one such patient.

The patient, a 38-year-old white man, appeared at the hospital with a complaint of crushing chest pains. He reported some sweating, shortness of breath, and numbing and tingling of the left arm and fingers. He was described as "a good historian with an unfortunate past history." This history, as he gave it, included transurethral resection for nonvenereal prostatitis in 1947, an operation for a rectal fissure in 1950, excision of a pilonidal cyst in 1951, a laminectomy for a herniated disc in 1953, hospitalization for treatment of osteomyelitis of the spine in 1953, acute myocardial infarction in 1954, and an orchiectomy for malignant teratoma in 1960—which treatment was supposedly followed by 6000 roentgens of x-ray therapy to the abdomen and groin. These hospitalizations were reported to have occurred in New York, Nebraska, Utah, and Texas. In addition, the patient reported that his mother had diabetes mellitus and that he had been told that he had a borderline glucose tolerance test; his father had carcinoma of the prostate; an older sister had recurrent skin infections as did the patient; two uncles died of myocardial infarction, and one uncle died of carcinoma of the prostate. Furthermore, the patient claimed to be allergic to aspirin, Darvon, penicillin, Pyridium, Furadantin, erythromycin, sulfa drugs, Novocaine, tomatoes, and strawberries.

The patient was admitted to the Medical Service with the presumptive diagnosis of myocardial infarction and was treated with bed rest and narcotics. Physical examination revealed that he appeared to be in acute distress and perspiring; his temperature was 99.4° F., blood pressure 88/60, pulse 100, respirations 18. There were multiple abscesses in both hips and buttocks, and he had a well-headed appendectomy scar, a scar in the lumbar region, and two right inguinal scars. The right testicle was missing. Other than this the examination was within normal limits. X-ray and laboratory examinations which included a wide variety of blood chemistries were all within normal limits. A series of EKG's showed no evidence of abnormality other than a slight tachycardia.

As the laboratory evidence was gathered, it became increasingly apparent that the patient had neither the myocardial infarction nor any of the other ailments (such as pancreatitis) which had been considered. Munchausen's syndrome was suspected and this diagnosis was supported by the nurse's observation that the patient seemed to be in distress only when others were in the room. At this point, letters and telephone calls to other hospitals established the fraudulent nature of much of his past history. The testicle had been removed not for a teratoma but for "neuralgia." Whenever actual pathology had been discovered in his various hospitalizations, it was usually the result of self-instrumentation. Between hospitalizations, he had had extensive contacts with outpatient clinics. He had submitted to a variety of diagnostic procedures and had had abdominal and back surgery, both of which had revealed virtually no pathology.

As the story became clearer, attention shifted from his chest (the "pain" had now subsided) to the demonstrable lesions—the abscesses. With this shift in emphasis, the patient's story changed and he spoke of the chest pain as an incidental factor. He said that all along he had insisted that the chest pain was probably "gas" and not a myocardial infarction; indeed, he had come to New Haven in search of a skin specialist who might clear up his baffling problem of recurrent infections and easy bruisability.

When I came to interview him, he was quite indignant at the psychiatric referral; however he was pleased to have the opportunity to talk into the tape recorder. The information which he gave was generally vague and so internally inconsistent that it cannot represent an accurate history. His manner was evasive, alternately ingratiating and boastfully contemptuous, and he constantly attempted to get me to assume the guilt for the "bungling" medical profession. When told that he would be referred for psychological testing, he demanded to be discharged. Although given follow-up appointments at the surgical clinic, he was not heard from again.

This patient exhibited what I see as the three main features of Munchausen's syndrome. First, he very dramatically presented a variety of medical complaints. The emphasis here is on the drama; whether it be the acute medical emergency or the highly interesting obscure diagnostic problem, these patients seem to be able to gauge the staging of their illnesses in such a way that they maximize audience (staff) response.

The second feature of this syndrome has been called "pseudologia fantastica" (Frankel, 1951); I prefer the term deception.[2] The medical history, present and past, is fraudulent, and while its elaboration depends on the contents of the patient's fantasy as well as the interest of the staff, the patient is well aware of his deception. When confronted with the inconsistencies in their stories, these patients often get indignant and angry, and they leave.

The third aspect of this syndrome, which our patient also displayed, is wandering. They have no geographical roots; they travel from hospital to hospital, from city to city. This feature differentiates them from more settled patients who use medical hospitalization from time to time to help resolve an acute psychosocial crisis (Bursten, 1965a, 1965c).

What could possibly motivate a person to wander from place to place seeking brief hospital admissions and painful procedures under false pretenses, not as an occasional frantic search for help but as a way of life? Several suggestions have been offered in the literature (Asher, 1951; Abse, 1959). The syndrome has been attributed to narcotics addiction, a desire to escape the police or criminal prosecution, a wish for free board or lodging, a need to be the center of attention and interest, and a "grudge against doctors and hospitals" which is satisfied by frustrating or deceiving them. Undoubtedly, these wishes are often involved. Our patient admitted intermittant addiction. He also freely described enjoying the attention he does not get "on the outside." His anger and contempt for doctors was very much in evidence. He complained that it was "perfectly all right for a doctor to make a mistake or to make the wrong diagnosis, treat a person for a year on the wrong diagnosis and never apologize . . . it's all right for the doctor to lie to the patient . . . but if the patient lies to the doctor, God help the patient."

However, the patient offered these explanations a little too easily, a little too glibly. When pushed to elaborate, he became anxious and acknowledged that addiction was not the "real reason"

2. For the considerations involved in the role of reality-testing in deception, see chapters 5 and 10.

behind his behavior. "I don't know what the real reason is—there are always reasons and reasons and reasons." If we consider carefully the explanations which are usually offered, we must agree with our patient that they do not suffice. These patients differ from other drug users in that they are not usually addicted. They are clever enough to obtain drugs without the repetitive hospitalizations and sometimes painful procedures. Nor could they just be looking for lodging; again, they usually shun long-term psychiatric hospitalization in favor of a situation which will bring them medical manipulation. Indeed, hospitalization itself is not crucial. Between hospitalizations, my patient baffled clinic doctors with a false but intriguing urological problem. In typical fashion, he underwent a variety of diagnostic procedures as an outpatient, and when confronted with the falsity of his medical history, he became angry and never reappeared at the clinic. What we see, then, is that these clever patients could probably satisfy the needs and wishes usually offered as explanations of this syndrome without resorting to the painful procedures and the wandering.

The point from which we may start to understand these people is that of manipulation. I see their actions as manipulative in the sense used in this book. There is clearly a conflict of goals between them and the medical staff which becomes apparent as soon as the hoax is revealed. The patient desires hospitalization and diagnostic procedures which would ordinarily be denied him. Thus he intends to influence the staff by his deception (and succeeds). That all this includes the satisfaction of having put something over on the staff can be seen from some of my patient's comments. While he did not directly admit that he had been trying to put something over on the medical staff, the component of contempt for physicians was quite apparent. "I know many doctors socially," he said, "and some of them are real fools. I've learned as much medicine without going to medical school as some of them have learned with going to medical school—and I know more about life than they do." And, at another point, "If you knew anything about drug addicts, doctor, you would know that when an addict is on drugs, sex means very little—if you knew anything about drugs." [3]

3. This interview antedated by several years my formulations about manipulation and putting something over. At that time, it did not occur to me to

It is clear that many of the manipulations of people exhibiting Munchausen's syndrome are impelled largely from within. They are driven to repeat, again and again, the deceptions leading to "medical care." They have primarily manipulative personalities.[4] Our patient was glib and evasive, deceptive and full of contempt. He was keenly aware of what would impress the staff and he used language more in the service of drama than in the service of actual and logical verbal communication. His past records revealed a chronic history of mendacity, bad checks, and an ability to impel others to get him jobs, pay for his lodgings, etc. The intriguing and perplexing question is why he had settled on this particular mode of expressing his need to manipulate.

The striking feature of patients with Munchausen's syndrome is that they are impostors (Michaels et al., 1964). Characteristically, the impostor is a perigrinator with no firm roots. He assumes a false identity and resorts to various machinations to support it. Our patient's false identity was "chronically ill and acutely ill"; in addition, he often used a false name. Indeed, as Deutsch (1955) has noted, the denial of the patient's real identity seems very important, and when the imposture must be given up, the patient has a high degree of anxiety. Impostors have high, unattainable ego-ideals and use their imposture as a means of defending against the anxiety aroused by their inferiority feelings. Consistent with Greenacre's (1958) view that the impostor's feelings of inferiority stem from fancied defective genital development, our patient spoke of the ridicule he received from his sister when he could not maintain an erection during childhood sexual play.

This line of analysis, however, raises a serious problem. The concept of falsely assuming a glorified role to defend themselves against the anxiety of inferiority feelings may be quite adequate

---

inquire about his feeling-state when the deception worked. If I had, I might have obtained more direct data about the exhilaration of putting something over. Spiro (1968) reported a patient with Munchausen's syndrome who used to regale people at bars with made-up stories of his experiences as a physician, private investigator, etc. Often, he would end the evening by revealing the fraud and laughing at the other patrons for their gullibility.
4. See chapter 10. Spiro (1968) has questioned the validity of including all people with Munchausen's syndrome under one characterological diagnostic heading.

to account for the usual impostors described in the literature. These impostors pretend to be scientists, heroes, and men of influence and affluence. However, patients with Munchausen's syndrome do not assume such glorious roles—on the contrary, they appear as victimized, pitiful, and (as with our patient) literally genitally defective. What is the relationship between this type of imposture and the more usual type? Immediately, the possibility of a counterphobic maneuver is suggested to us. Does the patient, fearing he is weak, inadequate, and genitally defective, attempt to master this fear by inviting the very thing he fears and "rising above it?" Listen to our patient, who in one of his deceptions induced a surgeon to remove one of his testicles. "I'm able to have an orgasm three or four times a day even when I'm 38, even with the removal of one testicle!" If my speculation is correct, we are beginning to traverse familiar ground. Our patient's attitude has in it the elements of the "flight forward" which plays so prominent a role in Reik's (1949) discussion of masochism. With his imposture, the patient actively invites what he fears; at the same time, while pretending to submit to the doctor, he is secretly defiant. He may be bloody, but he is unbowed.[5]

It can hardly surprise us to come upon masochism in the imposture of Munchausen's syndrome. Even on the surface, the syndrome suggests a masochistic approach to life. Reik has described two forms of masochism: sexual and social.[6] The sexual masochist consciously and intentionally seeks bodily pain, and by being beaten, he achieves gratification through orgasm. The social masochist is driven to seek social misfortune rather than bodily pain. There is no culmination in orgasm, and he is not aware of his part in provoking the misfortune. The patient with Munchausen's syndrome seems to occupy an intermediate maso-

5. A somewhat similar mechanism is described by Spiro (1968) who has adopted Grinker's (1965) postulation of mastery as a key factor in imposture. Spiro's patient had been hospitalized at the age of four and one half due to an automobile accident. He had experienced a variety of painful procedures. As an adult, the patient no longer remembered the unpleasantness; he recalled only that it was rare, in such a large family as his, that he could gain adult attention. Spiro has speculated that the repeated hospitalizations were attempts to master the pain of the earlier hospital confinement, but in a situation where the patient could control things.
6. I prefer Reik's term "social masochism" to that used earlier by Freud (1924)—"moral masochism."

chistic position. By his imposture, he actively and consciously seeks out bodily pain while presenting himself as the victim of an unkind fate. Thus, the house staff said that our patient had an "*unfortunate* past history." The procedures are not generally obviously sexual in nature and do not culminate in orgasm.

Masochism represents a reversal of subject and object (Reik, 1949, pp. 319–20; Brenman, 1952). The sexual and aggressive impulses which were once directed outward are now "given" to the other person to be directed toward the masochist. In this light, the imposture of Munchausen's syndrome appears to be a reversal of the more usual type of imposture. Rather than being the self-assured and "successful hero," the patient is the "hapless victim." Can we see the opposite—the desire to be the physician—through the imposture? Several patients reported in the literature had gone through a phase wherein they had posed as a physician or a health worker in an allied field. Our patient had briefly posed as a doctor when he was younger; at another time he posed as a trained surgical technician. On one occasion, he had been arrested for stealing medical instruments.[7] Certainly, in his fantasy life, the doctor's role was obvious. With his medical knowledge, he did not appear as a patient coming to the doctor in helpless confusion; his account of his "medical history" could rival an intern's report to the attending physician.

Of course, the impulses which have reversed their objects go much deeper than turning the desire to play the doctor into the desire to play the patient. Why the underlying sexual and aggressive impulses take the specific form of playing the medical patient is unclear. Simmel (1926) has drawn our attention to the Oedipal aspects of "doctor-games" and doctoring. I believe that the vicissitudes of the Oedipal period and its resolution in latency are of critical importance in determining that the manipulative tendencies will express themselves as Munchausen's syndrome.[8] Unfortunately, I do not have the clinical data to give firm support to this belief or to be more specific about the determining mechanisms. I have

7. In the original form of this section published in 1965 (n. 1), I could only speculate on this patient's medical impostures. Records which became available to me at a later time confirmed these speculations.
8. I do not mean to imply that developments later in life are not pertinent. Nonetheless, the Oedipal period and its resolution and the identifications of latency are of particular importance in setting the stage.

only the most scanty data about our patient's family situation. In general, his accounts were too vague and too unreliable to allow us to reconstruct with any confidence what his home life was like. However, there is one tantalizing passage in the report of a social worker who had seen the patient and his parents some twenty years ago. The parents were described as being "consciously protective of the patient" and anxious to conceal personal aspects of the household. Apparently his mother was protective to the point of being indulgent. Even when he was older, she referred to him in letters as "baby" and "sweetheart." She seems to have demanded a good deal of attention from him and tended to chide him for not being a dutiful son. There is a hint in this report that she may have been somewhat seductive towards the boy while demanding that he remain the cared-for child in the relationship. Perhaps this is in part what is reflected in his method of expressing his manipulative tendencies.[9]

Before leaving the subject of Munchausen's syndrome, we should briefly consider its relationship to factitious illnesses, as this relationship may illustrate a point made in chapter 10. In that chapter, I contrasted those who manipulate under certain social circumstances in order to achieve pleasure or avoid discomfort with those who do it as a life-style, impelled primarily by an inner need to manipulate.

People with factitious illness come to hospitals with demonstrable pathology which they themselves have surreptitiously produced. I agree with Spiro that Munchausen's syndrome "represents a special pattern within the group of factitious illnesses." The two features which make it special among factitious illnesses are the wandering and the chronicity. Others with factitious illnesses seem to have more stable lives. They probably resort to "illness" at times of stress. It may be that their characterological mechanisms are other than manipulative whereas these whom we classify as Munchausen's syndrome are driven more persistently from within by the forces of the manipulative personality.

9. Spiro's (1968) discussion of mastery of the anxiety and pain of childhood illness offers another possibility for the setting in which the manipulative tendency turns to Munchausen's syndrome. I do not know if a traumatic childhood illness is necessary. I doubt if it is sufficient. I believe it must be supported by the roles within the family which make the patient-role an acceptable resolution of the Oedipal situation.

THE SPECIAL-PROBLEM PATIENT

Several types of circumstances may result in a patient's being seen as unusual or exceptional. Some of these stem primarily from his own internal dynamics and the impact that these have on the staff. Other circumstances may involve particular events in the life of the institution during the patient's stay. For example, patients who might not ordinarily have been viewed as unusual may "present particular problems" when there are massive changes in ward personnel or when the census drops to a point where a budgetary crisis looms. Or, the attention focused on a patient with whom a new therapeutic measure is being explored may propel him into a position of prominence. Still other circumstances arise in the context of a particular patient's connections with prominent and influential people. In this section, we shall examine a type of situation arising largely from the patient's internal dynamics and the impact of these dynamics on the staff.

The special-problem patient was first described in detail in 1957 by Main. This patient has enormous needs for love and nurturance, which, as Burnham (1966) has noted, are experienced with intense ambivalence. The anxiety generated by this primitive ambivalence is handled by the patient's splitting the staff into "all good" and "all bad" people. She[10] can insulate herself from those "bad" people who are not on her side while appealing to the "good" people for love, nurturance, and, at times, a feeling of fusion. The hospital staff, reacting to the patient's needs, frequently becomes badly split over issues of the patient's management. Some staff members—the "good" ones—feel particularly protective and understanding of the patient. Indeed, the patient will often appeal to a "good" staff member by making him feel that he is the only one who can understand and help her. She will provoke guilt by alluding to the "bad" people who are "impossibly insensitive and demanding." The "good" staff is forced to deny its anger at the patient and at her incessant demands; instead, the anger is vented toward the cruel "bad" staff for its insensitivity. The "good" staff member develops a sense of omnipotent pride. The "bad" staff

10. Most of the "special-problem patients" described in the literature have been women.

members resent the "indulgent" actions of the "good" people and tend to feel that the "good" staff is naïve, over-involved, and too vulnerable to the patient's manipulations. As the staff becomes split, the patient becomes increasingly distressed (Stanton and Schwartz, 1954) and the process is intensified, leading ultimately to the exhaustion of everyone and the feeling on the part of the patient that she has been betrayed.

It is not at all uncommon to see the ward staff split over the issue of whether the patient is manipulating. Some (the "good" ones) see the patient's actions as neediness and "cries for help," while others (the "bad" ones) condemn the patient for her manipulations. Joan, a young woman of 23, had been in the hospital for over five years. This, in itself, was unusual for that particular hospital, which tended to keep patients for two to three years. It was well known that the clinical director had developed a special interest in Joan, as had certain other staff members including the resident who was her therapist. Other staff members resented her special position in the hospital and felt that she was allowed far too many "privileges." They knew that other, less appealing patients who had shown no appreciable progress and who were the center of repeated ward upheavals would have been transferred to another hospital long ago.

Joan was a good-looking, bright, and talented girl. She was cultured and had a quick, if somewhat biting, wit. She was easily aroused to anger if thwarted, and her rages could vary from yelling and temper tantrums to icy scorn which left one feeling about two inches tall. If she liked you, she could be a charming conversationalist and would sometimes surprise you with thoughtful gestures or gifts. She had a shadowy and fluctuating sense of her own boundaries; she craved interviews with sodium pentathol to which she responded with what seemed to be affectionate gestures—leaning on the therapist and stroking his arm. This was a kind of closeness she never showed when not under the influence of pentathol. The "bad" staff condemned the use of pentathol as evidence of the patient's seductiveness, and they expressed concern that the relationship was too sexual. They saw the therapist as being manipulated into using the pentathol by the "sexual" advances the patient made and by the patient's obvious distress and "inability" to talk in interviews without it. The therapist, on the other hand, felt that the touching was not primarily sexual, but rather an expression of her ambivalently held need for closeness. He felt that the most meaningful therapeutic contacts were made under these circumstances; Joan was certainly better able to talk about things which bothered her in contrast to other times when she was aloof.

Was Joan manipulating by our definition? The answer must be "yes and no." This was a very hungry, needy girl and I believe that her caressing under the influence of pentathol was an expression of her need for contact, if not for fusion. I do not think that she intended, by these actions, to arouse or seduce her therapist, even though it is entirely possible that he may have been aroused by the contact. Hence I do not see the contact as manipulative; however, she was bright and alert enough to manipulate the therapist and certain other people in the hospital to give her the pentathol in order to satisfy her desperate craving for contact. It is probable that she so desperately needed this and other equivalents of closeness that she sometimes manipulated staff into giving it to her. Although it is difficult to make a clinical distinction, at least on a theoretical basis, we can differentiate the needy, desperate appeal, which Main described, from manipulation. The appeal is a relatively primitive response similar to that of an appealing or suffering infant who, without the level of anticipatory thought or deception of the manipulator, stimulates the parent to care for it. On the other hand, there are times when the special-problem patient might crave the nurturance and be sufficiently organized to manipulate in order to obtain it. We can postulate two types of situations arising when the patient needs nurturance. First, the patient expresses this need by the appeal; this is an "honest," not deceptive, expression. If satisfaction is not forthcoming the patient may fly into a rage which is a relatively primitive response to frustration and deprivation and represents a further expression of her neediness. Secondly, again if nurturance is not forthcoming, or if the patient anticipates that it will not be forthcoming, she may contrive a deception in order to obtain it; this is manipulation. I would hypothesize that the second condition can arise only when the neediness is not very great. When the craving is strong, it probably represents a more regressed state of affairs—a state where the peremptory quality of

the neediness severely limits even the temporary delay of gratification which anticipatory thought and deception would require. In
the more primitive condition, the sense of self is probably less
firm than is required for rigorous intentionality. It is entirely
possible, of course, for the patient to move from the second condition to the first, and I believe that we encounter this move frequently. When the craving for nurturance is not strong, the patient may attempt to manipulate in order to obtain it. If the
manipulation is thwarted, the patient's narcissism is undercut. The
satisfactions of putting something over with its unconscious message of reunion and fusion are not achieved. The purging of the
bad introject is likewise thwarted. Under these circumstances, the
insecurity and the neediness (for nurturance and symbiosis) may
intensify to the point where manipulation is no longer possible
and the more primitive appeal takes over.

Let us explore a bit further the relationship between manipulation and the appeal. Both processes rest on infantile narcissism
and are fueled by the patient's need for reunion with a benevolent
and loving parent. In both cases the anger is expressed by scorn
and contempt for others and probably represents, in part, a repro-
jection of the bad introject. Why, then, do special-problem patients
become special-problem patients rather than manipulative personalities? A partial answer must lie with the nature of the mother-
infant relationship. Lomas (1962) has pointed out how the
mothers of special-problem patients demand that their infants have
an exclusive relationship with them. "Thus, in his search for identity, he is dependent not on his capacity to form relationships, but
on his capacity to form one particular relationship, and the qualities which would lead him to have confidence in himself are not
his real qualities but only those which happen to have importance
in one person's eyes." It may be that the mothers of these patients
demand the exclusive relationship because of their own poor ego-
boundaries; by promoting a symbiotic relationship they discourage
the degree of individuation necessary for a firm sense of self. The
child develops an expectation of the magical communication of
infancy where one's needs are either immediately seen or even
anticipated by the mother, or a catastrophic frustration is felt.
The mother of the patient with a manipulative personality, on
the other hand, may have a better capacity to allow her child to

differentiate from her. It is possible, for example, that during her infant's earliest life, she too places enormous value on the symbiotic relationship, but that as the infant grows older, she is either "spontaneously" capable of allowing a greater degree of individuation or that circumstances (such as the arrival of another child on which to focus a symbiosis) foster a degree of separation. The mother's high investment in the child continues and thus supports his narcissism but in a somewhat more object-differentiated milieu.

I have no evidence whatsoever to support these speculations. I present them more as a paradigm of the *types* of mother-infant relationships which might tend to result in one person's becoming a special-problem patient while another becomes a person with a manipulative personality. Clearly much more is involved in the difference, such as the sense of identity, propensity for activity and passivity, identification models, etc. which the family fosters. And many events in later life will help determine how solidly the person can maintain an independent sense of integration or how vulnerable he will be to a regression to the level of the appeal. As Lidz et al. (1965) have reminded us, any attempt to oversimplify the types of relationships involved in "producing" persons belonging to a clinical grouping must result in inaccuracies. This is an enormously complex area interwoven with many subtleties; our speculations and paradigms must be viewed only as first and rather gross approximations.

Staff members often have difficulty in gauging how much of the behavior of the special-problem patient is appeal and how much is manipulation. The "bad" staff all too often mislabels the patient's behavior as manipulative and uses the term in a pejorative sense. The "good" staff is liable to err on the side of seeing all behavior in terms of the appeal, and to overlook the occasions when the patient is truly being manipulative. And, even if a staff member is reasonably accurate in his differentiation of the manipulation from the appeal, we must consider the question of what to do about the manipulation, particularly when the manipulation may be largely in the service of gratifying deeper needs and when thwarting the manipulation may lead to the regressive state of the appeal. These considerations will be discussed in chapter 13.

Let us turn now from the discussion of a manipulator who is special because of his internal dynamics to a type of unusual patient who receives special attention because of the situation surrounding his coming to the hospital or office and because of the difficulties this situation causes for the staff. I refer to the patient who achieves unusual status because of his connection with other important people. Close relatives of physicians, for example, come to us as V.I.P. patients, set somewhat apart from other patients not necessarily by their special pathology but by the family from which they come. A review of the charts of one hospital made this fact very clear to me. Typically, the resident's case reports began with, "Y is an 18-year-old girl who comes to the hospital because of . . ." Only several paragraphs later were we introduced to the father. However, in the cases of three physicians' children, the charts read, "Y, the son of a prominent (medical specialist), is an 18-year-old . . ."

V.I.P. status is not limited to physicians or their relatives. To a greater or lesser extent, this status can be held by people in various situations. Other medical personnel—especially from the same medical center where the hospital is located—are viewed exceptionally. Political figures, famous people, friends of the hospital director, etc. can all be the reason for red-carpet status.

Such patients and their important connections pose particular problems for those involved in their ward-management and their psychotherapy. At the very least, the staff is likely to be distracted from the therapeutic focus by the tendency to look for the reaction of the important relative out of the corner of his eye. This distraction occurs, of course, whether the patient in question is particularly manipulative or not. While our focus here will be on manipulative patients, some of the staff reactions we encounter will be seen to occur in similar V.I.P. situations where the patient is not manipulative.

Often, the V.I.P. situation is low-key. The important connection may be unobtrusive and may wish to leave the treatment in the hands of the staff. While this may reduce the manifest pressure, the V.I.P. situation remains. I recall one situation where the patient's parents were away and a very prominent physician, a friend of the family, took a parental interest in him. The physician made only one phone call to the hospital to express his interest and potential availability if needed. His interest occupied the major portion of the staff meeting during which the resident insisted (more than he needed to) that the physician was not interfering, and the rest of the staff refused to believe him. Virtually no time was spent discussing the patient.

However, there are many situations where the pressure is much more overt. A patient was admitted to the ward of a Veterans Administration Hospital and was immediately felt to be "sociopathic." This hospital had a rule that no one with charges pending in court could be admitted. Because the admitting resident felt this man's story was suspect, he specifically asked about court charges and was assured by the patient that there were none. The patient claimed depression and severe anxiety attacks.

On the ward, the patient quickly lost his "depression" and seemed to settle in comfortably. He tended to keep somewhat to himself and while he attended the various ward meetings, he participated only minimally. He did form one or two friendships, and we soon became aware that he had been sneaking out of the hospital in the company of another patient on a few occasions. In the meantime, his records arrived from another hospital and revealed an eight-month hospitalization marked by repeated manipulative struggles. It was clear from that record that the patient, together with his somewhat overbearing father, had been very demanding and difficult to deal with. Shortly after we received this record, the resident was contacted by the police who had traced him to the hospital. They revealed that the patient had "breaking and entering" charges pending against him and that his case was soon to be heard. The patient was confronted with this report and was told that unless and until the charges were cleared up, he could not receive treatment in the hospital. He was further informed that the police wanted him, and he was advised to remain on the ward until they came. He readily acknowledged that it would be better not to compound his troubles by fleeing; further, he was certain that the "misunderstanding" would be cleared up. Then, he promptly persuaded another patient to leave with him. They were apprehended in another part of the state when, after having had a few drinks, they had an auto accident.

Within a day, the hospital director's office received a call from a legislator's office expressing interest and concern about the case. The patient's father had complained about how his sick son had been mistreated. The father was now badgering the resident to acknowledge the boy's sickness, and to change the diagnosis from "sociopathy" to schizophrenia. He made no secret of the fact that, through political influence, he had been able to change his son's disciplinary discharge from the armed forces to an honorable discharge. As the ward chief, I had backed my resident's actions in this case and I soon received telephone calls from my superiors expressing their concern. I was urged to contact the father—a most unusual procedure as I tended to rely on various other members of the ward staff for such contacts. Under the circumstances, I agreed to talk with the man to see if I could cool the situation down.

The father most ingratiatingly thanked me for my interest and then embarked on a whirlwind spiel which could briefly be summarized as follows: His son was sick—schizophrenia in its early stages was a likely diagnosis. Doctors who could release such a boy from the hospital had better be exceedingly certain of their diagnosis because they might be charged with malpractice. I should give him a statement testifying to his son's psychosis which he might show to the judge. With all of this, he might overlook his son's mistreatment at the hands of the resident. And, most important, he (the father) was a significant person in the world of politics and he knew political figures who would take up his cause.

I made a brief and unsuccessful effort to show him how his behavior played a role in the perpetuation of his son's difficulties. He responded with a shocked, "But I'm a FATHER!" (The record belied the suggestion that he really took fatherhood so seriously.) I then indicated to him that while we might legitimately disagree on the diagnosis, my diagnosis—and my resident's—would remain as we saw the case. If he felt that his son should not be prosecuted because of insanity, or that he should not be convicted because of it, he should so indicate to the judge. At any rate, his lawyer could advise him what to do and he could always arrange an independent psychiatric evaluation. We would not take him back while charges were pending; after the charges were cleared up, we would be willing to re-evaluate him if he sought admission, but at this time we could not guarantee admission. I acknowledged that I was aware of his political connections, that I supposed I would be hearing further from him and them, and that, with his son's permission, I would be happy to explain my position to them. He stormed out angrily and we heard nothing more from him.

I believe that to have bent the hospital rule and yielded to the father's pressure would have fostered an increasing amount of manipulation on the part of the patient. In addition, the staff would have been very resentful and would have taken its resentment out on the patient, perhaps by hardening its stand and refusing to grant even some of his reasonable requests. A continual conflict of goals might have been set up.

I was very fortunate in this situation to be in that particular hospital. The hospital director's office was quite prepared to back up my medical judgment as long as I kept them informed about the progress of the situation. My superiors on the medical staff were equally supportive. The legislator, to his credit, did not go beyond the inquiring phone call, and he was apparently willing to leave the running of the hospital to the professionals. And there can be no doubt that I was fortunate also in the fact that the father was a minor, rather than a major, political power.

Even knowing all these things, I found myself in a very uncomfortable position. The resident and other staff members were looking to me to protect them from what they felt was a harsh and dangerous political and administrative system. I had always insisted that clinical considerations had to be foremost—would I now practice what I had preached? On the other hand, the clinical decision was making waves, and administrators do not like waves, especially political waves. It would probably have been possible to work out some compromise with the hospital rule. At times during the few days in question, I could feel my own resistance harden. Were the phone calls from my superiors really just inquiries, or were they exerting pressure? How dare they overrule my clinical decision? It is easy to let one's fantasies grow and to become a crusader in this situation. Then came the counter-reactions. As I recognized my resentment and some of the Oedipal dynamics behind it (we all have our dragons to slay in the name of honor), I began to take a second look. Perhaps, because of my resentment, I was being unduly harsh with the patient. Maybe I was overlooking something in the diagnosis, or missing an opportunity effectively to help this patient. Fortunately, the doubt was short-lived, and, with the support I described above, the situation was handled adequately. I remain impressed, however, by the practical and psychological forces which operate in such situations.

Not all administrators are so supportive in such situations, and certain connections of the patients have more political clout or prestige than did our patient's father. A head nurse in another hospital recently described a patient who had been constantly in trouble, was clearly using the hospital to escape prosecution, and showed absolutely no inclination to give up his indiscriminate use of drugs. His brief hospital stay was marked by considerable turmoil and, when the danger of prosecution had passed, he signed out of the hospital. The nurse told me, "He was no patient for us. We never would have taken him if he were not Dr. X's son." (Dr. X is a prominent physician.) It is difficult for me to see how either staff or patient can engage in therapeutic work when a patient is admitted under these circumstances.

No situation arising in the real world of psychiatric life is a pure example of anything, and the next illustration has a plethora of factors all contributing to the staff's difficulty in managing this very manipulative patient. However, the comments of the staff regarding her V.I.P. status are rather illuminating.

Cynthia was 22 years old when she was admitted to the hospital because of anorexia nervosa. Although her condition had been chronic, once her parents decided she needed medical attention, events moved rapidly. Her father was a nationally prominent attorney who knew many of the senior members of the hospital personally. Even those staff members who did not know him personally were aware of his prominence and of his reputation both as a highly skilled lawyer and as a defender of the underdog. Conceivably, any one of them could have needed and received his services—at least so did their fantasies run. Thus, when the family became sufficiently concerned about Cynthia's vomiting and loss of weight, the father called his friend on the senior staff and an immediate admission was arranged. This in itself was quite exceptional as the typical procedure involved a series of evaluative interviews before a patient was accepted in the hospital; this patient was guaranteed admission before the admitting officer had even seen her.

Once in the hospital, she exhibited many of the characteristics of the special-problem patient described in the preceding section. The staff easily became split into "good" and "bad," and certain staff members had the feeling that only they understood the patient. They were struck by her loneliness, emptiness, and the desperation behind her anorexia. The "bad" staff were much more impressed with her manipulations.

The staff had enormous difficulties in dealing with Cynthia's weight. "Good" staff members were afraid that she was wasting away to the point of imminent death while some "bad" staff members were less concerned. After innumerable discussions, the staff decided, by no means unanimously, that Cynthia would be tube-fed if she failed to gain "some" weight every day. Then came painful discussions about whether one ounce was sufficient in terms of the rule, whether the scales were accurate in terms of the single ounce, etc. Looking back at these discussions, one is inclined to feel that they were silly quibbling, but anyone who has seen the intensity of staff dissension created by the special-problem patient will recognize that this type of quibbling was merely the surface manifestation of severe staff splits.

Cynthia herself was extremely manipulative in all of this. She would occasionally talk a nurse into not weighing her. She would take a drink of water just before weighing in order to produce the weight gain. She would put a heavy object in her mouth or in her clothes. It was extraordinary how she managed, day after day, to "gain" a barely perceptible amount—just enough to avoid the tube feeding. Then, having "gained" a certain amount, she would prepare herself for the tube feeding. The weights would be relinquished and massive vomiting would be induced. The staff would notice the "weight-loss" of a pound or two, tube-feed her once, and the whole process would start again.

This behavior was clearly manipulative. Cynthia intended to deceive the staff. Even when confronted with the fact that she was observed drinking the water, she would deny it. When the weights were discovered in her clothes, she claimed no knowledge of how they had gotten there. I have no direct information indicating that Cynthia derived satisfaction from having put something over on the staff in this manner, but it is quite likely that she did. In other situations, her "playful" and gleeful contempt was obvious. For example, after reading about one of her father's current activities in the newspaper, she took the article to her therapist and said, "Look, here's a man with the same name as my father." Told that this was her father, she feigned disbelief and induced her therapist, in all seriousness, to tell her that her father was a famous man and an important attorney. As he continued his explanation, he became gradually aware of the contemptuous look he was getting from the patient. She walked away from him and began to tell other patients how her "stupid" therapist actually believed that she didn't know who her father was.

Now, all of these problems[11] could be encountered with any special-problem patient. However, the reactions of the staff in this case occurred against the background of her V.I.P. father. Several staff members whom I interviewed started the conversation by saying, "Well, you know, she's Y's daughter—the famous lawyer." Did this fact influence her treatment? We know that it influenced the fashion in which she was admitted. Some of the staff members felt that nursing personnel could not be firm with Cynthia because of a lurking fear that she would complain to her father who would transmit the complaint to the senior staff. Others had the impression that some nurses catered to her wishes with the fantasy (and hope) that she would report to her parents how well she was treated and that this message would get back to the senior staff.

There was also a tendency among some nurses (and probably other staff members as well) to want to talk with Mr. Y when he visited. At times, this was more than the usual contact between a parent and the nursing staff. One nurse clearly remembered how jealous Cynthia had been when she observed her talking with her father. The nurse felt that the father had some particular interest in talking with her and she felt flattered. Some of the nurses made

11. In this case we again see how the patient may employ manipulation in an attempt to cater to an underlying conflict. Cynthia manipulated partly because she could not allow herself to gain weight.

a special case out of Mr. Y, allowing him visiting privileges which other parents did not have. This, too, became an issue in the staff dissension. We can speculate that Cynthia's contempt was fostered by her seeing these exceptional privileges.

Some of the staff members felt that they themselves were not affected by Cynthia's V.I.P. status, but almost all were quick to point out how other staff members had been affected. There was general agreement that it was more difficult to set limits in a reasonable fashion. Some nurses tended to be too lenient while others bent over backwards not to be swayed by the V.I.P. status, and they tended to be unreasonably strict. We encountered a dichotomy similar to this one earlier in my discussion of my own feelings and fantasies when confronted with the father with political influence.

In addition to the nurses' fantasies and the observations of other nurses, from time to time there was concrete evidence of Cynthia's V.I.P. status. Mr. Y was not a dramatic or blustering intruder on the medical scene, but every so often he would express his concern to his friend, a high-ranking member of the senior staff. This doctor would communicate his concern to the staff, who became increasingly irritated at the interference. After all, they were faced with the problems day after day: Was there an implication that they were not concerned? Was there an implication that they were mistreating Cynthia? "Concern" without concrete suggestions about how better to treat the patient can be a type of innuendo which must make the staff more self-conscious and even less free to use its clinical judgment.

After Cynthia had been in the hospital for a year without having made any appreciable progress, her resident therapist left. She was not assigned to a new resident; she was selected by a member of the senior staff as his private patient. Although this was occasionally done in this hospital, many of the staff members felt that Dr. Z had selected Cynthia primarily because of her father. The reasoning ran this way: Cynthia had been here a year with no progress. Mr. Y had been expressing his concern. It might be that the resident had not been doing a good job. Dr. Z felt that he owed it to Mr. Y to give his daughter every chance. Some people even felt that the dean of the medical school might have been influential in having Cynthia treated by Dr. Z rather than by another resident. I heard this line of reasoning from a sufficient number of staff members to suggest to me that they had discussed it among themselves at one time.

Interestingly enough, Dr. Z was the only staff member with whom I talked who did not mention that Cynthia was Mr. Y's daughter. When I finally called this to his attention, he did not seem to grasp the point I was making until I asked him directly whether the fact that Mr. Y was so prominent and so friendly with some senior staff members influenced either his choice of Cynthia as a patient or his treatment of her. He did not think so. He was aware of who Mr. Y was and the influence he wielded, and he readily acknowledged the possibility that Mr. Y's status might have played some subtle role, but he was not conscious of it.

When Cynthia became Dr. Z's patient, she became a V.I.P. patient in an additional respect. Dr. Z himself was a V.I.P. in the hospital. Residents were quite resentful of the fact that Dr. Z's opinions about Cynthia's management carried far more weight than did their opinions about their own patients. It was extremely rare in the hospital for anyone on the staff to continue to treat a patient who left the hospital against medical advice. Yet, when Cynthia left in this manner, Dr. Z remained as her therapist on an outpatient basis.

It was not possible for me to verify the assessments the staff members made about each other's motivations. Nonetheless, at the very least, staff members felt this way about each other and thus contributed to the dissension. And it is clear that her V.I.P. status added to the difficulties of ward management of this manipulative patient.

Why are staff members influenced by the V.I.P. status of a patient? Some of the more obvious reasons have already been touched on. There is the desire to make a good impression and the fear of reprisal from one's superiors or from the important person himself. I believe that there is another factor, less practical in nature and more psychological. The circumstance of doctor, patient, and V.I.P. is a triadic[12] situation and as such it is likely to have Oedipal overtones. This is undoubtedly less conscious

12. The triadic situation is also seen when the patient changes therapist (Scher, 1970).

than the more obvious practical considerations, and its influence is subtler but probably just as powerful. The doctor, flattered to be treating the V.I.P.'s relative, tends to develop rescue fantasies which, as Freud (1910) indicated, involve both saving the mother from dangerous situations and identifying with the father. It is now the patient who needs saving (treating) and the V.I.P. with whom the doctor partly identifies. For there is little doubt that V.I.P. status rubs off onto the doctor; he becomes more important by treating the V.I.P.'s relative. At the same time, the V.I.P. is the powerful and feared figure who will punish the doctor for transgressions and disobedience. And probably in some cases the doctor feels that he is directly in competition with the V.I.P. After all, when the patient was in his hands she got sick, but in the doctor's hands she will get well.

Again, evidence for this formulation is hard to come by. I have never had in analysis a doctor who was treating a V.I.P. patient. Two fragmentary remarks by staff members who worked with Cynthia are relevant, however. I have already mentioned one of these—the remarks of the nurse who felt that Mr. Y had a particular interest in talking to her and that Cynthia became jealous when she observed this. In a discussion with one of the male staff members, I asked him why he felt the management of Cynthia was so difficult. "Are you kidding?" he answered. "When you date the boss's daughter—she might tell the old man on you."

I do not know if problems of this magnitude are encountered with all patients who have V.I.P. connections. Not all V.I.P. patients are also special-problem patients. Some hospitals attempt to neutralize the V.I.P. effect by *insisting* that all patients undergo the same routine procedures. The very process of insisting must serve to underscore the V.I.P. nature of the patient's status. However, it may be possible in this manner to minimize some of the practical effects of V.I.P. status—especially if the V.I.P. is truly cooperative and unobtrusive. Nonetheless, the more subtle Oedipal factors are probably untouched by either the routinization of procedure or the unobtrusiveness of the V.I.P.

There are three types of situations involving manipulation by the family of the patient which we may encounter in our clinical practice. One of these, where overt or covert manipulation is a regular part of the family milieu of the patient, has been discussed in chapter 7. The other situations involve manipulation of the doctor or hospital staff by a family member and manipulation of the patient by one of his relatives.

In each of these latter two situations, we evaluate the relative's behavior, using the same criteria of manipulation that we employ in evaluating a patient's actions. This evaluation may be even more difficult than it sometimes is with the acknowledged patient because we usually have less access to the relative and his thoughts and feelings. Whether the deception is intended or whether the relative experiences the exhilaration and contempt involved in putting something over may not be at all apparent to us because we may not have sufficient contact with the relative to enable him to let us know. From a theoretical point of view, we should distinguish between the relative who manipulates and the one who (like some V.I.P.'s) influences by exerting pressure, but who does not employ deception and derive pleasure therefrom. From the practical standpoint, we may often not be able to do much about either, although the manipulator, if found out, is probably less likely to receive the high-level support afforded the influential V.I.P. This may not result in better overall treatment, however, because the hospital staff may easily develop such a pejorative attitude toward the manipulating family that rational treatment may become impossible.

The manipulating relative often tries to influence the staff in terms of the treatment program. He will come up with a variety of reasons why hospital rules and policies should be modified. He may lie about his financial resources in order to be charged a lower fee. He may plead special hardship in order to miss required family meetings. He may create an atmosphere of urgency and crisis in order to procure a visiting pass for a patient who might be better off not going on passes. He may collude with the patient's acting out, even to the extent of deceiving the staff in order to cover it up. For example, the manipulative parents of a schizophrenic girl were told by the staff that they could not visit their daughter. They "agreed" that this decision made sense; their daughter was too disturbed, and the parents, ingratiatingly, "wished to cooperate with the hospital in every way possible." They agreed to see the social worker on a weekly basis and to have no contact with the daughter until the staff felt it was wise. The social worker was impressed with the conscientiousness of these parents and their hard work in their sessions with her. The nursing staff verified that they had made no attempt to see the patient. All seemed to be going well until the patient, unable to contain herself any longer, confessed to the staff that her parents had been coming once a week between their sessions with the social worker. They stood on the sidewalk outside the hospital and waved to the patient who had been instructed to appear at her bedroom window. In addition, the parents had arranged a small network of other patients to meet them and carry notes to the patient.

There are, of course, many factors which contributed to the patient's need to confess. At the very least, she was put in an impossible situation—torn between the hospital and her parents. She both admired her parents' cleverness and was ashamed of their dishonesty. She felt many obligations to those patients who served as secret couriers. She deeply resented her parents' interference in "her" therapy and, almost in a mirror of her masturbation struggle, she enjoyed the excitement but she knew it "wasn't good for her."

When the disclosure had been made, the staff reacted very angrily. The patient group was roundly chastised for their collusion and the parents were confronted with the manipulation. They easily shrugged off the confrontation by saying that they did not think that just waving would hurt. And as for the notes, they were just notes telling the patient they loved her; they were not the same as personal visits with an ongoing dialogue between them and the patient. However, if the staff thought it advisable that this activity stop, they would comply. We will never know if yet another mode of secret communication was set up.

It is easy to adopt the view that these relatives are "sabotaging" the treatment. The anger which this provokes in the staff is augmented by its feeling of having had something put over on it. Indeed, their activities make treatment very difficult, but it is probably more helpful to consider these activities in the same light that we consider a patient's resistance; it makes no therapeutic sense to adopt a pejorative attitude toward either. Fleck et al. (1957) and Fleck (1965) have outlined some of the stresses that families may have when one of their members is hospitalized. Rather than blaming these families for being unreliable or for undermining the treatment, we must be ready to consider the psychological factors which lie behind the manipulation. Is the manipulation predominately a feature of a manipulative personality and thus to be understood chiefly in terms of the relatives' need for narcissistic repair? Or is it a manipulation brought into play primarily to subserve some other parental need, such as guilt, fear of separation, etc. If we approach the behavior from this viewpoint, there may be a chance that we can work with the parents, allay their fears, or gratify some of their needs so that treatment may proceed.

There is another reason for viewing the family's manipulation as a psychological phenomenon fired by the relatives' needs rather than as a sabotage of the treatment. Elsewhere (Bursten, 1969) I have considered some of the theoretical and technical issues involved in discussing patients' relatives with them. I do not feel it is helpful to patients to condemn their relatives. When I find it necessary to talk about relatives to patients, I discuss the relatives as human beings with their own problems, needs, and fears, rather than as "good" or "bad" people.

While the relative's attempt to manipulate the staff can produce very trying circumstances, manipulation aimed at the patient himself can also jeopardize the course of therapy. A middle-aged woman was discovered by her husband to be unresponsive. She had taken an overdose of sleeping medication and vodka. She was comatose on admission to the hospital, and shortly thereafter she developed pneumonia. When she responded to medical treatment, a psychiatric consultant was called. His examination revealed a somewhat exhibitionistic woman, covered with bruises inflicted by her husband. She did not appear significantly depressed.

The marriage had been a relatively stable tempest for many years. The husband criticized her and demanded that she clean the house and do secretarial chores for him. She responded by doing both poorly, which roused him to anger. Both of them were sporadically heavy drinkers, and periodically the husband beat the patient up. This type of excitement characterized the homeostatic balance point of the marriage—a marriage which was held together in great measure by the sado-masochistic relationship of the partners. Recently, the husband had openly flaunted his affair with another woman in front of his wife, but after an agonizing, dramatic scene he had agreed to give the other woman up. On the day of the suicide attempt, the wife had learned that the husband was still seeing the other woman. She had confronted him with this knowledge, he had become angry at her "spying," had beaten her up, and left the house. The patient acknowledged that she had wanted to die and had taken the pills and the vodka with that intent. However, when the psychiatrist saw her, she was no longer actively suicidal.

The patient readily discussed her situation with the consultant and seemed to have some potential for psychotherapeutic work. She was vaguely able to realize how angry she had been at her husband. She readily acknowledged how hard her current mode of living was for her, although this acknowledgment may have been more of a proud, masochistic display than an insight. She readily agreed that she needed further help and when the prospect of being transferred to the psychiatric service was raised, she accepted the offer.

The husband, slightly older than the wife, was a dapper, smooth-talking man who showed only the barest traces of a life of dissipation. He was bright and quick, and he had been in a variety of successful business ventures. He took over immediately. Even before the psychiatric consultant was able to talk with the patient, the husband insisted on meeting him. He claimed the status of a needy and suffering person. He grimaced and held his side while telling the consultant that he had been injured in an automobile accident a year previously. He was disdainful and contemptuous of the hospital staff whom he felt were incapable of treating his wife correctly. However, when the consultant attempted to elicit from him a discussion of the marital situation, he revealed very little. He preferred to gloss over their problems and to present an image of marital harmony. He had no explanation for his wife's suicide attempt. The wife reported that her husband had suggested that she divulge very little to the doctors—whereupon she launched into a running, complaining account of the marriage.

Shortly after the patient had indicated her desire for transfer to the psychiatric ward, the consultant held a joint meeting with the patient and her husband. The husband asked her if she really wanted to go to the psychiatric ward, and she became less certain. The decision was left up in the air. Although the husband had said that the decision was up to the patient, he later told the psychiatrist that he did not feel that the transfer was in her best interest. He repeatedly said that he "did not want to be conned into anything." Ultimately, he revealed that he had other plans for his wife. He was starting a new business venture and he needed her assistance with some of the chores. He suggested that a week with her in the mountains might be even better than psychiatric hospitalization.

On the following day, the psychiatric consultant received a long letter from the husband indicating that he felt it important to keep the marriage together. The letter ended with the statement that if the wife stayed in the hospital she would surely worry about his returning to his girl friend, and this worry would not help her at all.

That afternoon, in another joint meeting, the husband appeared markedly disheveled, as if to underline how badly he needed his wife at home. He maintained that psychiatric hospitalization seemed the best course for her, and all the while he massaged his side—the site of the injury. He managed to "reassure" his wife that he would not be seeing the girl friend during her absence.

The patient responded by saying that she was needed at home and, really, it was the feeling of being needed which would repair the marriage. She became determined to leave the hospital and he "reluctantly" agreed.

A follow-up telephone call by the consultant a few weeks later found the marriage equilibrium quite well restored. The wife was doing the new chores for her husband and was being criticized for her performance. "Things have not changed much," she said. She alternated between feeling proud that she could help her husband and feeling used. Perhaps, someday, she thought, she might see a psychiatrist for prolonged therapy.

I cannot tell from the record or from my discussions with the psychiatric consultant whether the husband had a manipulative personality. He did seem to have many narcissistic traits, together with a pervasive contempt and an ability to use other people to his advantage. Indeed, it was probably some of these characteristics which had attracted the masochistic wife to him. She was fair game for his manipulations. If he had been more considerate she very possibly would not have married him or stayed with him. It may thus be a moot point whether it was his manipulativeness or her masochistic needs which prevented the psychiatric hospitalization. More probably, it was the "fit" of these two personalities (Spiegel, 1957; Ackerman, 1958) which prevented the transfer to the psychiatric ward. Thus, when we consider the effect of manipulative relative on the acknowledged patient, we must ask ourselves, "What does the patient get out of it?" and "What does the couple, or the family unit, get out of the manipulation?" Where the manipulative aspects of one family member are a crucial aspect of the fit with personality features of the other family members, change is difficult indeed.

CHAPTER 13

TREATMENT ISSUES: GENERAL

I do not know of any chemical or pharmacological agent for which manipulative behavior is a specific target. True, there is a variety of substances which may result in a lessening of manipulation in various situations. A psychotic patient whose manipulation is a desperate attempt to maintain distance and boundaries may be less driven to manipulate if treated with phenothiazines. Anxiety, restlessness, hyperactivity which may promote activity that puts the patient in conflict with staff and thus leads to manipulative activity can be allayed by several types of drugs. The manipulative behavior of some addicts can be appeased by narcotics. And sedatives, narcotics, and psychotomimetic agents can blur the sense of self and the ability to plan which underlie intentionality. But these agents, with the exception of the last group, strike at some of the causes of manipulation rather than directly at its processes. And while the group of agents which undercut intentionality may aim more directly at manipulation, they are not specific enough; not only manipulative intentionality but all intentionality is compromised. Thus, even if we wished to undercut manipulative behavior chemically, these agents could not be used without undercutting the intentionality in many other behaviors as well.

If there were a drug which was specific to manipulation, our task would be somewhat easier. We would still be beset by problems of diagnosis—problems of some magnitude, as we have seen—but at least, having decided that this or that particular patient should be treated for his manipulation, we could calculate a dose of the drug and give it to him. We could even delegate the actual drug administration to other reliable persons; after all, 10 mg. of chemical X are 10 mg. of chemical X no matter who gives it to the patient. However, this state of affairs is rarely realistic in psychiatry. Human beings, rather than chemicals, are the chief agents of change in most of the psychiatric situations involving manipulation. And "10 mg." of Dr. A or Nurse B or Ward C on Monday is not at all equivalent to the "same dosage" on Tuesday. On the basis of our diagnostic assessment, we can suggest a therapeutic approach but its implementation will vary from individual to individual and from situation to situation. Thus, it would be futile for me to prescribe a set of rules to be followed in the treatment of manipulation even if I had such a fine record of success in this area that I really knew what worked—and I do not claim such a record. What I can do more realistically is discuss the issues which might be considered when we decide to attempt to alter manipulative behavior. These treatment issues, filtered through the personalities and technical skills of workers who may keep them in mind, may be of some help in treating the patient who manipulates.

The first issue in any treatment procedure is knowing with what condition we are faced. Diagnosis of manipulation, as I have noted several times in the preceding chapters, is frequently a difficult task. Let us briefly review the four components by which I define manipulation. There must be a conflict of goals perceived (accurately or inaccurately) by the patient. The manipulator must intend to influence the other person. Intentionality, as I have defined it, is a conscious phenomenon—or at least one readily accessible to consciousness, and it requires anticipatory planning and a sense of self as actor. Deception as the means of influence is the third element and here I refer to the situation where the patient's reality-testing is sufficiently intact for him to know that he is deceiving the other person—even though he may, for a moment, lose himself in the deception. The fourth element, and the one which we do not have a chance to observe directly in many clinical situations, is the sense of satisfaction in having put something over on the other person. At times, all of these elements may be very clear to us, while at other times we may reasonably infer some of them when we observe the others. Furthermore, since the diagnosis hinges so much on accessibility of the elements to consciousness, there are many behaviors which will lie in the "grey" area between manipulation and the expression of an unconscious wish.

It is here that the distinction I discussed in chapter 2 becomes important. In that chapter, I pointed out that some psychiatrists reduce virtually all of our conventional diagnostic categories to issues of manipulation. Conversion reactions, depressions, mania, and masochism have all been described as if the central feature were manipulation. Indeed, there are some who do not concern themselves with the differences in mental processes which make up our various diagnostic categories; they choose to see all behavior as transactional "games" played between manipulators (including, I suppose, themselves). They constantly confront the patient as if they were in a chess match where one must always be ready to block the opponent's attempts to control the board. There are two assumptions behind this approach which I challenge.[1] Firstly, there is the explicit assumption that in all our patients the prime issue is a manipulative struggle for control. Sometimes this is put in terms of the patient's need to remain dependent and his coercive effort to have us take care of him. Secondly, there is the implicit assumption that, even where the patient's coercive wishes are significant, they are always reasonably accessible to consciousness. For, only under this latter condition would it make sense for us to "point it out" to him—unless, and this is a crucial "unless"—we do not care whether he understands us or himself, and we want only to get him (make him, control him) to change his behavior. Thus, it could be argued that when we tell him that he is manipulating, he will get the message that he had better act differently, and he will stop doing whatever we characterize as his illness, even if what we say makes no real sense to him. As one patient put it, "If you can figure out what they (staff) think is wrong with you and prove that they are right but that you are getting better, you are halfway home."

If this method does alleviate distressing symptoms, and it some-times does, why not employ it? Or, in the case of characterological problems, if this method changes behavior that society feels is offensive, why not use it if we have agreed that the behavior must be changed? After all, we have an analogous situation with regard to medications. They do not, in themselves, lead the patient to a correct understanding of himself, but they do clear up some distressing symptoms. Likewise, setting limits may lead to salutory results even when the patient thinks the limit is unjust. Perhaps it is

1. The grounds for these challenges have been discussed elsewhere in this book, particularly in chapters 2, 4, and 6.

precisely the incorrect clarification which so stiffens the resistance of some patients that some forbidden impulse becomes less peremptory and a symptom disappears. Or perhaps the anger which the accusation of manipulation raises may in some way alter the patient's inner dynamics. Or the punishment value of the accusation may satisfy the needs of, say, the masochist, or may sufficiently threaten the dependency needs of the oral-dependent character for behavior to be changed. Other factors, such as the need to please the therapist or to belong to a ward group, may also play a part.

Like every "technique" in psychiatry, confrontation of the patient with the label of "manipulation" does seem to work in some cases while it fails to achieve the desired result in others. When it does produce the desired behavioral change (and just whose desire that is is an interesting question), I believe it is often not because that patient has fully grasped a basic truth about his mental processes; what he may have learned is a code of action which brings him some gratification. At times, this may be sufficient. However, there are also often instances where this "technique" is not satisfactory. I have seen patients driven out of treatment because of the hostility generated by the "accusation." I have seen others who put up a facade of compliance in the relatively controlled ward situation but who revert to their former behavior patterns in the less controlled wider world. There are those who revel in the "mea culpa!" possibilities of confession again and again that they have been guilty of manipulation. And there are those to whom the label "manipulation" makes no sense. They understand the word not as unwitting attempts to influence other people but as I define it in this book; they feel accused of willful attempts to control others by unfair means. And if the desire to control is not conscious, or not even a prominent part of the unconscious motives of a patient's behavior, we do not increase our credibility or our efforts to collaborate with him by telling him that he is manipulating.

Certainly in any therapeutic endeavor aimed at helping the patient explore his own mental processes, interpretations and clarifications which are correct in terms of both content and timing are crucial. (Glover, 1931; Fenichel, 1941.) With this approach, which is the one I generally prefer, we may forego the possibility of quickly training behavioral change, in the hope of widening the patient's horizons as he increases his self-knowledge. And here, the incorrect clarification that the patient is manipulating may be quite antitherapeutic.

A hospitalized schizophrenic scientist had been working part-time in a laboratory in the medical school. He had been in treatment with me for about two years when the following incident occurred. He came into my office one day bristling with anger and announced that he did not want to go to work for a while.

"What's up?" I asked.

"I was scratched by a rabbit in the laboratory the other day, and yesterday I was sure I would get tuleremia." He went on to say that he felt that one could get elephantiasis from tuleremia, and that this would result in his legs being swollen. With this thought in mind, he had started to take a bath. Looking at himself in the bathtub (probably under water) he was convinced that his legs were swollen and that he was no longer himself. "I yelled out to the nurse, 'there's a different person in my body.' And do you know what she said to me? She said, 'You're saying that because you want to accomplish something; you want to act crazy so you won't have to go to work.' "

"I didn't say anything," he continued, "but I thought of taking a kitchen knife and murdering her, or maybe of operating on my legs. I couldn't sleep all night, I was so upset."

I asked the patient what the swollen legs were like.

"Like this," he replied. He took out a pen and a scrap of paper and drew the following figure:

I pointed out to him that it was not the legs that were swollen in the figure. We both agreed that the figure resembled a fertility doll and this opened up for discussion his fear of impregnation and his feelings of carrying around within his body alien and hostile people. After our discussion, he did go back to work.

At a much later time I understood further that the patient must have perceived the nurse's comment as a hostile accusation—a jab, an attack on his bodily integrity. Rather than be invaded by yet another alien force, he had better take a knife to her and ward off the danger. Or was it too late? Should he, perhaps, cut himself to let the poison or poisonous introject out?

There is a marked difference in the approaches taken by the nurse and myself. She saw his call as an attempt to control her, to manipulate her. Perhaps she perceived it this way because she was frightened and needed to reassert her own sense of control in dealing with her psychotic patient. Perhaps she had learned to approach all behavior in terms of a distorted "game theory" which asks only, "How are you trying to fool me now?"

My approach was based on my impression that the patient was not manipulating. He was trying to communicate some very frightening experiences—experiences which he knew would not be real in my world but which were very real in his. The question I asked myself was not, "What is he trying to put over on me?" but "What is frightening him so badly?" And with that approach, he was able to tell me. The nurse never knew what really concerned him nor was she aware of his impulse to defend himself by murdering her.[2]

Even when we can be reasonably certain that a patient is manipulating, we must still make further diagnostic assessments. These are geared toward determining some of the factors which impel the patient to manipulate. We can conveniently, if arbitrarily, separate these factors into three groupings: reality factors, intrapsychic factors reflecting some perceived danger or desired goal, and factors reflecting the peremptory quality of a manipulative personality. We shall consider the first two groups in this chapter while the third group will be discussed in chapter 14.

2. This type of situation frequently arises in the evaluation of suicidal behavior. Some workers tend to see all such behavior as "gestures"—designed to coerce others into helping them. While I can agree that these patients need help, some of them make genuine if unsuccessful suicide attempts, and to treat these patients as if they were manipulators is to court disaster.

The diagnostic problems associated with reality factors have been discussed in chapter 8. Because of the staff's therapeutic orientation and zeal, its position of power, and the desire to maintain the status quo, staff personnel most often are unable to analyze the reality situation on the ward in a dispassionate manner. Even when the manipulation might be justified and adaptive on the part of the patient, it is frequently treated as a piece of pathology and the staff's provocation and oppression go unnoticed.

Even when the manipulation is not primarily an adaptive response to an oppressive environment but is more clearly an expression of the patient's inner conflicts, a variety of reality factors should be considered. Some of these factors have also been reviewed in chapter 8. The organization of the value-system of the ward, the need of the staff for the excitement of the public "trial" of a manipulator, the manipulative collusion of certain staff members, and a whole gamut of neurotic reactions on the part of staff and other patients may all contribute to the evocation of the manipulation.

These considerations lead us to the following principle: Not every patient manipulation should be automatically opposed or even focused on as a major area for discussion with the patient. At the outset, a judgment should be made about whether the manipulation should be a focus for the patient's treatment or the ward's treatment (or both). Indeed, this principle raises the question whether a particular manipulation need call for any treatment at all. You will recall our discussion earlier in this chapter about those who see psychiatric treatment as a continuous struggle for control. It is not necessary to see every manipulation as requiring a countermove. In terms of some ward ideologies, a certain amount of manipulation might be expected as a part of daily living. In terms of the individual patient, as we shall see, the manipulation may be relatively less important than some of his other problems.

We should not oppose every manipulation? What effect will this have on the whole ward? Many staff members are concerned that "if you let some patients 'get away' with manipulating, how can you limit the manipulations of others?" This concern reflects in part an exaggerated sense of fairness (or perhaps guilt). Our treatment approach must be as flexible and adaptable to each individual problem as group living allows. To feel that we must oppose every manipulation is to treat by formula rather than by an attempt at rational understanding. In our own families, if two of our children have planned to go to the movies and one of them has a bad cold or is being punished or has not completed his homework assignment for tomorrow, we do not ordinarily feel it unfair to limit that child while we let the other one go to the movies. In one case, the manipulation may reflect the psychic equivalent of the "bad cold" while in another case it may not.

Admittedly, this calls for a degree of sophistication exceeding that required to pick up the fact that a patient is deceitfully putting something over on you. I suppose that it demands that we be psychiatrists rather than moralists. And, if there are those on our hospital staffs who, because of less training or because of different types of training, are unable to apply this degree of sophistication, it demands that we unashamedly teach them, guide them, and direct them.[3]

Patients, even more than staff, lack psychiatric sophistication, and it is a bit much to expect them automatically to understand the subtleties of ego-organization. They, too, will raise the question of "fairness" based on the more easily perceieved manipulative behavior of various patients. In part, this is a reasonable protest based on what they observe and what they understand; in part it is also defensive because, by focusing on the obvious aspects of behavior, they can avoid the dangers of considering the less obvious and more anxiety-provoking aspects. It is sometimes helpful to explain to the patients, perhaps in a group or community meeting, the basis on which we distinguish between various behavioral manifestations which to them may appear to be similar. We do not have to guard our psychiatric knowledge jealously, nor should we conduct teaching sessions or employ technical terms. We could say, for example, "Yes, Mr. Jones fooled us by saying he was looking for a job and then getting an apartment behind our backs in the hope that we would discharge him. And Mrs. Smith did the same thing. But you remember what brought Mr. Jones in here in the first place was the trouble he got into by fooling people. This

---

3. I cannot subscribe to "democratic" or "team" approaches if this means that the treatment will sink to the lowest level of staff sophistication. These approaches make sense only when they provide a relaxed staff atmosphere which tends to raise the level of psychiatric sophistication.

has been a lifelong problem with him and we've seen it again and again on the ward. This is why we feel that he should not leave the ward unless he is accompanied by another person. Mrs. Smith hasn't had this sort of problem. As a matter of fact, she's always been afraid of doing something unless she asked permission first. It seems as if you're beginning to feel a little more independent, Mrs. Smith." This type of discussion may be helpful to some patients by conveying to them that we are less interested in some of the surface manifestations of behavior than in the people who exhibit the behavior. We cannot, of course, expect all patients (or staff) to go along with these kinds of distinctions. If we recall Piaget's (1932) line of moral development[4] we will recognize that I am recommending a "justice" based on "equity"—a relatively mature sense of justice to which many people find it impossible to subscribe.

A ward with a "rule" against manipulation—whether an overt or covert rule—is setting a standard of behavior or discipline probably more geared to social control in the interest of maintaining a functioning ward unit; it is not *treatment* of the individual manipulator.

Some psychiatrists who have been concerned with autocratic government of patients by staff have attempted to democratize the management of the ward society by giving patients as a group a major role in community decisions. This does not solve the problem of the need for flexibility, however. One patient, having needs quite different from those of another, may still find himself subordinated to the larger group of patients who exert the decision-making function and who may be as rule-conscious and need as much "fairness" as staff.

What we have gotten into in this discussion is related to the age-old problem of individual man versus the state (society). This political-philosophical problem has been grappled with through the ages—beginning long before psychiatrists were given the power to construct "therapeutic communities" (Rubenstein and Lasswell, 1966; Mayer, 1969). The point is that our reaction to the manipulator in some instances may be "treatment" of the ward society by discipline of the individual, but it may not be therapeutic (or antitherapeutic, for that matter) for the particular individual.

4. See chapter 7.

Having considered the various ward factors which may be involved in the manipulation, we are faced with the question of how to deal with these factors when we feel that the incident is of sufficient significance to warrant intervention. I do not have any prescription for changing staff attitudes other than constant discussions. Some people are very limited in their potential for adopting a flexible approach. We must recognize that various members of our staff have been selected for a variety of reasons, not all of them on the basis of their suitability for this kind of work. Where possible, all staff should be selected with an eye to their potential for working within the particular ward ideology.

In instances where they encourage or collude in patient manipulation, it is a difficult matter to help the staff avoid either the collusion or focusing on the patient and punishing ("treating") him for the manipulation. The noncolluding staff members may tend to turn the patient into a scapegoat, in this case as a relatively safe way of expressing their anger toward those staff members who have encouraged the manipulation. Those who have colluded may be chagrined when the manipulation comes to light, and they may attempt to displace the blame and undo the manipulation by focusing on the patient-manipulator. It is sometimes helpful if these facts are borne in mind during staff and patient-staff discussions of the manipulation. In some extreme cases where a staff member repeatedly encourages or colludes in seriously disruptive manipulations despite the fact that his collaboration has been repeatedly discussed with him, it may be necessary to remove him from decision-making roles with a particular patient or even from participation in the ward community.

It is a fairly common practice for clinical directors and chief residents to refer those staff members whose inner conflicts interfere seriously with a therapeutic approach with patients for their own psychotherapy. While this makes sense from a humanitarian point of view, and while it may eventually pay off professionally, it cannot usually be considered as "treatment" of the reality situation in which the patient-manipulator finds himself. The staff member may change very little over the short range; in fact, during his own treatment he may act out his inner conflicts even more blatantly than he did before. Thus, while the referral may have given the administrator the sense of having done something in a difficult ward situation, he may, in fact, have accomplished very little. Nor do I suggest that we remove all those whose neurotic conflicts interfere with a therapeutic approach. If we did that, we might be left with no staff at all. We must accept as a fact of life that our wards are manned by human beings and that there will always be those who encourage patients to manipulate. Staff discussions and good communication among staff members are important; good supervision is helpful. However, it is vital to the treatment program of the individual patient that we avoid making a scapegoat of him under the guise of "treatment" in order to preserve the illusion that the staff played no part in the manipulation.

If we should look to the environment of the ward for its part in producing the manipulation, perhaps we should also look beyond the ward to other environmental factors evoking the manipulation by the patient. Some of these factors, such as cultural differences, manipulative family values, and the desire to manipulate a society which is felt to be oppressive have been referred to in chapters 7, 11, and 12. When the family impels the patient to manipulate us, we become quite concerned. A situation such as this was described in chapter 12, where the patient's parents had arranged to see their daughter surreptitiously and were using other patients as secret messengers while they pretended compliance with the hospital's rule that they should have no contact with their daughter. Often our reaction in such a case is precisely what I recommended for extreme cases of staff collaboration with the patient-manipulator; we remove the family from the scene by increasing attempts to separate them from the patient. There are no good guidelines that I know of to tell us when a family should be prohibited from visiting a hospitalized patient. Some psychiatrists hold to the view that certain families are so upsetting to patients that they become so disorganized that they can do no useful therapeutic work. They recommend separation. Others maintain that this is precisely the situation in which the family must be involved, but only under supervision (chaperone) or in a family therapy situation. Without this involvement, they say, the important reality issues will not be confronted. Still others hold the view that family visits should not be restricted; what goes on in the unsupervised visits will be grist for the individual and family therapy mill. Obviously, the situation I refer to here is much more complex than the mere occurrence of manipulation, and it involves therapeutic issues far beyond the scope of this book. What I can point out, however, is that very often when the family collaborates with the patient to manipulate the staff, it may be a sign of their pain. There is probably little to gain in adopting a punitive attitude toward them. If possible, they should have a chance to explore the anxieties that may underlie their actions. Are the parents so attached to the patient that the separation is unbearable? If so, perhaps we should reconsider the separation to see which plan offers the best chance of treating the patient-family unit. Do the parents fear loss of control and need to manipulate in order to reassert themselves in the face of a frighteningly powerful professional staff? Perhaps we can help them understand that and be less frightened, or perhaps we can offer them some role in decision-making which they will find reassuring. It is not inconceivable that, in some instances, we might acknowledge that we are aware of the manipulation, discuss its implications, and advise the family against its continuance and then leave it up to the family whether they choose to continue. After all, we are not in this profession to win points, to save face, or to beat anyone in a game; we are in it to devise the most helpful approach in any particular situation.

Understandably, we are less concerned when the target of the manipulation is not we but lies outside of the hospital. We rarely become terribly excited if, for example, the family helps the patient manipulate in order to get into college. Such a manipulation does not directly threaten either the treatment or our personal authority. Nevertheless, as with every bit of behavior which commands our attention, we may wish to explore what it tells us and can tell the patient and his family about themselves and their relationships and values.

At times, psychiatrists view instances where the patient manipulates others outside of the treatment situation not merely with lack of concern but with enthusiasm—even with collaborative enthusiasm. This is particularly likely where the psychiatrist shares the patient's view that some segment of our society has been particularly oppressive. The appropriateness of this attitude depends to a great extent on what the psychiatrist sees as his task. If he is interviewing the patient with a view to helping him avoid the draft or promoting her right to an abortion, such enthusiasm is appropriate. Where the treatment is conceptualized in terms of reinforcing self-assertion or reactions which the psychiatrist considers adaptive, such enthusiasm may help accomplish these goals, although he must not then punish such responses of the patient when they are in the service of accomplishing goals with which the psychiatrist is in disagreement. For example, a white outpatient may engage in a manipulation designed to help a black family buy a house from a seller who would not sell to black people. The psychiatrist who believes in equal opportunities for all people may applaud this manipulation as a sign of his patient's increasing self-assertiveness. Later, this patient may engage in some manipulation designed to prevent his employees from organizing and gaining improved wages and working conditions. What now? Shall the psychiatrist applaud this manipulation also as a sign of increasing self-assertiveness, even though he disapproves of its goal? It is hardly likely that he would do so. In fact, he might punish this manipulation by subjecting it to an aggressive "analysis" designed to show that it is the product of the patient's neurosis. This approach is indeed based largely on reinforcement, but I fear it is political therapy rather than psychotherapy.

The charge has been leveled at psychoanalysis that it attempts to get patients to conform to a society which, at times, may not be worth conforming to (Fromm, 1970).[5] Actually, many in the contemporary mental health movement attempt to persuade or coerce their patients into conforming to their own values—values which sometimes focus around the reform if not the revolution of society (Tullipan and Feldman, 1969). Sometimes this is done in the relatively subtle manner described above; sometimes it is more direct. One community mental health center called a meeting of all patients recently discharged from its outpatient clinic. Ostensibly this meeting was to organize a "follow-up" group. Actually, it became an attempt, under the guise of "treatment," to mobilize citizen participation in an attempt to effect some social changes.

If we are to attend to the psychotherapy rather than the political

5. In this book, Fromm levels many criticisms at psychoanalysis. While I maintain that this important criticism is invalid, I do not imply that all his criticisms, especially against organized psychoanalysis in America, are without merit.

therapy of patients, we will discuss their manipulations with them where it makes sense in terms of expanding their knowledge of themselves, or supporting their self-esteem, their sense of intactness, etc. It is a mistake to consider only these manipulations which we feel are neurotic (or undesirable) while not commenting on those which we feel are adaptive. There exists a widespread misconception that to analyze an adaptive response is to undercut it. This misconception proceeds from a pejorative view of therapy. Any bit of behavior has the potential for telling the patient something about himself. If the discussion is conducted skillfully and uncritically, the adaptive behavior will not be challenged despite the fact that some of its underlying motivations may be uncovered.

It can readily be seen that while I have attempted to separate reality factors from intrapsychic factors in our discussion, this attempt has not been entirely successful. The groupings, as I have indicated, are somewhat arbitrary. This reflects the fact that good diagnosis and good treatment must be geared to a "mix" of these factors.

When we survey the array of reality factors which can evoke manipulation by a patient, we may be tempted to conclude that there should be no "patient" at all. Paraphrasing a slogan about parents of disturbed children which was popular in the 1930's, we could say, "There are no sick people; there are only sick societies." I do not subscribe to this view. While I applaud the thoughtful advances made by the field of social psychiatry, I am not at all hopeful that prevention of crippling inner psychological states can occur on a large scale. There will always be the need for specialized help for those who wish to change themselves, not necessarily to conform, but to improve their functioning and sense of well-being. And some of these people will gain optimal benefit from a clinical psychiatry which focuses on them as individuals within a social system.

The question which arises, then, is how we arrive at the proper mix of a focus on the reality (social) factors and a focus on the intrapsychic factors in any given instance. This is a question which is currently being hotly debated in psychiatric circles; some psychiatrists hold that virtually only social factors should be considered, others maintain that any pronounced focus on reality factors will reduce the intensity of the transference to the individual psychotherapist and/or provide the patient with rationalizations with which to keep from looking at himself. There is no doubt that a focus on reality factors can shore up the defenses the patient erects against examining his own conflicts, while a focus on the patient's inner conflicts can conviently prevent examination of the ward and the possibility of making the patient a scapegoat.

I am convinced that the basic task of the clinical psychiatrist is to help individuals called "patients" to move toward positions of more nearly optimal functioning and that our chief method must be the alleviation of inner conflicts which limit their functioning. Nonetheless, we must avoid reality situations which, by forcing the patient to repeat his neurotic or psychotic patterns, prevent him from experimenting with new ways of thinking and action even when his internal dynamics may be sufficiently altered to make such experimentation possible. Thus, when we identify a patient's manipulation, I cannot give a general rule about what the "mix" of attention to him as manipulator and to the community at large should be. Psychiatrists of differing persuasions will have their various recommendations. However, while there is no defined optimal "mix," the perceptive clinician must be aware, at least, of all the issues.

Let us turn more directly to the treatment issues involved when we focus on the individual patient's intrapsychic situation. We will refer here generally to situations where the manipulation is in the service of avoiding some perceived danger or gaining some desired goal rather than predominately an expression of a manipulative personality. Here we come to the second part of our "principle," and we may again raise a question. Even if we do not oppose every manipulation, should we not at least take up every manipulation as a topic of discussion with the patient? Again I would answer in the negative. We do not, indeed we cannot, discuss every bit of behavior which comes to our attention. Even in psychoanalysis, we exercise selectivity in our comments. While all of the patient's behavior is of importance and interest to us (or, at least, all of it that we can humanly observe and keep in mind) we tend to confine our remarks to those that will serve some therapeutic purpose. While I adhere to the proposition that clarification and interpretations should touch on material relatively accessible to consciousness—and manipulation is, by definition, relatively accessible—we must be aware that there may be other themes just as accessible and of greater pertinence.

What will move therapy forward depends on one's therapeutic point of view and goals. From the vantage points of psychoanalytically oriented psychotherapy, we may find it necessary to help the patient break through a period of resistance; if the discussion is likely to further this end it should be undertaken. If not, such a discussion might only further strengthen the resistance. At another time, the patient may be struggling with his fear of passivity. To discuss his manipulation *qua* manipulation might distract him from that struggle, whereas to focus on some of the determinants of his intentionality having to do with activity and passivity might be more to the point. You will recall the case of Cynthia, the anorexic girl described in chapter 12. Certainly her manipulations to simulate weight gain were important, but the focus on that theme at the expense of downplaying her fears of gaining weight and her desire to control the timing of her tube feeding (a very sexualized activity) led to an impossible contest and probably helped her avoid a consideration of these other vital issues.

At still other times, the manipulation might signal a desperate attempt on the part of a psychotic patient to differentiate himself from his therapist. We might elect to clarify for the patient what he is doing or we might feel at this point that the patient's observing ego is not in a sufficiently solid position to make use of such a clarification. The possibilities are limitless and there can be no general rule about whether a manipulation should be discussed or which aspect of the manipulation or its underpinnings should be taken up. It is here that intrapsychic considerations, such as those discussed in chapters 3–6, are of prime importance. By assessing what the manipulation means in terms of where the patient is and where the therapy is, both we and the patient may learn something important about him. And even if we do not directly comment about the manipulation, we gain some important knowledge about the patient's pressing concerns by, for example, the content of the lie or the timing of the contempt. In this case, we may feel that it is premature for a comment and we may save our remarks for a more opportune moment.

Now, the hospitalized patient spends comparatively little time with his individual psychotherapist; the bulk of his time is spent with other staff members. They provide much of the atmosphere in which the patient's change is expected to take place. I see their role generally as providing highly sensitive reactions to and interactions with him. These reactions and interactions will be enhanced by their ability to understand what is going on in the patient's mind. It is this sensitivity which may lead them away from the repetitive and stereotyped charge of "You're manipulating!" It is the same sensitivity of reaction and interaction which comprises much of the work of the individual psychotherapist with, say, the schizophrenic patient. Here is a hypothetical illustration. Let us suppose a schizophrenic patient, struggling to keep ego boundaries intact, has manipulated us partly in the service of reinforcing his sense of separateness. He may have complained of a stomach ache in order to avoid going to the group calisthenics session which was compulsory on this ward. The staff member who is insensitive or who has a morbid fear of patient "regression" may accuse the patient of manipulating or malingering. Often this is done more to preserve the integrity of the ward rule than to help the individual patient. The highly sensitive staff member might say nothing and allow the patient to miss the meeting. (Indeed, forcing the patient to go to the calisthenics at this time might provoke more regression than allowing him time to consolidate his sense of separateness.) Or, he might attempt some clarification with the patient, such as, "Does the calisthenics session make you feel crowded?" Or, he might discuss the possibility of some type of "compromise" based on his knowledge of the patient's internal status. Perhaps he could arrange for the patient to attend the session but not participate unless he felt up to it. Or perhaps he could arrange for the calisthenics instructor to give the patient some modified, individualized exercise. The skilled and inventive staff member will think of a variety of ways to promote the patient's participation to the degree that such participation is comfortable for him. He will avoid a showdown and will not engage in a senseless challenge of the actual state of the patient's stomach. Understanding the dynamics of lying, he will realize that the "stomach ache" (even if it is unreal) is expressing something very real to the patient. Understanding something about the state of the schizophrenic ego, he will recognize that when the patient says "stomach ache" he may mean something very different from what the staff member means; thus he will realize the foolishness of arguing the point. He may even surmise that the patient's use of the words "stomach ache" may indicate the pressure of a poisonous introject and that it is the explosive threat of the need to reproject this introject that makes the patient so fearful of the annihilation of everything that his ego-boundaries are in danger. He may then decide to be gentle and to give the patient some distance and some time. He will base his reactions on his understanding of the social and intrapsychic forces which contribute to the manipulation, but at the same time he must avoid competing with the therapist by displaying his psychiatric virtuosity to the patient. This bid for the patient's admiration would lend itself to the splitting which we have already encountered in the case of the special-problem patient (see chapter 12).

Of course, not all of our patients are schizophrenic and not all instances of manipulating, even with schizophrenics, will be handled in the same manner. In some instances, we may feel that the patient's prime need is for control, either to help him grapple with his disturbing inner impulses or, as we shall see in our discussion of the treatment of the manipulative personality, to provide him with a powerful identification figure. In situations such as these, it may be therapeutically wise to set limits by directly confronting and opposing the patient's manipulations (Abrams, 1968; Cohen and Greenspoon, 1963). This opposition, however, should proceed not from our need to follow some pejorative rule, but from our psychiatric assessment of the requirements of the individual patient.

Frequently a patient manipulates as he asks permission to do something. This situation occurs not only in hospitals but also in outpatient practice. For example, the patient may distort his income or not reveal that he has insurance coverage, in order to have the therapist set a lower fee. Or the patient may request some special "privilege" and fortify this request with a lie. In this discussion, I assume that the deception is transparent and that we realize that the patient is manipulating. Generally, I react to the request separately from the manipulation. If the request is reasonable both for the patient and for me and/or the hospital, I will grant it; if it is unreasonable, I will not. Most often I will, in addition, indicate that I am aware of the deception, and I will attempt to explore it with the patient. However, I do not ordinarily refuse the request merely because it was posed in a manipulative manner. I do not believe that punishing manipulations in this fashion will lead to their extinction. More probably, they will lead to even more subtle and successful manipulations, and what might have developed as a collaborative relationship will degenerate into a detective game.

CHAPTER 14

TREATMENT ISSUES:
THE MANIPULATIVE PERSONALITY

In the preceding chapter, we have discussed general issues to be considered when we encounter manipulative behavior in the course of treatment of a variety of psychiatric patients. When that patient is a manipulative personality, there are special problems because the manipulation is no longer primarily a behavioral event in the life of the patient; rather it is more central to the very fabric of the patient's personality itself. Even the patient's presenting problems are different. Other patients are clearly suffering and come to us for help, albeit they may want a different kind of help from that which we have to offer. Or, in the case of some psychotic patients, the ability to function may be so severely hampered that we must intervene in order to prevent imminent tragedy.[1] Many manipulative personalities do not come to our attention under either of these circumstances. They do not usually have a degree of suffering which would impel them to seek treatment of any duration, and their minds are clear enough to allow them to function quite well (and cleverly). Indeed, the person with a manipulative personality whose pattern conforms to the expectations of the larger community, such as the successful businessman or administrator, does not usually seek help. However, the person with a manipulative personality who comes into conflict with others may come for "treatment." Often, the request for treatment itself is part of a manipulation such as in the situation where a wife threatens to leave unless the patient "straightens out" or the threat of jail for some criminal offense is met by the patient's pleading sickness and requesting

1. There are those (Szasz, 1961, 1963) who maintain that we should never intervene if the patient does not want treatment. I do not hold to this view, although I do feel that we should limit such intervention to situations of *imminent* danger.

hospitalization. Often, it is not the patient but the community which sends him to us, or even commits him to our care in the hope that we can do something for him that prison can not ([British] Mental Health Bill, 1959; Jones, 1962). Schmiedeberg (1949b), referring to the "psychopath," noted that he rarely wishes to change. He uses doctors to get himself out of trouble. Craft (1968, p. 817) has written "In contrast to many other forms of mental disorders, success (in the treatment of psychopathic disorders) in terms of personal well-being may conflict with success in the community." He has pointed out that there are often two treatment targets for the psychopath—the security and protection of the community at large and the rehabilitation of the psychopath in order that he may re-enter this community. Often, the first target is pre-eminent.

What we are encountering here is the interplay of psychiatric and sociological factors which were discussed in chapter 10. You will recall that I recommend a psychiatric classification based on the patient's personality organization. The particular dynamics of the manipulative personality have been described and serve as the basis for our discussion here. Accordingly, we shall not consider the treatment of "psychopaths" or "sociopaths" because these diagnoses are usually so heavily influenced by the existence of criminal offenses. Our interest is not in criminality, but in the manipulative personality.

The importance of differentiating between the manipulative personality and the criminal is pointed up in an article by Maddocks (1970). He was interested in evaluating the commonly accepted proposition that as "psychopaths" grow older their pathology "burns out." He de-emphasized criminal offenses as a criterion and placed emphasis on such factors as charm, lack of ease in stable situations, frequent changes of jobs and sexual partners, lying, unreliability, etc. He found that although some untreated psychopaths settle down as they get older, most do not. The illusion that "psychopaths" mature later in life has been created by the fact that as they get older, they tend to be convicted for offenses less often. "While psychopaths may leave the prison circuit they may enter the hospital circuit, and . . . improvement in conviction figures nevertheless hides a good deal of unhappiness and maladjustment" (p. 514).

Thus, if we confine our interest here to the treatment of the manipulative personality, we will learn little from examining results of treatment methods reported in the literature, however valuable these reports may be in assessing the "treatment of sociopathy." For example, Whiteley (1970) noted a 40% improvement in "psychopaths" treated by the group-oriented therapeutic milieu of the Henderson Hospital in England. The criteria of improvement were no further convictions or hospitalizations within two years of discharge. While we can applaud even this degree of success with a group constituting such a social problem, we do not know if those of their group who had manipulative personalities have had significant alterations of these personalities, or if they became more successful or more adaptive manipulators. Again, Craft et al. (1964) attempted to contrast the effect of an authoritarian ward with that of a group therapy ward patterned after the Henderson Hospital on two groups of "psychopaths." Those treated on the authoritarian ward had fewer offenses and seemed slightly better able to take I.Q. tests. They reported more subjective improvement. They seemed more impelled to try to please and comply with requests at the time of discharge. Now this may indicate a change in their tendency to be manipulative; they may be more straightforward in their approach to life. However, it could just as well indicate that they have learned the rules and, as a part of their deceptiveness, they seem to follow the expectations of others.

To the degree that society calls on us to treat or control its criminals, we may continue to focus on "sociopathy"—but I am not very optimistic that psychiatry is up to this task, or indeed am I certain that this task is the proper business of clinical psychiatry.[2] To the degree that we have an interest in the manipulative personality—with or without criminality—we may fruitfully look for ways of modifying it.

Now, although evaluative studies of the treatment of sociopathy or criminality have little value to us with our focus on issues involved in the treatment of the manipulative personality, we

2. This is not to say that clinical psychiatry has no role in the management of criminality. For example, to the degree that we understand the manipulative personality, we may *contribute* to the management of those criminals with that type of personality.

should not altogether discard these studies without a closer look. Many criminals and delinquents do have a manipulative personality core and some of the techniques which have been developed to deal with "sociopaths" are directed towards the manipulative aspect of the personality. We should examine some of these studies and techniques in search of what seems to have had some therapeutic impact on the manipulative personalities of these people.

Inasmuch as manipulative behavior often leads to consequences which we find offensive, treatment approaches have sometimes focused on the issue of control of this behavior. On the one hand, Craft has felt that the firm, authoritarian approach has a modicum of success. Likewise, certain therapeutic communities, organized to treat drug addicts, many of whom have manipulative personalities, have a tough, no-nonsense approach. One such community is Daytop. Here, from the very outset, the resident (patient) is inserted into a rather rigid social hierarchy; he has his place and his jobs to do, and he is not supposed to "step out of line." He must discontinue his previous addictive and deceptive behavior or face community censure and ultimately be expelled from the community.

Compare this approach with that used by Aichhorn and other psychoanalysts (Aichhorn, 1925; Schmiedeberg, 1949a; Eissler, 1950) in their treatment of delinquents. Aichhorn (pp. 124 f.) has written, "To the dissocial child, we are a menace because we represent society, with which he is in conflict. He must protect himself against this terrible danger and be careful what he says in order not to give himself away. . . . One thing they all have in common; they do not tell the truth. Some lie stupidly, pitiably; others, especially the older ones, show great skill and sophistication. . . . The inexperienced teacher or adviser is easily irritated, especially when the lies are transparent, but he must not let the child be aware of this. He must deal with the situation immediately *without telling the child that he sees through his behavior*" (italics mine). Some of Aichhorn's adolescents were permitted to go through a phase of such aggressive destructiveness that the very existence of the institution was threatened. Now this approach contrasts very markedly with that of Daytop where, from the outset, the resident is confronted with his deceptiveness. In the

Daytop group meetings there is a premium placed on honesty, not only about what the resident does but also about how he feels. His attempts at deception are met with expressions of annoyance and ridicule.

Somewhat in between these contrasting approaches is the atmosphere prevailing at the Henderson Hospital in England. This hospital unit, primarily devoted to the treatment of antisocial people within the context of a therapeutic milieu, allows considerable latitude to its residents. Although it does not permit drugs or violence in the unit, and it will call into question the usefulness of the hospitalization when residents persistently miss group meetings or activities, it does not scrutinize so much of the residents' everyday activities, both on and off the unit, as does Daytop. Deviant behavior, often manipulative, is confronted, but not with anything like the pejorative intensity found at Daytop.

All of these approaches apparently meet with some measure of success, although, as Greenacre (1947) has warned, early alterations of behavior may be illusory. Further, we must remember that success is often measured not in terms of the alteration of the manipulative personality but in the diminution of the social deviance for which the patient was referred. How can we account for the fact that apparently significantly different approaches all lead to some enthusiastic appraisal? It might be that each approach is dealing with a different type of person. In psychoanalytic treatment at Daytop and at the Henderson Hospital, treatment is voluntary on the part of the patient and selective on the part of the therapist. While there may be various social constraints impelling the patient toward treatment, he is not locked up and he can escape and go elsewhere if he wishes. He need not have applied for treatment in the first place. On the other hand, the therapist in each of these situations screens the applicant and forms some kind of judgment about whether the applicant is suitable for treatment. Thus there is a selection process which may weed out the poorest risks but which also may tend to steer the applicant into the type of treatment situation most appropriate for him.

While there undoubtedly are differences among the patients in the three situations, they do generally share in the predominance of manipulative personality characteristics and I believe that the fact that each of these treatment situations succeeds even in holding these patients, let alone significantly changing some of them, has more to do with what is similar about the situations than what is different among them. And where can we find the similarities? They do not lie in the area of behavior control, restrictiveness, or permissiveness. They lie rather in the nature of the relationship of the patient to the therapeutic other.

As we have seen in chapter 10, the manipulative personality forms narcissistic object relationships. In order for a useful engagement to take place, the patient must be able to identify with his therapist. Let me recount for you an interview I had with members of the screening group for Daytop. A few years ago, out of curiosity, I went to NARCO[3] in order to learn what they had to offer drug addicts. Entering the storefront office, I introduced myself as a local psychoanalyst who was interested in their approach to addiction. My reception was friendly enough, but I was somewhat taken aback when they led me down a dingy flight of stairs to a dimly lit room in the basement of the building where we could "talk better." The cultural gap was immediately apparent as I was convinced that I could talk much better in the protective comfort of my consulting room. Nor was I more at ease when they embarked on a vituperative harangue against psychiatry. Psychiatrists were stupid, soft, gullible. They didn't know the first thing about "dope fiends" and con-men. Every one at NARCO had known people who had seen psychiatrists for months or even years, and it was laughable how psychiatrists swallowed lie after lie. Here we can recognize the contempt which is so prominent a part of the manipulative personality. But over and above the contempt, I knew that there was much truth in what they said. I listened with interest, sipped the coffee they served, and asked them why else they felt that psychiatry had such poor success with addicts. They insisted that psychiatrists would never have success because the "dope fiend can't relate to

3. NARCO—Narcotics Addiction Research and Community Opportunities, Inc.—is an organization in New Haven, Connecticut, which is devoted to drug information and educational programs. At the time of this interview, NARCO was also involved in the screening process for the local Daytop community.

him." ("Relate" in the jargon of NARCO and Daytop does not mean merely a relationship. "I relate to what you are saying" means "I see some of myself in what you are saying; you and I are similar." Thus, even the word carries the concept; the relationship for the narcissistic person implies identification.) They pointed out that only another "dope fiend" could be helpful because he knew all the tricks, having used them himself. One dope fiend could identify with another and would listen to him. I was to hear this theme reiterated time after time in my subsequent visits to NARCO and Daytop. "Identify" and "relate" (in the special sense of the word) were the keys to the possibility of a meaningful relationship.

I believe that much the same essential ingredient exists in the Henderson Hospital. The effect of the therapeutic milieu is that residents (patients) are not treated by staff but by each other and the "community." While the staff tends to oversee the trends, directions, and limits of the community, decisions and most of the discussion, advice, rewards, and punishment come from the total community which is predominantly comprised of the residents. Thus, a new resident can identify with the particular people who collectively represent the "organization"—the residents.

I observed an example of this process of identification during a session at Henderson Hospital where four applicants were being screened. The screening committee consisted largely of residents, with a sprinkling of staff. The first applicant to discuss her situation was Florence, a buxom 18-year-old girl with pretty but already hardened features. Her dress left her somewhat inappropriately exposed. Her appearance and manner suggested less the seductiveness of the hysteric and more the cold exhibitionism of the phallic narcissistic woman. She denied having any real problems or being dissatisfied with her life. She planned to get married in a few weeks and was not at all concerned that she had been "engaged" to five different boys that year. She was uninterested in the proceedings and she blandly told only as little information as she felt we probably already knew.

Her parents had accompanied her. The mother, prim and proper, was obviously mortified, partly at having so disgraceful a daughter and partly at being in this old, shabby building together with so many "criminals." The father was painfully patient and didactically condescending towards his daughter. It was a terribly unhappy family.

The questioning was quite unsuccessful. Ultimately it degenerated into a sequence where a resident would ask her (for example) if she ever got into financial trouble. She would blithely deny or minimize. Father would say, "But Florence, what about the money you owe the bank?" Florence would acknowledge that she owed the bank money but would maintain it was unimportant as she planned to pay it back anyway. Father would add bit by bit to the story until we learned of a long history of cheating, petty thefts, provacativeness, unstable relationships, etc. Throughout the proceedings, Florence remained cool, aloof, and unconcerned.

Somewhat later, another applicant was being questioned who was considerably more open than Florence. He acknowledged that he had inveigled his girl friend into taking care of him even when she knew he would repeat the same patterns of getting into trouble. He felt pleasure at getting her to stick by him again and again. Florence leaned forward. "You mean you like having power over her?"

"Yes," he acknowledged. "It's hard to explain. It's a feeling, you know."

Florence was obviously engaged in the conversation now. "Yes," she beamed, "I feel that way too, lots of times. And what about . . . ?" There followed a brief interchange where both applicants shared their pride in putting something over. Unfortunately, the committee had "given Florence her turn" and was now screening the other applicant. They directed their questions only at him, and she drew back into marvelous isolation once again. In retrospect, I felt that from that point at least, if the applicants had been screened as a group instead of in succession, we could have learned more about Florence and she would have shown an interest and willingness to engage herself with the group—or part of it. As it was, the community was left with the impression of her lack of investment and she was not selected for admission. What is important, here, however, is that it took a person with whom she could identify to engage her at all.

There is another aspect of identification and narcissism which occurs at Daytop and Henderson. Once engaged, the resident has the prospect of moving up the social hierarchy. Soon he is not a new resident but an old one, and he is asking the questions. Thus, in some ways, he can move up to the more powerful position of the person who is as he would like to be. There is considerable narcissistic gratification in this. In addition, it provides an outlet for the narcissistic repair of the manipulative personality. At Daytop, I chatted with John, an older resident. He was discussing the value of the small group confrontations. He emphasized how a resident had benefited from ridicule. Every time the resident was phoney, John would sarcastically make fun of him: "You're a baby, you're a nothing, you're afraid to face your real feelings, that's why you're a phoney." While John knew this made the other resident uncomfortable, he pointed out that ultimately the resident saw that he couldn't get away with phoneyness and he became more honest with himself.

My next question took John by surprise.

"How did you feel when you were ridiculing him?"

"It was for his own good," he replied defensively.

"Sure, it may have helped him, but how did *you* feel?"

He smiled, rolled his eyes toward the ceiling and his face was sheer bliss. "Man," he said, "I really liked it!"

In the psychoanalytic situation, the prospects for such identification are much slimmer because often the analyst's life style is so dissimilar to that of the manipulator that there is little basis for identification. Several authors (Aichhorn, 1925, 1936; Eissler, 1950; Hoffer, 1949) have emphasized the importance of the narcissistic object relationship by recommending that the analyst be cleverer and more powerful than the patient so that the patient will wish to emulate him.

Some manipulative personalities, especially those who have been quite adaptive and successful in life, do share many aspects of their life styles and cultures with the psychoanalyst. Here, the identification problem may be less formidable. In addition, even among manipulative personalities, the capacity to sustain relationships, to control impulsivity, and to endure frustrations, and the nature of the value systems vary considerably. Thus, it should not surprise us to find that some people with manipulative personalities can be analyzed in the usual manner from the outset rather than, as Eissler has suggested with delinquents, only in the usual manner after a long first phase where the analyst actively seeks to become an identification figure. Zaritzianos (1967) has presented the case of a delinquent whose analysis from the beginning utilized the standard technique. The case of the businessman presented in this book is one which also illustrates this point. His analysis with me proceeded in a standard fashion. Yet there is no doubt that he identified with me as an ideal figure early in the analysis. He had dreams of stealing my books and appropriating my sexual prowess. Very soon after the analysis had started, his dreams, which were full of absurdity, alerted me to his need to have a pseudoanalysis, a parody of analysis which would represent a massive joke on me. You will recall the instance described in chapter 6 where he attempted to bait me by linking a "fear of buses" to a fear of vaginas. I did not "fall for it" and he felt stupid in comparison with my cleverness. This type of sequence was repeated countless times. And cleverness had exceedingly high value for him; if he were clever, he was masculine, powerful, and he was carrying on the family tradition.

There were other factors which kept him coming in the early days. He was propelled by his desire to defeat the analysis, the analyst, and all those relatives who had so much stake in his coming. There are many things which bring a person to treatment and keep him in place for a while. But I doubt that without his ability to identify with me and my cleverness, he would ever have had the interest to engage in therapeutic effort.

The standard psychoanalytic technique, built upon the analyses of neurotic people and dependent on the repetition of the Oedipal situation, requires the ability to form complementary object relationships. People with manipulative personalities have primarily narcissistic object relationships, perhaps rather thoroughgoing or perhaps as a stable characterological defense against the dangers of complementary object relationships.[4] It is on the level of identification that we can begin to engage these people.

Common to Daytop, Henderson, and psychoanalysis, then, is the fact that they engage the manipulative patient through his narcissism. We must consider the technical implications of this type of relationship in common clinical situations, such as prob-

4. See chapter 10.

lems of trusting the patient, attempting to win the patient's affection through gift-giving, and making our verbal interventions
meaningful.

I have often heard members of a hospital staff plan the therapy
of an antisocial person in terms of trust. "Of course he's un-
trustworthy," they say. "No one trusts him; everyone expects him
to violate trust and he does what is expected. We must trust him;
we must tell him we trust him and we will measure up to our
trust." I have yet to see a manipulative personality become trustworthy under such a regimen. From what we have learned about
the manipulative personality, we can see that he will need to
prove and improve his worth by purging. He will be contemptuous
of our trust and we will be reduced in his eyes. When he violates
trust, the staff often reacts in anger or tries to provoke his guilt
("Look what you did after I trusted you.") These staff responses
may create an uncomfortable situation for him but they can have
no real impact. Staff members are merely exploitable objects; the
exploitation does not always work, but perhaps next time it will.

I believe that Aichhorn did not make an issue of trusting the
patient. Rather, he concentrated on being clever himself in order
to serve as a narcissistic object for the patient. Trusting involves
the recognition of a separate other whom you value and from
whom you expect something. It implies dependence, and the adult
trusting relationship requires the ability to be guided by guilt.
These attributes, the attributes of a person who can form complementary object relationships, are not at all prominent in the manipulative personality. The approach to this patient cannot be
through love or guilt; it must be through narcissistic identification.
What stance, then, should we take toward the patient's unreliability? If we are not to trust the patient, neither should we play
detective unless we are sure that we can do a very good job at
it. If the patient knows we have an intense interest in catching
him and he evades us, he again raises his self-esteem by being
contemptuous of us. I gather that in some places, such as Daytop,
the residents are pretty good at catching each other; they do know
the ropes. However, I do not think that it is the being caught
that is effective. Rather it is the being outwitted by someone who
is admirable which paves the way for a narcissistic attachment.
Other limit-setting hospital programs can be successful only to

the degree that they can so restrict the activities of the patient that he is virtually constantly under scrutiny. I have not been impressed with the results of such attempts in many hospitals where the patient may be demonstrably cleverer at outwitting the staff than the staff is at catching him. These situations provide much material for discussion at staff meetings but produce little change in the patient.

An alternative stance for those of us who lack such skill and intimate knowledge of the styles of the antisocial manipulative personality is to get out of the detective business altogether. We can always take the position that since the patient has had such a long history of lying, it is reasonable to suppose that he will continue. We may show that we do not consider this a personal affront, but rather something which may be understood. While this will help us avoid undue reliance on a complementary relationship, it is not sufficient; we must also have some important aspects of our personality with which the patient may identify or no working relationship will be established.

Another affectionate gesture often employed in the attempt to win over the manipulative personality is the granting of favors or the giving of gifts. If we merely attempt to gratify these patients in this manner—a procedure which would have holding power with someone needing a complementary relationship—they will use and abuse us but will not be genuinely interested in us.

Eissler (1950) has maintained that delinquents need special gifts as evidence of love and friendship. According to his observations, male delinquents need gifts of money while female delinquents need gifts of sexual attention. He felt that the giving of these gifts repeats the early oral situation where love is measured in terms of gifts of food. I doubt that these gifts are necessary in the treatment of all delinquents and they certainly are not necessary in the treatment of all manipulative personalities. Especially in the early stages of the therapeutic relationship, such transactions probably do not directly serve the complementary function of the giving of love; if the transactions are to be therapeutically useful rather than exploitative on the part of the patient, the usefulness is to be found in the narcissistic aspect of the relationship. The relationship cannot survive if the gift is given by a devalued object; it is a truly worthwhile gift only if it is given by someone who has the magic power and other qualities which represent what the patient feels he has or would like. "He *gave* me something" may lead to transient gratification, but "*he* gave me something" raises the promise of a more permanent attachment. This was amply illustrated by the businessman whose dreams showed that while in part he wanted to be my little girl and passively receive love and sexual gifts from me (complementary), the predominant trend was narcissistic; in the analytic hours he was envious of my intellect and cleverness, and in his dreams he wanted to take my books. Eissler's technical suggestions about giving (pp. 115 f.) seem to imply much the same line of thought developed here. "The analyst must never make the giving of money a routine matter because then he becomes, in the delinquent's eyes, a person of whom he can take advantage. . . . The money must be given without any conditions being attached to the gift. . . . Nor must the concrete support be given in a situation in which the delinquent thinks he has pressured the analyst into surrendering money. . . . It must be so given as to conform to the imagery of a mother who gives freely from her abundant supply. . . . Probably for the first time in his life, the delinquent has the experience of obtaining something he is ardently striving for without a corresponding decrease in the omnipotence of the person who is ready to share an advantage with him."

Our understanding and our verbal interventions should also be guided by the narcissistic nature of the relationship. The content of our remarks should focus primarily on the mechanisms of narcissistic repair rather than, for example, on Oedipal or dependency themes. The illustration in chapter 6 wherein I showed how the businessman was trying to bait me is a case in point. This clarification was important because it helped to focus on his need to put something over on me, a focus which would eventually lead to the interpretation of his narcissism. The manner of the clarification was important inasmuch as I conveyed my conviction that the baiting was a subject for our mutual psychological study; I invited a working alliance (Greenson, 1965) I was not pejorative. I exercised my skills and my cleverness in the course of the analytic work without trying to display virtuosity. If he had felt that I had some stake in impressing him, he would have focused on that rather than on my cleverness, and I would have been devalued in his eyes. Without my skills, I could never have served as an object with whom he could identify. And the areas in which I am clever are ones which count for him—he sees value in them. Another patient might have other values and I might be a stupid bungler on his turf. We probably would not work well together because he could not identify with me, and our association would dissolve.

In every therapeutic endeavor, it is important that our clarifications and interpretations be on target so that they will not be used defensively to increase the resistance. But with manipulative personalities, the accuracy of our intervention is even more important because it enhances our stature and shows a similarity between our thought and the patient's thought. If we are on the same wavelength, he can identify with us. Often we are presented with situations which offer possible clarifications along either complementary or narcissistic lines. The narcissistic focus is preferable. I shall present three illustrations drawn not from psychoanalysis but from my observations at the Henderson Hospital.

At this hospital, there is a community fund to which all residents contribute. Ordinarily, the fund is used to provide loans for transportation for residents who are looking for jobs or to give other types of personal assistance in situations of need. One Saturday, when many patients were away for the weekend, the remaining residents called a community meeting, decided to have a picnic, and voted themselves the right to use community money to get food.

At the Monday morning community meeting, several residents objected. John replied that they had obtained approval at the Saturday community meeting.

"Yes," Dick responded, "but a lot of us weren't there."

"Well, it's community money and we used it for the community."

Jane: "But only for part of the community. Most of us weren't here. I don't see why you didn't ask at the meeting on Friday when we were all here."

John became very exasperated. "It was bloody well cloudy on Friday—we didn't ask for the fuckin' money because we didn't think of having a fuckin' picnic on Friday."

Cheryl: "Well, I don't see what harm was done. We had a little blast, is all."

Tom brought up a new point. "Well, I was at the meeting. You said you wanted the money for carfare. If I'd known you'd spend it on food, I'd have voted against it."

There was continued bickering back and forth. A staff member ventured a clarification: "It does sound like there was some jealousy. You figured that most of the residents were out having a good time on the weekend, so you wanted your own good time."

A second staff member continued, "And maybe those who were out for the weekend were jealous that they missed the picnic." These comments brought general disagreement from both of the resident factions. The bickering continued, and everyone left the meeting feeling that the discussion had not led anywhere.

In the staff meeting which followed, the theme of jealousy was pursued. Someone recalled that the staff had had a picnic on Friday and some of the patients had been obviously envious. Then one staff member brought up the fact that they really did not need the money for the food—they could have gotten the food from the hospital.

Now, Monday morning quarterbacking (or in this case, Monday afternoon) is a safe and pleasant pastime. We should not overlook the fact that these residents were sitting at a meeting, talking and letting others talk, disagreeing, bickering, but they were not hitting, stealing, setting fires, or dealing with their tension in the extreme forms of action which had characterized their prehospital lives. This is the chief meaning of the meeting, and from this point of view it was successful. But I was left with the questions, "Could a little more have been done? Why did we all leave feeling that nothing had been settled?"

The whole tone of the picnickers' remarks, of course, revealed the familiar features of people with manipulative personalities: the unconcern, the explosive angry outburst designed to make the other person feel he is being unreasonable, the minimizing of the action, the deceptive withholding of information, etc. And there were two puzzling features about the story. Why had they asked for carfare when they wanted to spend it on food? They undoubtedly had enough votes to use the money for whatever they wished. And why was the whole problem raised anyhow when they could have gotten the food from the hospital? I believe that oral supplies and jealousy, while important, were not the most prominent issue, and this is why clarifications along this line met with general disagreement and the discussion led nowhere. I believe that what was important to these manipulative people was the fact that some of them felt taken advantage of; they had been used and abused by the others, and their narcissism was bruised. Likewise, the others had had to support their narcissism by taking advantage, by deception, by putting something over on the rest of the community. Several hours after the meeting, I wondered if there would have been more of a sense of resolution if the focus of the staff's remarks had been on the feelings of being taken advantage of and the need to arrange the picnic in a shady way.

The second illustration could come from any hospital, almost any week. It involves the flaunting of some undesirable behavior or attribute. Very frequently, the staff believes that if a patient exhibits his undesirable behavior, it is a plea for control, possibly because the patient feels guilty about what he is doing. In many cases, this may well be the case. Some patients do become terrified if they feel at the mercy of their impulses and they ask for our help in controlling them. Others, masochistically oriented, exhibit their misbehavior in order to evoke punishment. However, I do not think that either of these paradigms reflects the predominant narcissistic position of the person with a manipulative personality. His indiscreet behavior may have more the function of contempt and a kind of defecating on the other person than the function of asking for control. I have often felt that hospital staff members seize upon the "plea for control" explanation indiscriminately, perhaps as a justification for their desire to control or to alleviate their guilt when they set limits. Here is the illustration:

In a small group meeting Tim, a new patient, was telling the others about his trouble on the job. "I got the job as the manager of a small restaurant. It was confusing because I had to lead two lives. At home with my roommate I was homosexual. All my friends were homosexual. But on the job I was straight. I worked well and I got praise for the job. They wouldn't like it if they knew I was homosexual. Sometimes, I just wanted to shout it out —to see what their reaction would be. But I knew what it would be—they'd fire me."

While this does seem to have the elements of the need for punishment, or perhaps the need to avoid success, I suspected that such complementary object relationships were not a prominent part of Tim's personality. I asked him why he had wanted to shout it out.

"I wanted to throw it in their faces; I wanted to say, look, I'm not really straight at all, I'm homosexual. I'd be laughing at them, because I fooled them!"

The third illustration involves Mary, a pretty but cold and haughty prostitute who was exceedingly manipulative. She was masterful at interpreting her behavior in Oedipal terms in the group therapy sessions without any resultant modification in her behavior. In a sense, she participated in therapy as she did in her more overtly sexual encounters. She gave the men what they wanted but she was not really involved, and thus she could defeat them and laugh at them.

Mary had tested and strained most of the rules of the hospital. Told she could bring no liquor into the hospital, she would come back drunk and proudly state that the liquor was inside her.

On this occasion, Mary had left the hospital. According to the rule, if a resident leaves for more than 72 hours, upon his return, he is referred for community discussion to consider whether he should continue as a patient. In almost predictable fashion, Mary came back after 72 hours and 25 minutes.

In the community meeting on the following morning, Mary sat poker-faced, with no evidence of remorse. She gave a rather stock excuse, "I wasn't making it here, I really want to try, but I can't seem to do well. That's why I left." She did indicate that she wanted to try once again in the hospital community, and she hoped they would take her back. Her lateness, "only half an hour," was due to poor bus connections; she had really tried to get back on time.

Some people analyzed Mary's situation in terms of her need to lose. As one nurse put it, "She put herself in a predicament by coming back late; she loses both ways. If we bend the rule, she loses because it's not good for her to break the rules and she knows it. If we stick strictly to the rules and discharge her, she loses because she needs the help and she's been rejected." I suggest an alternative interpretation. Mary created a situation where she could win both ways. If we bent the rule, especially out of our need to "trust" her, believe her, or rescue her from her "terrible life style," she would laugh at us and our weakness and gullibility. If we adhered to the rule and discharged her, she would devalue the hospital—"who needs that place and its silly rules, anyhow?"—and she would still laugh at us. With the narcissistic manipulator, the name of the game is not "losing"; it is "winning." And even before the decision has been made, she has "won" because she has thrown the community into such a dilemma. She is not struggling with the problem; the rest of us are struggling, and she is a cool onlooker.

This type of situation, which arises so frequently in the hospital treatment of people with manipulative personalities, indeed poses a dilemma, and I do not have any ready-made solutions. It is helpful to remember that the patient's object relationships are largely narcissistic and not complementary. His predominant aim is to test his superiority and his object-need is to find someone magically superior, someone like himself or his ideal. We can only fulfill this role if we take ourselves out of the dilemma. If we have rules we should stick to them. Where possible, we should avoid rules which are unenforceable or which will place us in these dilemmas. And we should bear in mind that the need to be punished or the cry for help is not the primary issue. Nor is the rule the issue. The issue is the patient's need to defeat us. If we undertake any clarification at all, it must be along the lines of his narcissism. Perhaps in that way we can demonstrate our worth by ignoring the false issues which he presents to us and showing him our oneness with his feelings. "It must be awfully important for you to make us squirm," said with interest and an invitation to self-scrutiny is better than "You want us to punish you," "I really want to give you every opportunity," or a show of over-concern with "the rules."

Aichhorn (1936) has written about another technique geared to the theme of the narcissistic relationship. By being utterly unpredictable, by surprising the patients, he made them uneasy and attempted to demolish their self-confidence. In one case, he made a particularly haughty young man wait for an hour, at the end of which time the patient was completely undone. In this way, Aichhorn felt that his own superiority and desirability as an object—an ideal figure—would be enhanced. Interestingly enough, some of the same types of initial relationships occur at Daytop where, in pointed and painful confrontations and in his low position in the organizational hierarchy, the new resident is sharply reduced in stature and pride. I cannot evaluate these techniques as I have not tried them. I do not set out to *make* my patients uneasy (although I do not hesitate to let them be uneasy) nor do I try to reduce people in stature. I am not sure this is necessary. It is necessary to be unimpressed by the patient's haughtiness, but whether the added maneuver of degrading the patient is necessary is unclear to me.

With some manipulative personalities, and I suspect they are the more socially adapted patients who have the better prognoses,[5] we may observe complementary aspects of their object relationships. However, these aspects (such as Oedipal themes) will have strong narcissistic coloration and, especially early in the work, the greater emphasis must be on the narcissistic themes, both to catch the patient's interest by providing him with a kind of relationship which is meaningful to him and by talking about things he is experiencing.

What happens next? I cannot say for certain what happens in the nonpsychoanalytic therapeutic communities. It may be that the identification is sufficiently strong for some of the patients to take on the communities' values. It may be that some patients learn more adaptive ways of expressing their manipulative personalities or otherwise gratifying their narcissistic needs. Often, especially at Daytop, patients stay with the organization, thus cementing an identification in a socially useful manner and remaining in an organization which can be narcissistically quite gratifying. Still other patients may be adolescents whose manipulative personalities are not so firm. It may be that some of these patients have had the manipulative aspects of their personalities magnified by the vicissitudes of adolescence (see chapter 6), or, if they have firmer manipulative personality structures, the need to act in an antisocial manner during adolescence may have emerged (see chapter 10). For these patients, the therapeutic

5. These people probably correspond to what Henderson described as "creative psychopaths" (Henderson and Batcheler, 1962). Whiteley (1970) has pointed to their better prognoses.

community may provide a moratorium wherein the storms of adolescence can subside.

In the psychoanalytic treatment, we can sometimes see the unfolding of the characterological defence of manipulativeness. After an "initial" phase of three years during which time the businessman and I increasingly clarified his need to put something over, we were able to do some deep interpretative work which traced his manipulative behavior to its infantile sources of defecating out the "possessed by the devil" bad object and the desire to be elevated to Heaven (the reunion). Then, for the first time, the patient thought of his sister who had been the object of such contempt, and he said "poor kid." This was the first compassion he had shown for anyone during the analysis, the first expression that there could indeed be a separate and worthwhile other. Gradually, the need to put things over subsided and was replaced by more complementary relationships and feelings of need. The anal and Oedipal issues were again brought up with much greater significance, and for the first time the patient began to feel hungry in the analytic hours.

Much of what I have said about the analysis of the manipulative personality is consistent with Kernberg's (1970b) broader discussion of the analysis of narcissistic personalities in general, and the pathway I have described here is similar to that which he has discussed. "Actually, these patients develop a very intensive transference [if we let them] . . . what appears as distance and uninvolvement on the surface is an active process of devaluation, depreciation, and spoiling. The undoing of this transference resistance typically brings about intense paranoid development, suspiciousness, hatred, and envy. Eventually, after many months and sometimes years of treatment, guilt and depression may appear in the patient; awareness of his aggression toward the analyst may develop into guilt over it, and more human concern for the analyst as a person in combination with a heightened tolerance of guilt and depression in general" (pp. 71 f.). I am not convinced that all manipulative patients must go through a frankly paranoid period, although projection of infantile rage does appear. Some manipulative personalities, possibly those with a greater component of complementarity in their object relationships, enter a depressed period without the development of overt paranoia when their narcissistic defense has been weakened.

Thus, the analysis of the manipulative personality is part of the larger problem of the analysis of narcissistic personalities.[6] It is exceedingly difficult work; from the outset it is difficult to engage these patients in the treatment enterprise, and as the work progresses, the intensity of the dangerous rage and longings against which the manipulations have defended them gives ample justification for the firmness with which this characterological defense has been held. It is little wonder that these patients are so therapeutically elusive.

6. The reader is again referred to Kohut (1971) for a detailed discussion of the analysis of narcissism.

REFERENCES

Abraham, K. 1924. A short study of the development of the libido viewed in the light of mental disorders. Reprinted in *Selected papers on psychoanalysis*. New York: Basic Books, 1953.

————. 1925. The history of an impostor in the light of psychoanalytic knowledge. Reprinted in *Clinical papers and essays on psychoanalysis*. New York: Basic Books, 1955.

Abrams, G. M. 1968. Setting limits. *Arch. Gen. Psychiat.* 19:113–19.

Abse, D. 1959. Bed for a night. *Med. World* 90:79–84.

Ackerman, N. 1958. *The psychodynamics of family life*. New York: Basic Books.

Aichhorn, A. 1925. *Wayward youth*. Reprint. New York: Viking Press, 1935.

————. 1936. Zur Technik der Erziehungsberaten. Der Uebertragung. Chap. 5. Die narzissistiche Uebertragung des "jugenlichen Hochstaplers." *Zeitschr. f. psychoanal. Paedegogik* 10:61–73.

Alexander, F., et al. 1946. *Psychoanalytic therapy*. New York: Ronald Press.

Altschel, S. 1968. Denial and ego arrest. *J. Amer. Psychoanal. Ass.* 16:301–18.

Arieti, S. 1955. *Interpretation of schizophrenia*. New York: Brunner.

Asher, R. 1951. Munchausen's syndrome. *Lancet* 1:339–41.

Bak, R. C. 1953. Fetishism. *J. Amer. Psychoanal. Ass.* 1:285–98.

Bergler, E. 1944. Psychopathology of impostors. *J. Crim. Psychopath.* 5:696–714.

Blos, P. 1962. *On adolescence*. New York: The Free Press of Glencoe.

Bonime, W. 1960. Depression as a practice: dynamic and psychotherapeutic considerations. *Comprehen. Psychiat.* 1:194–98.

————. 1966. The psychodynamics of neurotic depression. In *American Handbook of Psychiatry*, vol. 3, ed. S. Arieti. New York: Basic Books.

Brenman, M. 1952. On teasing and being teased: and the problem of "moral masochism." *Psychoanal. study of the child* 7:264–85.

Breuer, J., and Freud, S. 1893. Studies on hysteria. Stand. ed. Vol. 2. London: Hogarth Press.

Brill, H. 1966. Classification and nomenclature of psychiatric conditions. In *American Handbook of Psychiatry,* vol. 3, ed. S. Arieti. New York: Basic Books.

(*British*) *Mental Health Bill.* 1959. London: H. M. Stationery Office.

Burnham, D. L. 1966. The special-problem patient: victim or agent of splitting? *Psychiat.* 29:105–22.

Bursten, B. 1965a. Family dynamics, the sick role, and medical hospital admissions. *Fam. Proc.* 4:206–16.

──────. 1965b. On Munchausen's syndrome. *Arch. Gen. Psychiat.* 13:261–68.

──────. 1965c. Psychosocial stress and medical consultations: some mediating mechanisms. *Psychosomatics* 6:100–06.

──────. 1967. Motility in the establishment of boundary. Unpublished thesis presented to the Western New England Institute for Psychoanalysis.

──────. 1969. Discussing relatives with the borderline patient. *Psychiat.* 32:324–33.

──────. 1972. The manipulative personality. *Arch. Gen. Psychiat.* 26:318–21.

Chapman, J. S. 1957. Peregrinating problem patients—Munchausen's syndrome. *J.A.M.A.* 165:927–33.

Cleckley, H. 1955. *The mask of sanity.* St. Louis: C. V. Mosby.

──────. 1959. Psychopathic states. In *American Handbook of Psychiatry,* vol. 1, ed. S. Arieti. New York: Basic Books.

Cohen, R. E., and Greenspoon, L. 1963. Limit-setting as a corrective ego experience. *Arch. Gen. Psychiat.* 8:74–79.

Coleman, J. V. 1969. The no-patient. Unpublished paper presented at the Connecticut Mental Health Center.

Craft, M. 1968. Psychopathic disorders. A second trial of treatment. *Brit. J. Psychiat.* 114:813–20.

Craft, M.; Stephenson, G.; and Grange, C. 1964. A controlled trial of authoritarian and self-governing regimes with adolescent psychopaths. *Amer. J. Orthopsy.* 34:543–54.

Deutsch, H. 1944. *The psychology of women,* vol. 1. New York: Grune and Stratton.

──────. 1955. The impostors: contribution to ego psychology of a type of psychopath. *Psychoanal. Quart.* 24:483–505.

Diagnostic and statistical manual of mental disorders, 3rd ed. 1968. Washington: Amer. Psychiat. Ass.

Dreikurs, R.; Shulman, B. H.; and Mosak, H. M. 1952. Patient-therapist relationship in multiple psychotherapy: I. Its advantages to the therapist. *Psychiat. Quart.* 26:219–27.

Durandin, G. 1957. Recherche sur les motifs et les circonstances du mensonage. *Ann. Medico-psychologiques* 115/1:209–42.

Eck, M. 1965. *Lies and truth.* London: Macmillan.

Edelson, M. 1970. *Sociotherapy and Psychotherapy.* Chicago: Univ. of Chicago Press.

Eisnitz, A. J. 1969. Narcissistic object choice, self representation. *Int. J. Psychoanal.* 50:15–25.

Eissler, K. R. 1950. Ego-psychological implications of the psychoanalytic treatment of delinquents. *Psychoanal. Study of the Child* 5:97–121.

————. 1951. Malingering. In *Psychoanalysis and Culture,* ed. G. B. Wilbur and W. Muensterberger. New York: Int. Univ. Press.

Eissler, R. 1949. Scapegoats of society. In *Searchlights on delinquency,* ed. K. R. Eissler. New York: Int. Univ. Press.

Erikson, E. H. 1962. Reality and actuality. *J. Amer. Psychoanal. Ass.* 10:451–74.

————. 1968. *Identity, youth, and crisis.* New York: W. W. Norton.

Erikson, K. T. 1957. Patient role and social uncertainty—A dilemma of the mentally ill. *Psychiat.* 20:263–74.

Fenichel, O. 1939. The economics of pseudologia phantastica. Reprinted in *The collected papers of Otto Fenichel.* New York: W. W. Norton, 1954.

————. 1941. *Problems of psychoanalytic technique.* New York: The Psychoanalytic Quarterly, Inc.

————. 1945. *The psychoanalytic theory of neurosis.* New York: W. W. Norton.

Ferenczi, S. 1913. Stages in the development of the sense of reality. Reprinted in *Contributions to psycho-analysis.* Boston: Richard G. Badjer, 1916.

Fleck, S. 1962. Psychiatric hospitalization as a family experience. Reprinted in T. Lidz; S. Fleck; and A. Cornelison, eds., *Schizophrenia and the family.* New York: Int. Univ. Press, 1965.

Fleck, S.; Cornelison, A.; Norton, N.; and Lidz, T. 1957. The intrafamilial environment of the schizophrenic patient. II. Interaction between hospital staff and families. *Psychiat.* 20:343–50.

Fliess, R. 1942. The metapsychology of the analyst. *Psychoanal. Quart.* 11:211–27.

Frankel, E. 1951. Munchausen's syndrome. *Lancet* 1:911.

Freud, S. 1900. The interpretation of dreams. Stand. ed., vol. 5, chap. 7. London: Hogarth Press.

————. 1910. A special type of choice of object made by men. (Contributions to the psychology of love, I). Stand. Ed., vol. 11. London: Hogarth Press.

————. 1911. Formulations on the two principles of mental functioning. Stand. ed., vol. 12. London: Hogarth Press.

————. 1914. On narcissism. Stand. ed., vol. 14. London: Hogarth Press.

————. 1915a. Instincts and their vicissitudes. Stand. ed., vol. 14. London: Hogarth Press.

————. 1915b. The unconscious. Stand. ed., vol. 14. London: Hogarth Press.

————. 1917. Introductory lectures on psychoanalysis. Stand. ed., vol. 16. London. Hogarth Press.

————. 1923. The ego and the id. Stand. ed., vol. 19. London: Hogarth Press.

————. 1925. Negation. Stand. ed., vol. 19. London: Hogarth Press.

————. 1926. Inhibitions, symptoms, and anxiety. Stand. ed., vol. 20. London: Hogarth Press.

————. 1927. Fetishism. Stand. ed., vol. 21. London: Hogarth Press.

————. 1930. Civilization and its discontents. Stand. ed., vol. 21. London: Hogarth Press.

————. 1932. New introductory lectures on psychoanalysis. Stand. ed., vol. 22. London: Hogarth Press.

————. 1938a. An outline of psychoanalysis. Stand. ed., vol. 23. London: Hogarth Press.

————. 1938b. Splitting of the ego in the process of defense. Stand. ed., vol. 23. London: Hogarth Press.

Fromm, E. 1970. *The crisis of psychoanalysis.* New York: Holt, Reinhart, & Winston.

Fromm-Reichmann, F. 1950. *Principles of intensive psychotherapy.* Chicago: Univ. of Chicago Press.

Gatenby, P. B. 1955. Munchausen syndrome. *Brit. Med. J.* 2:1207.

Geelard, E. R. 1965. Two kinds of denial: neurotic denial and denial in the service of the need to survive. In *Drives, affects, behavior,* vol. 2, ed. M. Schur. New York: Int. Univ. Press.

Gesell, A., and Ilg, F. L. 1946. *The child from five to ten.* New York: Harper.

Gill, M. M. 1963. Topography and systems in psychoanalytic theory. *Psychological Issues.* Monograph No. 10.

Gill, M. M., and Brenman, M. 1959. *Hypnosis and related states.* New York: Int. Univ. Press.

Glover, E. 1931. The therapeutic effect of inexact interpretation; a contribution to the theory of suggestion. *Int. J. Psychoanal.* 12:397–411.

Greenacre, P. 1945. Conscience in the psychopath. *Amer. J. Orthopsy.* 15:495–509.

————. 1947. Problems of patient-therapist relationship in the treatment of psychopaths. In *Handbook of correctional psychology,* ed. R. M. Lindner and R. V. Selinger. New York: Philosophical Library.

————. 1950. General problems of acting out. *Psychoanal. Quart.* 19:455–67.

————. 1958. The relation of the impostor to the artist. *Psychoanal. Study of the Child* 13:521–40.

Greenson, R. R. 1965. The working alliance and the transference neurosis. *Psychoanal. Quart.* 34:155–81.

————. 1967. *The technique and practice of psychoanalysis,* vol. 1. New York: Int. Univ. Press.

Grinker, R. J., Jr. 1965. Imposture as a form of mastery. *Arch. Gen. Psychiat.* 13:261–68.

Guterman, S. J. 1970. *The machiavellians.* Lincoln, Neb.: Univ. of Neb. Press.

Hartmann, H. 1939. *Ego psychology and the problem of adaptation.* New York: Int. Univ. Press, 1958.

Hartmann, H., and Loewenstein, R. M. 1962. Notes on the superego. *Psychoanal. Study of the Child* 17:42–81.

Hartshorne, H., and May, M. 1928. *Studies in deceit.* New York: Macmillan.

Heimann, P. 1950. On counter-transference. *Int. J. Psychoanal.* 31: 81–84.

Henderson, D. 1939. *Psychopathic states.* New York: W. W. Norton.

Henderson, D., and Batchelor, I. R. 1962. *Henderson and Gillespie's textbook of psychiatry.* 9th ed. London: Oxford Univ. Press.

Hildenrich, C. A. 1968. *A dictionary of personality.* Dubuque, Iowa: William C. Brown.

Hoffer, W. 1949. Deceiving the deceiver. In *Searchlights on delinquency,* ed. K. R. Eissler. New York: Int. Univ. Press.

Hollingshead, A. B., and Redlich, F. C. 1958. *Social class and mental illness.* New York: Wiley.

Irvine, R. E. 1955. Munchausen syndrome. *Brit. Med. J.* 2:1207.

Jacobson, E. 1946. The effect of disappointment on ego and super-ego formation in normal and depressive development. *Psychoanal. Rev.* 33:129–48.

———. 1957. Denial and repression. *J. Amer. Psychoanal. Ass.* 5: 60–92.

———. 1961. Adolescent moods and the remodeling of psychic structures in adolescence. *Psychoanal. Study of the Child* 16:164–83.

———. 1964. *The self and the object world.* New York: Int. Univ. Press.

James, W. 1907. *The principles of psychology,* vol. 2. New York: Henry Holt.

Janowsky, D. S.; Leff, M.; and Epstein, R. S. 1970. Playing the manic game. *Arch. Gen. Psychiat.* 22:252–61.

Johnson, A. M., and Szurek, S. A. 1952. The genesis of antisocial acting out in children and adults. *Psychoanal. Quart.* 21:323–43.

Jones, M. 1952. *Social psychiatry. A study of therapeutic communities.* London: Tavistock Publications.

———. 1953. *The therapeutic community.* New York: Basic Books.

———. 1957. The treatment of personality disorders in a therapeutic community. *Psychiat.* 20:211–20.

———. 1962. Society and the sociopath. *Amer. J. Psychiat.* 119:410–14.

Kernberg, O. 1967. Borderline personality organization. *J. Amer. Psychoanal. Ass.* 15:641–85.

————. 1970a. A psychoanalytic classification of character pathology. *J. Amer. Psychoanal. Ass.* 18:800–22.

————. 1970b. Factors in the psychoanalytic treatment of narcissistic personalities. *J. Amer. Psychoanal. Ass.* 18:51–85.

Klein, G. S. 1970. *Perception, motives, and personality.* New York: Alfred A. Knopf.

Klerman, G. L. 1969. Mental health and the urban crisis. *Am. J. Orthopsy.* 39:818–26.

Knight, R. P. 1946. Determinism, "freedom," and psychotherapy. *Psychiat.* 9:251–62.

Kohut, H. 1971. *The analysis of self.* New York: Int. Univ. Press.

Krauss, F. S. 1913. Der Vogel. *Int. Zeitsch. f. artzl. Psychoanal.* 1:288–89.

Kris, E. 1952. *Psychoanalytic explorations in art.* New York: Int. Univ. Press.

Levine, M. 1952. Principles of psychoanalytic treatment. In *Dynamic psychiatry,* ed. F. Alexander and H. Ross. Chicago: Univ. of Chicago Press.

Lewin, B. D. 1950. *The psychoanalysis of elation.* New York: W. W. Norton.

Lewis, H. B. 1971. *Shame and guilt in neurosis.* New York: Int. Univ. Press.

Lidz, T.; Cornelison, A. R.; Singer, M. T.; Schafer, S.; and Fleck, S. 1965. The mothers of schizophrenic patients. In *Schizophrenia and the family,* ed. T. Lidz, S. Fleck and A. Cornelison. New York: Int. Univ. Press.

Linn, L. 1967. Clinical manifestations of psychiatric disorders. In *Comprehensive textbook of psychiatry,* ed. A. W. Freedman and Harold I. Kaplan. Baltimore: Williams & Wilkins.

Lomas, P. 1962. The origin of the need to be special. *Brit. J. Med. Psychol.* 35:339–46.

Lustman, S. L. 1969. Mental health research and the university. *Arch. Gen. Psychiat.* 21:291–301.

Maddocks, P. D. 1970. A five year followup of untreated psychopaths. *Brit. J. Psychiat.* 116:511–15.

Mahl, G. F. 1968. Gestures and body movements in interviews. In *Research in psychotherapy,* vol. 3, ed. J. M. Schlein. Washington: Amer. Psychol. Ass.

Mahler, M. S., and Gosliner, B. J. 1955. On symbiotic child psychosis. *Psychoanal. Study of the Child* 10:195–212.

Main, T. F. 1957. The ailment. *Brit. J. Med. Psychol.* 30:129–45.

Marmor, J. 1970. Social action and the mental health professional. *Amer. J. Orthopsy.* 40:373–74.

Mayer, M. 1969. *On liberty: man vs. the state.* Santa Barbara, Cal.: Center for the Study of Democratic Institutions.

McCord, W., and McCord, J. 1964. *The psychopath.* New York: D. Van Nostrand.

Michaels, A. D.; Domino, E. F.; and Moore, R. A. 1964. The case of the feverish impostor: psychiatric and neurological puzzle. *J. Neuropsy.* 5:213–20.

Miller, W. B. 1958. Lower class culture as a generating milieu of gang delinquency. *J. Soc. Issues* 14:5–19.

Moustakas, C. E. 1962. Honesty, idiocy, and manipulation. *J. Hum. Psychol.* 2:1–15.

Murphy, G. 1947. *Personality. A biosocial approach to origins and structure.* New York: Harper and Brothers.

Novey, S. 1959. The technique of supportive therapy in psychiatry and psychoanalysis. *Psychiat.* 22:179–87.

Ollendorff, R. H., and Adams, P. L. 1971. Psychiatry and the draft. *Amer. J. Orthopsy.* 41:85–90.

Parsons, T. 1951a. Illness and the role of the physician; a sociological perspective. *Amer. J. Orthopsy.* 21:452–60.

————. 1951b. *The social system.* Glencoe, Ill.: The Free Press.

Piaget, J. 1932. *The moral judgement of the child.* London: Rutledge and Kegan Paul.

Piers, G., and Singer, M. B. 1953. *Shame and guilt.* Springfield, Ill.: Charles C. Thomas.

Platt, S. L.; Rappaport, R. G.; and Barglow, P. 1969. Follow-up of therapeutic abortion. *Arch. Gen. Psychiat.* 20:408–15.

Rado, S. 1926. The psychic effects of intoxicants. *Int. J. Psychoanal.* 7:396–413.

————. 1928. The problem of melancholia. *Int. J. Psychoanal.* 7: 420–38.

————. 1933. The psychoanalysis of pharacothymia. *Psychoanal. Quart.* 2:1–23.

Rapaport, D. 1951. States of consciousness. *Transactions of the second conference.* New York: Josiah Macy, Jr., Foundation.

————. 1953. Some metapsychological considerations concerning activity and passivity. Reprinted in *The collected papers of David Rapaport,* ed. M. M. Gill. New York: Basic Books, 1967.

Rapaport, D., and Gill, M. M. 1959. Points of view and assumptions of metapsychology. *Int. J. Psychoanal.* 40:153–62.

Rapaport, R. N. 1959. *Community as doctor.* London: Tavistock Publications.

Redlich, F. C., and Freedman, D. X. 1966. *The theory and practice of Psychiatry.* New York: Basic Books.

Reich, A. 1960. Pathological forms of self esteem regulation. *Psychoanal. Study of the Child* 15:215–32.

Reich, W. 1949. *Character analysis.* New York: The Noonday Press.

Reik, T. 1937. *Surprise and the psychoanalyst.* New York: E. P. Dutton.

————. 1941. *Masochism and modern man.* New York: Farrar & Reinhart.

Riessman, F., and Miller, S. M. 1966. Social change versus the psychiatric world view. In *Issues and problems in social psychiat.,* ed. B. S. Bergen and C. S. Thomas. Springfield, Ill.: Charles C. Thomas.

Robins, E. 1967. Personality disorder, II. Sociopathic type. Antisocial disorders and sexual deviation. In *Comprehensive textbook of psychiatry,* ed. A. M. Freedman and H. I. Kaplan. Baltimore: Williams & Wilkins.

Rosenfeld, H. 1964. On the psychopathology of narcissism: a clinical approach. *Int. J. Psychoanal.* 45:332–37.

Rubenstein, R., and Lasswell, H. P. 1966. *The sharing of power in a psychiatric hospital.* New Haven: Yale Univ. Press.

Ruesch, J. 1959. General theory of communication in psychiatry. In *American handbook of psychiatry,* vol. 1, ed. S. Arieti. New York: Basic Books.

Schafer, R. 1959. Generative empathy in the treatment situation. *Psychoanal. Quart.* 28:343–73.

———. 1968a. *Aspects of internalization.* New York: Int. Univ. Press.

———. 1968b. On the theoretical and technical conceptualization of activity and passivity. *Psychoanal. Quart.* 37:173–98.

Schecter, D. E. 1968. Identification and individuation. *J. Amer. Psychoanal. Ass.* 16:48–80.

Scher, M. 1970. The process of changing therapists. *Amer. J. Psychother.* 25:278–86.

Schmiedeberg, M. 1949a. The analytic treatment of major criminals: therapeutic results and technical problems. In *Searchlights on delinquency,* ed. K. R. Eissler. New York: Int. Univ. Press.

———. 1949b. The treatment of criminals. *Psychoanal. Rev.* 36:403–10.

Searles, H. F. 1963. Transference psychosis in the psychotherapy of chronic schizophrenia. *Int. J. Psychoanal.* 44:249–81.

Segal, H. 1964. *Introduction to the work of Melanie Klein.* New York: Basic Books.

Seidenberg, R. 1970. Catcher gone awry. *Int. J. Psychoanal.* 51:331–39.

Simmel, E. 1926. The "doctor game," illness and the profession of medicine. *Int. J. Psychoanal.* 7:470–83.

Singer, J. E. 1964. The use of manipulative strategies; machiavellianism and attractiveness. *Sociometry* 27:128–50.

Small, A. 1955. Munchausen syndrome. *Brit. Med. J.* 2:1207.

Spiegel, J. P. 1957. The resolution of role conflict within the family. *Psychiat.* 20:1–16.

Spiegel, J. P., and Bell, N. W. 1959. The family of the psychiatric patient. In *American handbook of psychiatry,* ed. S. Arieti. New York: Basic Books.

Spiro, H. R. 1968. Chronic factitious illness. *Arch. Gen. Psychiat.* 18:569–79.

St. Clair, H. R. 1966. Manipulation. *Comprehen. Psychiat.* 7:248–58.

Stanton, A., and Schwartz, M. 1954. *The mental hospital.* New York: Basic Books.

Stern, R. 1970. Standard operating procedures and institutionalization in the psychiatric unit. *Amer. J. Orthopsy* 40:744–50.

Stewart, W. A. 1970. The split in the ego and the mechanism of disavowal. *Psychoanal. Quart.* 39:1–16.

Stone, L. 1961. *The psychoanalytic situation.* New York: Int. Univ. Press.

Sullivan, H. S. 1956. *Clinical studies in psychiatry.* New York: W. W. Norton.

Szasz, T. 1961. *The myth of mental illness.* New York: Hoeber-Harper.

———. 1963. *Law, liberty, and psychiatry.* New York: Macmillan.

Thursz, D. 1966. Social action as a professional responsibility. *Social Work* 11:12–21.

Tomalin, N., and Hall, R. 1970. *The strange voyage of Donald Crowhurst.* London: Hodder and Stoughton.

Tulipan, A. B., and Feldman, S., eds. 1969. *Psychiatric clinics in transition.* New York: Bruner/Mazel.

Von Bertalanffy, L. 1966. General system theory and psychiatry. In *American handbook of psychiatry,* vol. 3, ed. S. Arieti. New York: Basic Books.

Webster's third new international dictionary. 1969. Springfield, Mass.: G. and C. Merriam Co.

Weiss, E. 1942. Emotional memories and acting out. *Psychoanal. Quart.* 11:477–92.

Whiteley, J. S. 1970. The response of psychopaths to a therapeutic community. *Brit. J. Psychiat.* 116:517–29.

Williams, B. 1951. Munchausen's syndrome. *Lancet* 1:527–28.

Winnicott, D. W. 1953. Transitional objects and transitional phenomena. *Int. J. Psychoanal.* 34:89–97.

Wittels, F. 1938. The position of the psychopath in the psychoanalytic system. *Int. J. Psychoanal.* 19:495–509.

Woolf, M. 1949. The child's moral development. In *Searchlights on delinquency,* ed. K. R. Eissler. New York: Int. Univ. Press.

Zaritzianos, G. 1967. Problems of technique in the analysis of a juvenile delinquent. *Int. J. Psychoanal.* 48:439–47.

Date Due